UPSIDE DOWN LIVING

A TEMPLATE FOR CHANGING OURSELVES AND THE
WORLD FROM THE BOOK OF ACTS

UPSIDE DOWN LIVING

A TEMPLATE FOR CHANGING OURSELVES AND THE
WORLD FROM THE BOOK OF ACTS

GREG LAURIE

KERYGMA
PUBLISHING

UPSIDE DOWN LIVING

ISBN: 978-0-9801831-7-7
Published by: Kerygma Publishing—Allen David Books, Dana Point, California
Coordination: FM Management, Ltd.
Cover design: Christopher Laurie / Ross Geerdes
Photography: Trever Hoehne
Editor: Highgate Cross+Cathey
Interior design: Highgate Cross+Cathey
Production: Highgate Cross+Cathey

Printed in the United States of America

Dedicated to Levi Lusko and Pedro Garcia—
Two young men who are turning their world upside down.

CONTENTS

ONE
POWER TO CHANGE THE WORLD

In the years since I've been in ministry, I've seen the generations come and go. Boomers, Busters, Generations X, Y, and Z…they come in one door, enjoy their moment in the sun, and then make room for the ones coming behind them.

In the process, of course, music changes, terminology changes, and styles change. That's only to be expected. And it's only to be expected that previous generations won't like all the changes that the new generation brings with them.

As a matter of fact, during the recent political campaigns, we heard a lot about "change." The word was used so often, it almost became a new cliché.

But the one thing that must never change in the Church of Jesus Christ is our basic message and mission. It must not and cannot change, because the gospel is the gospel—"the power of God for the salvation of everyone who believes: first for the Jew, then for the Gentile" (Romans 1:16, NIV).

The fact is, however, that very gospel—the message that underlies our existence as believers—is under attack as I have never seen it attacked before.

Yes, the Church has always had its minor disagreements—over style, emphasis, and certain points of doctrine—but this is much more serious than that. This is not about how you might view the order of prophetic events, or even the never-ending debate concerning the sovereignty of God and the freewill of man.

This is life and death.

For in what we call the Church today, there is a debate among a growing number as to whether or not Jesus Christ is really the only way to salvation, or whether or not "all Scripture is given by inspiration of God."[1]

There are some Pied Pipers out there who are leading many unsuspecting believers or would-be believers down a wrong road. I see churches getting away from the simple declaration of the gospel, and focusing instead on issues like "global warming."

So instead of global warming, I want to issue a global *warning*. We had better get back to the basics, or we will lose what little influence we have as the Church.

The trend nowadays with some churches is to be cool, contemporary, and relevant. And it's not that my objective as a pastor has been to be lame, out-of-date, and irrelevant! But at the same time, relevance may be overrated. What matters most is truthfulness and accuracy—and a bold, unapologetic proclamation of the gospel.

Which Brings Us to...

That's why book of Acts will always define what is truly relevant. Why? Because it was and to this day remains as the original template for the Church of Jesus Christ. Within the pages of this book, penned by Luke the physician, we see the very blueprint of the Church that Jesus Himself laid down for all of us.

And we stray from it at our own peril.

This is the Church that changed the world through prayer and through preaching, and we need to get back to what these first believers received and experienced on the day of Pentecost.

Some would say, "Well, maybe we need another Pentecost."

No, we don't need another Pentecost any more than we need another Calvary. The first one was good enough! Let's just appropriate what was made available on that day when the Church of Jesus Christ was born. Let's tap into the power that was poured out on First century believers—and remains every bit as available to Twenty-first century believers—as we seek to bring the gospel to our generation.

It was said of the early Church that they turned the world upside down. And by the way, that was offered as a criticism, not a compliment.[2] When Paul and Silas were preaching the gospel in Thessalonica, an angry mob yelled, "Paul and Silas have turned the rest of the world upside down, and now they are here disturbing our city" (Acts 17:6, TLB).

May God give us more disturbances like this!

G. Campbell Morgan said, "Organized Christianity which fails to make a disturbance is dead." And frankly, that's what concerns me; we're *not* making much of a disturbance anymore. We're so worried about fitting in, about relating, and about being relevant and cool that we've forgotten what it is to make a stand for the truth. Instead of the Church turning the world upside down, my fear is that the world is turning the Church upside down.

Many years ago A. W. Tozer said, "If the Holy Spirit were taken away from the New Testament Church, 90 percent of what they did would come to a halt. But if the Holy Spirit were taken away from today's Church only 10 percent of what it does would cease."

That is a powerful statement. *How dependent on the Holy Spirit are we really?*

An old country preacher named Vance Havner once said, "We are not going to move this world by criticism of it nor conformity to it but by the combustion within lives that have been ignited by the Spirit of God."

So that's why we need to get back to this book-of-Acts template.

That's why we need to be involved in upside down living.

An Unfinished Book?

Here before us in the book of Acts is the story of a handful of men and women who did not leave their world the same way they found it. These were ordinary people who, empowered by the Spirit, were able to do extraordinary things. It was the beginning of a movement that continues to this very day. Because the book of Acts tells the story of God's Spirit changing the lives of those that encounter Him, you might call it an unfinished book.

In the opening chapter, Luke wrote to Theophilus, saying, "These are the things that Jesus *began* to do and teach." In other words, it's an unfinished story, with more chapters to come.

Now I'm not suggesting we literally write out new material to insert into the pages of our Bibles. But what I am saying is that we should never put a period where God has placed a comma. God is still working, and in that sense these "Acts of the Holy Spirit" are still being recorded in our day.

Covering a period of Church history spanning some thirty years, the book of Acts is basically nonstop action. In some cases one chapter ends with a miracle, and the next begins with one. Seeing this, we might falsely conclude that these First century believers experienced miracles every moment.

I don't think that was necessarily the case. I think they, like us, had many days of just walking by faith and applying biblical principles as they sought to obey God. Yet as you leaf through the pages of this exciting biblical record, you have to be in awe of the repeated, powerful intervention of the Spirit of God into human affairs.

Three Vital Elements

The book of Acts is a record of the Acts of the Holy Spirit covering about a thirty-year period, from A.D. 33-63.

That's important to note, because as we read the book itself, it seems like this era of the Church was in constant turmoil and non-stop action. And yes, there certainly were miracles, healings, and mighty works in this era. But not every day. Most of their days were lived out as we live ours, simply walking by faith through the normal ups and downs of existence.

In the pages of Acts, however, Dr. Luke focuses in on the dramatic and undeniable interventions of the Holy Spirit. And it was the work of the Holy Spirit that propelled them forward.

Over the years, emperors, dictators, and—more recently—academics and atheists have done their best to destroy the Church. Needless to say, they have failed. And *they always will.*

After this Church was established, waves of horrific persecutions rolled over these early believers. Secular historians are in agreement that there were ten great persecutions, ten major attempts to wipe out Christianity from the face of the earth. It began with the wicked Caesar Nero, and continued through the reign of Diocletian.

Believers were literally fed alive to wild animals in Roman arenas for sport. They were torn apart, tortured, and many were burned at the stake. Caesar Nero would cover Christians in pitch and use them as human torches in his gardens, lighting the way of his chariot as they cavorted naked. The Roman emperor Diocletian killed so many Christians the Church was forced to go "underground." Diocletian thought he had obliterated all of the believers, and celebrated the occasion by having a coin struck with the words: "The Christian religion is destroyed and the worship of the Roman gods is restored."

Obviously, he was wrong. Ancient Rome was reduced to ruins, but faith in Jesus Christ continues to blossom all over the world. Instead of being weakened and destroyed by Rome, the Church was transformed into a lean, mean, preaching machine! Rome lies in the dust, and the Church is triumphant. Jesus said, "The gates of hell shall not prevail against it!"

Dr. Luke, who also brought to us the Gospel of Luke, authored the book of Acts. A detailed, careful writer, Luke took time to research his subject, capturing eyewitness events with a dramatic flair. Most importantly, however, Dr. Luke wrote under the direct inspiration and guidance of the Holy Spirit.

The book offers three vital ingredients in the way God works. In the book of Acts, we see *the Spirit of God* working through *the Word of God* in the hearts of *the people of God.*

All three of those elements are crucial.

Sometimes you encounter churches that emphasize the Spirit of God. It's all about the Holy Spirit and the emotions, experiences, and phenomena that come along with His filling of individual believers. In some of these same churches, however, there is a lack of sound, systematic instruction in the Word, opening the door to out-of-balance teaching, or, in some cases, outright heresy.

And then on the other hand you have churches that focus all their energies on the Word of God. They're really into the Bible—teaching it, preaching it, analyzing it, and diagramming and dissecting it. Yes, they teach the Scriptures so very carefully, but sometimes there is no openness to any contemporary work of the Holy Spirit in these churches, and things can become staid and sterile.

In the book of Acts, however, you have all three elements in operation. Acts gives us the record of the Spirit of God working through the Word of God in the hearts of the people of God.

And think about this simple fact: In a relatively short period of time, perhaps three decades, this original group of 120 and their converts were able to turn the world around. That was no small task! Their world in that day, as with our world today, was messed up big time! We think conditions are bad in the Twenty-first century, and indeed they are, but the world of the First century wasn't a walk in the park, either. In fact, it was a most difficult time and place to bring the gospel. Believers in those days lived under the iron fist of the godless and powerful Roman Empire. Immorality was rampant, divorce widespread, slavery the order of the day, and infanticide a regular practice.

In city after city, prostitutes openly walked the streets and plied their trade. The religious establishment of the day was corrupt to the core. Thousands of people openly practiced idolatry, spiritism, and outright demon worship. Temples erected to false gods stood on seemingly every corner.

What's more, everywhere the believers went bringing this message they were harassed, ridiculed, physically assaulted, imprisoned, or—in some cases—put to death. Yet within three decades, those original 120 disciples had multiplied and changed the world.

Tertullian, an early Church father who wrote 200 years after the birth of the Church, made this statement about the impact of the gospel: "We have filled every place among you, cities, islands, fortresses, towns, market-places, the very camp, tribes, companies, palaces, the senate, the forum. We have left nothing to you but the temples of your gods."

Don't you love that? Tertullian is saying, "There is no stone that has been left unturned. There isn't one little crevice or corner where the gospel has not gone. We have invaded your culture." And as you look back, you see that the Roman Empire eventually crumbled, while the message of Christ spread across the world.

We have the same message—and the same task—before us today. So how were they able to accomplish it? They understood that ministry wasn't just for a select few apostles; no, ministry was for everybody. Everyone was to go and bring this message to their generation and sphere of influence.

In Acts, then, we see the work of God's Spirit in a band of people who shook their world. As we read through the book, some of what these early disciples did seem pretty radical at times. I think it may seem that way to us because we have settled for a watered-down version of what Christianity really ought to be.

This isn't "radical" Christianity that we read about in the book of Acts, this is *normal* Christianity. And this is what we should be asking God for in our brief slice of time on planet earth.

"Many Infallible Proofs"

The former account I made, O Theophilus, of all that Jesus began both to do and teach, until the day in which He was taken up, after He through the Holy Spirit had given commandments to the apostles whom He had cho-sen, to whom He also presented Himself alive after His suffering by many infallible proofs, being seen by them during forty days and speaking of the things pertaining to the kingdom of God.

And being assembled together with them, He commanded them not to depart from Jerusalem, but to wait for the Promise of the Father, "which," He said, "you have heard from Me; for John truly baptized with water, but you shall be baptized with the Holy Spirit not many days from now." Therefore, when they had come together, they asked Him, saying, "Lord, will You at this time restore the kingdom to Israel?" And He said to them, "It is not for you to know times or seasons which the Father has put in His own authority. But you shall receive power when the Holy Spirit has come upon you; and you shall be witnesses to Me in Jerusalem, and in all Judea and Samaria, and to the end of the earth."

Now when He had spoken these things, while they watched, He was taken up, and a cloud received Him out of their sight. And while they looked steadfastly toward heaven as He went up, behold, two men stood by them in white apparel, who also said, "Men of Galilee, why do you stand gazing up into heaven? This same Jesus, who was taken up from you into heaven, will so come in like manner as you saw Him go into heaven." (Acts 1:1-11)

In verse 3, Luke says to Theophilus, "Listen, we have many infallible proofs."

In other words, Christianity isn't some feel-good belief system that asks you to check your brains at the door or subscribe to misguided fairy tales. It is based on reliable and documented evidence on the life, death, and resurrection of Jesus Christ, thereby justifying His claims and promises.

Granted, there will always be an element of faith involved in being a believer. But it is a faith based on the clear facts! The Greek term Luke uses here for "proof" is a word that includes the idea of *convincing*.

Beginning only hours after the event itself, people denied that Jesus rose from the dead. Some have claimed it was all an elaborate hoax, concocted by the disciples. Or that all of those hundreds of witnesses the Bible speaks about experienced some kind of mass, simultaneous hallucination, and never saw His risen body.

Luke declares, right here at the top, "Listen to me. I have done primary research on this topic, and I have proof."

> He also presented Himself alive after His suffering by many infallible
> proofs, being seen by them during forty days…. (v. 3)

The word that Luke uses for "seen" here comes from the Greek word for *eyeball*. So they eyeballed the risen Lord Jesus.

Have you ever eyeballed someone? Let me restate the question. *Do you have a mother?* You know what I mean. You've been out with your friends, come in late, and your mother looks at you. She says, "Where have you been?"

And you say, "Uh-oh."

She's eyeballing you. Staring holes into you! That's what the disciples did when they first laid eyes on their risen Lord. And that's what you and I would have done, too. These disciples had seen Jesus crucified and put to death. They'd heard the blows of the hammer, and had seen the spikes penetrate His hands and feet. They had seen the Roman soldier pierce His side with a spear, to make sure He was dead, and the blood and water that spilled from His side as a result. They had seen His traumatized, beaten body taken from the cross, and they knew that no one could have those things happen to him and ever live again—much less walk and talk with them.

But suddenly, there He is! *Alive*. Breathing. Walking. Talking. Smiling. And He doesn't appear just once or twice; He's popping up everywhere! He shows up to Mary at the empty tomb…with two men on the Emmaus Road…with the disciples in the upper room…then back with them again in the upper room because Thomas hadn't made it the first time!

He shows up here, He shows up there, He shows up to more than 500 people at one time. But who is He really? Is He a man? Is He a phantom? Is He just a spirit? Can you put your hand through His body? No, He's solid. His flesh is warm to the touch. He eats a piece of fish in their presence (a very good menu choice, I think). He was a real man, alive in a real body. Yet at the same time, He could appear in a room and disappear again. He could traverse distances in the blink of an eye.

So Luke declares, "Listen to me, I've got proof! We saw Him. We know He is alive, and none of us could possibly deny it."

But what about those who claim the whole resurrection story was a hoax, somehow pulled off by the disciples on hundreds of people?

Not a chance. If the resurrection had been a con job, some sophisticated, elaborate swindle, then certainly one of them would have broken ranks under the terrible persecution that followed. Someone being led to executioner's block to have his head removed, someone being lowered into a vat of boiling oil, someone tied to a post over a pile of kindling and about to be burned alive, would have suddenly yelled, "Hey, time out here! I deny it all! We just made this whole thing up."

But no. The fact is that every one of the apostles except John died the death of a martyr. And it's not as though he got off easy! Tradition tells us that they lowered him in a pot of boiling oil—and he wouldn't cook! So he was banished to the island of Patmos.

Under the stress of torture, exile, or death, someone would have recanted. Men and women don't die for a hoax. But not one of them broke ranks, because they could not deny what they knew to be true.

Jesus was certainly alive. They'd seen Him. Eyeballed Him. His very Spirit had filled them to overflowing, and they wanted nothing more than to share this message, this great Good News, with others.

We tend to put these First century saints on a pedestal—stained glass people with halos over their heads. But they were real people just like you and me. Most were uneducated, with few of the social graces, and not much money to speak of. The men had calloused hands and very limited knowledge of the world. Some were outright outcasts.

Yet it pleased God to use these people to change the world.

They Still Didn't Get It

It's interesting to me that even though Jesus had been raised from the dead, even though they had touched Him, walked with Him and talked with Him, the disciples initially tried to circle back to an old idea.

> So when the apostles were with Jesus, they kept asking him, "Lord, has the time come for you to free Israel and restore our kingdom?" (Acts 1:6)

Free Israel? Restore our kingdom? In other words…*Is it time for You to overthrow Rome?* You see, they still didn't quite get it. They were excited that the Lord was alive again, and it's as if they were saying, "So…are we going back to business as usual, Lord? We really don't understand the whole crucifixion thing, but here You are, alive again, and everything is wonderful. Now it must be time to roll up our sleeves and get the kingdom established!"

That, you may remember, had been their firm belief. They thought Jesus had come to establish an earthly kingdom and break the iron manacles of Roman rule. And once again Jesus had to put that wrong idea to rest with a mild rebuke.

> "The Father sets those dates," he replied, "and they are not for you to know. But when the Holy Spirit has come upon you, you will receive power and will tell people about me everywhere—in Jerusalem, throughout Judea, in Samaria, and to the ends of the earth." (vv. 7-8, NLT)

Jesus was effectively saying, "Will you guys get off of that, finally? I'm *not* going to establish an earthly kingdom…at least not now. That's not why I have come, and that's not for you to worry about. The times and seasons are not your concern."

It's a similar scene today among people who are always studying Bible prophecy and end times passages, to the exclusion of the rest of Scripture. I too am a student of Bible prophecy, and believe the Lord could come back at any time. And I believe we truly have seen signs of the times and prophesies fulfilled before our very eyes. But at the same time, I've seen so many people over the years trying and trying to figure out dates and times and places—and then claim they have some previously unknown insight or have discovered some special Bible code that reveals the day of the Lord's second coming.

Yet Jesus Himself said, "But of that day and hour no one knows, not even the angels of heaven, but My Father only" (Matthew 24:36).

So here is what Jesus is saying to those disciples, and to us: "Don't be so worried about when I am coming. Focus instead on what you're to be doing while you await My coming. Don't concern yourself with the 'when.' It will happen precisely when it is supposed to happen. Just be ready, because it could happen at any moment."

Don't focus on the *when*, Jesus is saying, focus on the *what*.

And what is "the what"? It is proclaiming the message He gave us to proclaim. That's the most important thing.

> And He said to them, "It is not for you to know times or seasons which the Father has put in His own authority. But you shall receive power when the Holy Spirit has come upon you; and you shall be witnesses to Me in Jerusalem, and in all Judea and Samaria, and to the end of the earth." (vv. 7-8)

The words above were the last words Jesus spoke before His ascension.

I'm always interested in people's last words…the final statements they utter before exiting the planet. In Matthew 28:16, the gospel account gives these additional details of our Lord's last words before being taken up out of their sight:

> "All authority has been given to Me in heaven and on earth. Go therefore and make disciples of all the nations, baptizing them in the name of the Father and of the Son and of the Holy Spirit, teaching them to observe all things that I have commanded you; and lo, I am with you always, even to the end of the age."

How would this kingdom be established? "*Go into all the world and preach the gospel.*" And how, from a human standpoint, were they going to pull this off? The apostles were in no way ready for such a task.

There was still much they didn't understand. Their faith was weak. They had failed in their public witness and also in their private faith. Even Simon Peter, their acknowledged leader, had openly denied the Lord. If *Peter* could be intimidated and demoralized by the words of a servant girl in the high priest's courtyard, how could any of them be expected to go anywhere and preach anything?

Jesus answered that question, too.

How would they do it? They would do it with a power they had never known before. A power beyond anything they had yet experienced. A power to change the world. Verse 8. "*You shall receive power when the Holy Spirit has come upon you; and you shall be witnesses to Me] in Jerusalem, and in all Judea and Samaria, and to the end of the earth.*" Power to be a witness. Power to share your faith. Power to turn your world upside down. Power to do what God has called you to do.

Here is the fact that we need to realize: *The very same power that was poured out on the Day of Pentecost is available to us today.* On that day, Peter said it loud and clear: "This promise is to you, and to your children, and even to the Gentiles—all who have been called by the Lord our God" (Acts 2:39, NLT).

What promise? The promise of the Holy Spirit.

Given to whom? Given to us, right here, right now.

As we consider these things, we need to be careful about avoiding unbiblical extremes. One extreme is to go beyond Scripture, or even contradict it. And sadly, much of what is being done today in the name of the Holy Spirit has little or nothing to do with Him. Far too often when we see aberrant, bizarre, or freaky behavior it is attributed to the Holy Spirit. You know what I mean… "*The Holy Spirit made me do that.*"

Don't blame all of these bizarre activities and antics on God's Spirit. Many Christians and non-Christians alike recoil from such excesses. The danger occurs when people seek some experience or manifestation that's really not offered in Scripture.

The other danger (every bit as serious) is to *not* seek something that Scripture clearly offers. It is foolish to consider a biblical experience and say, "Well, because I don't have it, then it must not be real." The truth is, the Bible has promised a dimension of power for every believer who wants to be a witness for the Lord.

All we have to do is ask.

Have you asked for this power, to become a bold, effective witness for Jesus? When you refuse to receive all that God has for your life, that is what the Bible calls "quenching the Holy Spirit."

Dunamis

Did the disciples already have the Holy Spirit in their lives before the Day of Pentecost? Yes, because prior to His ascension and the Day of Pentecost, the gospel of John records this encounter with the resurrected Jesus:

> Again Jesus said, "Peace be with you! As the Father has sent me, I am sending you." And with that he breathed on them and said, "Receive the Holy Spirit." (John 20:21-22, NIV)

So the Holy Spirit came into the disciples at that time, *before* Pentecost.

Here's how it works. Before you are a Christian, the Holy Spirit is *with you*. In other words, He is working in your life to convince you that you need Jesus Christ and His saving work in your life. Then, once you receive Christ into your life, the Holy Spirit comes and lives *inside of you*. The Bible teaches that the Holy Spirit indwells every Christian. As believers we are sealed and led by the Holy Spirit.

In Acts 1:8, however, Jesus speaks of something more than the Spirit coming to indwell you. He speaks of the empowerment you will receive when the Holy Spirit *comes upon you*.

That's a very important distinction. When He comes upon you, it is to bring power.

The word Luke uses here for "power" is a fascinating term. It comes from the Greek word *dunamis*. A variation of that word entered the English language when Alfred Nobel made the discovery that would ultimately become his fortune. In 1867, Nobel discovered a power that was stronger than anything the world had known up to that time. But he didn't know what to call it. So he talked to a friend of his who happened to be a Greek scholar, and said, "What is the word in the Greek for explosive power?"

His friend replied, "It is *dunamis*."

So in 1867, Nobel received U.S. Patent Number 78,317 for his new invention…which he called *dynamite*. And that's where that word entered our vernacular.

In Acts 1:8, Jesus said, "You will receive *dunamis*." We also get our word "dynamic" from this same Greek term. So what was Jesus saying? "You will receive dynamic, explosive power when the Spirit has come upon you."

What kind of power? Not political power. We see the struggle for political power every night on the news. It seems like people will say or do almost anything to obtain such power. That's not the power Jesus speaks of here. It's not the power to overthrow Rome, or any other government. Jesus says, "No. I am offering you dynamic *spiritual* power. Power to preach the gospel. Power to change the world. Power that will come upon you."

If you are a Christian, the Holy Spirit already lives inside of you. *But has He come upon you?* Have you ever said something like this? "Lord, empower me with Your Holy Spirit to bring the gospel to my sphere of influence."

We spoke of Peter, being intimidated by a woman servant at a fireside into denying His Lord—not once, but three times! Yet after the empowering of the Holy Spirit on the Day of Pentecost, that same Simon Peter stood up and fearlessly addressed a large crowd of Jews from all over the world, ultimately seeing 3,000 people come to faith from that one message. What power!

Do you have this *dunamis* in your life? Are you one of those people who shrink back in fear at the mere thought of speaking a word out loud about who Jesus is and what He has done for you? Do you feel that "something must be missing" from your spiritual walk? Do you find the world turning you upside down, instead of you turning the world upside down? If you answered yes to any of those questions, then you are a candidate for the empowering of the Holy Spirit.

You might ask the question, "Well, what do I need to do to obtain this?"

I have a very simple answer for you: You just need to ask God for it.

"Can it really be that easy?" you ask.

Yes, it can. And is!

In Luke 11:13, "If you being evil know how to give good gifts to your children, how much more will your Heavenly Father give the Holy Spirit to them that ask Him?"

To those that ask Him.

Not…those that plead with Him.

Not…those that beg Him.

No, if you simply ask the Father, He will give that power to you, and He will give it freely and generously. If you have never received this gift, you can simply say, "Lord, empower me with Your Holy Spirit so I can have power to be a witness for Jesus."

You've already done that? Then maybe you need a refill!

Not long ago, as I was leaving a restaurant, I checked our bill before I got up to the counter to pay, and noticed it seemed a little higher than normal. I was somewhat stunned to see that they had charged us for every refill of iced tea!

Here's some good news for you. God does not charge you for a refill of the Holy Spirit. He will just give that refill to you. And oh, how we need it. How *I* need it! I need God's power to do what He has called me to do; because there is no way I can be a pastor and an evangelist on my own. And He will fill me again and again.

Actually, being filled with the Spirit is a *command.* We are told in Ephesians 5:18-19 (NLT), "Don't be drunk with wine, because that will ruin your life. Instead, be filled with the Holy Spirit, singing psalms and hymns and spiritual songs among yourselves, and making music to the Lord in your hearts."

The idea in the original language is be filled again and again and again. But what does that really mean? That particular word "filled" can be translated different ways. One picture is that of wind filling a sail, and carrying the boat along through the water. Another translation of the word speaks more of the way that salt permeates meat, and has the idea of influence or effect.

So we are not talking about some random surge of emotion here. Some people really get psyched up about being filled with the Spirit, and think they should expect some bolt of lightning out of heaven, or maybe some warm feeling that washes over them.

And yes, sometimes those things happen.

But at other times it will simply be the permeation of the Spirit in your life, changing the very flavor of who you are, or the Spirit filling your sails to get you moving. The point is, the Spirit provides you with power when you need it. Too many of us get hung up on the emotional aspect of this experience, or think we need to dim the lights and sing for an hour before He will fill us.

Instead we should simply say, "Lord, by faith may I just receive this power into my life." And He will fill you. Tomorrow morning, you can ask Him again and He will do the same.

Scripture says, "This promise is unto you, and to your children, to all that are afar off, even as many as the Lord our God shall call."[3]

That's another way of saying…this is for *you*.

TWO
The First Message of the Church

On the day of Pentecost all the believers were meeting together in one place. Suddenly, there was a sound from heaven like the roaring of a mighty windstorm, and it filled the house where they were sitting. Then, what looked like flames or tongues of fire appeared and settled on each of them. And everyone present was filled with the Holy Spirit and began speaking in other languages, as the Holy Spirit gave them this ability.

At that time there were devout Jews from every nation living in Jerusalem. When they heard the loud noise, everyone came running, and they were bewildered to hear their own languages being spoken by the believers. They were completely amazed. "How can this be?" they exclaimed. "These people are all from Galilee, and yet we hear them speaking in our own native languages! Here we are—Parthians, Medes, Elamites, people from Mesopotamia, Judea, Cappadocia, Pontus, the province of Asia, Phrygia, Pamphylia, Egypt, and the areas of Libya around Cyrene, visitors from Rome (both Jews and converts to Judaism), Cretans, and Arabs. And we all hear these people speaking in our own languages about the wonderful things God has done!" They stood there amazed and perplexed. "What can this mean?" they asked each other.

But others in the crowd ridiculed them, saying, "They're just drunk, that's all!" (Acts 2:1-13, NLT)

When it comes to God's work and God's ways in this world, don't ever think that we invented skepticism and cynicism in the Twenty-first century. In fact, people were just as likely to scoff at God's Word or explain away God's works in the days when the Bible was written as they are today.

Take this description of the coming of the Holy Spirit on the day of Pentecost, for instance. At least some of the first-hand, eyewitness observers of that phenomenon immediately tried to blow it off with a snide remark.

One translation says: "But there were others who laughed mockingly and said, 'These fellows have drunk too much new wine!'"[4]

As if drunk people do this sort of thing!

As it happens, I have a little firsthand knowledge about drunk people. In fact, I spent the first seventeen years of my life around them, because I was raised in an alcoholic home. So you need to take my word for this: *Drunk people don't speak in other languages.* Most of the time, they have enough trouble speaking in their own language! And if they do manage to say some things, they won't even remember it the next day.

What a ridiculous explanation of the supernatural intervention of the Holy Spirit.

"Roaring, Mighty Windstorm"

The Scripture speaks of a "sound from heaven like the roaring of a mighty windstorm." And it came *suddenly*.

The believers had known something was coming, because Jesus had told them He would send His Spirit. They simply had no idea what to expect.

So the sound emanating from that room—one translation describes it as "a sound like a strong wind, gale force"[5]—caught them by surprise. By noting that the sound came from heaven, Luke was emphasizing that this was a supernatural action.

In the third chapter of John, Jesus compared the Holy Spirit to the wind in His conversation with Nicodemus. The Jewish leader had been trying to wrap his mind around what Jesus was saying—particularly about being born again.

> "Men can only reproduce human life, but the Holy Spirit gives new life from heaven; so don't be surprised at my statement that you must be born again! Just as you can hear the wind but can't tell where it comes from or where it will go next, so it is with the Spirit." (John 3:6-8, TLB)

In other words, "Nicodemus, you can't see the wind but you can see its effects."

So…can what happened to those disciples at Pentecost happen to believers today?

The answer to that is yes and no. Nowhere else in the Bible do we read of a mighty rushing wind, and the Spirit coming among people in tongues of fire. But then again, we frequently read in the book of Acts of the Holy Spirit empowering, speaking to, and using the believers.

So here's what it comes down to. Pentecost was an event that was never to be repeated. Having said that, the power that was given by the Holy Spirit to the early Church in the First century at Pentecost is still available to the Church of the Twenty-first century. The power that was entrusted to them is also available to us. As you read through the book of Acts, you read of the Spirit filling His spokesmen again and again.

The Spirit filled Peter at the Beautiful Gate of the Temple, as he reached out to a crippled man and pulled him to his feet, well and whole again.

The Spirit filled Stephen as He boldly proclaimed the Lord's name to a hate-filled Sanhedrin, who had him on trial for his very life.

The Spirit filled Paul as he attempted to proclaim the Good News of Jesus Christ to a gentile governor, and found himself opposed by a sorcerer.

The Spirit filled a whole group of believers, as they knelt together to pray for boldness in the face of intimidation and persecution. "And when they had prayed, the place where they were assembled together was shaken; and they were all filled with the Holy Spirit, and they spoke the word of God with boldness" (Acts 4:31).

Why do I bring these things up? Because if you have ever been afraid to speak up for your faith, if you have ever been opposed or mocked as a Christian, then you are a candidate to be filled with the Holy Spirit.

In the last chapter, I mentioned that one way we could translate the Greek term of being "filled with the Spirit" is with the picture of wind filling a sail. So in Ephesians 5:18, when Paul says, "Be filled with the Spirit," he is essentially saying, "May the wind of the Spirit fill your sail and guide your course through life."

Have you ever been out in a sailboat and found yourself with no wind? It's a lot of work to row back to shore! And then a gust of wind comes along, you quickly hoist your sail, and find yourself cruising across the waves again. And you say to yourself, "Ahh…now this is the way it ought to be."

That's a pretty good picture of what it's like in the Christian life when we try to do what God has told us to do in our strength. It's like rowing a sailboat! You know, we grit our teeth, and really dig in, saying, "I've got to obey the Lord, and keep my thoughts pure, and witness to my neighbors, and love my spouse, and resist temptation…." And it's hard going! We find ourselves with blisters on our blisters.

But then we come to our senses, and say, "Lord, I can't row this boat on my own. I ask that Your Holy Spirit will fill my sail and help me accomplish what I can't accomplish in my own strength."

When we do that, what has seemed like duty to us begins to feel more like delight.

To be filled with the Spirit means that I am carried along by and under the control of Jesus Christ. I fill my mind and heart with His Word, so that His thoughts become my thoughts. To be filled with the Holy Spirit is to walk thought-by-thought, decision-by-decision, act-by-act, under the Spirit's control.

"This is What Was Spoken..."

As the Holy Spirit was poured out on the Day of Pentecost, we read that the believers spoke in tongues or languages they had never known previously. A diverse international audience was gathered in Jerusalem at this particular time, and to the amazement of all, each of them heard the Good News of salvation in Jesus Christ being declared in his or her own language.

The gift of tongues, given by the Holy Spirit on the Day of Pentecost, is still available to believers today. And the purpose of the gift of tongues is to build you up spiritually. The apostle Paul says, "For he who speaks in a tongue does not speak to men but to God, for no one understands him; however, in the spirit he speaks mysteries" (1 Corinthians 14:2).

What happened on the Day of Pentecost was not a normal use of the gift of tongues, because the disciples spoke in languages that were understood by all these other people.

After the sound of that hurricane had drawn a great crowd of alarmed and curious people to where the disciples had been staying, Peter took his stand before them all and began to fearlessly declare what God was doing.

"Men of Judea and all who dwell in Jerusalem, let this be known to you, and heed my words. For these are not drunk, as you suppose, since it is only the third hour of the day. But this is what the prophet Joel spoke:

'And it shall come to pass in the last days, says God,
That I will pour out of My Spirit on all flesh;
Your sons and your daughters shall prophesy,
Your young men shall see visions,
Your old men shall dream dreams.
And on My menservants and on My maidservants
I will pour out My Spirit in those days;
And they shall prophesy.
I will show wonders in heaven above

And signs in the earth beneath:
Blood and fire and vapor of smoke.
The sun shall be turned into darkness,
And the moon into blood,
Before the coming of the great and awesome day of the LORD.
And it shall come to pass
That whoever calls on the name of the LORD
Shall be saved.'"

Peter is saying, "Come on, guys, give me a break. These men aren't drunk. Hey, it's only 9:00 in the morning. The bars aren't even open yet!" And he goes on to say, "This is what was spoken by the prophet Joel…"

This reminds us that if we can't say, "*This is what was spoken of,*" we should not seek it or practice it! I bring this up because every now and then someone comes along and says, "Hey, you can have this great new experience with the Holy Spirit…." Then they go on to describe some unusual phenomenon—whether it be screaming, shrieking, laughing uncontrollably, or making animal noises. And my response is, "Excuse me. Where is that in the Bible?" Because frankly, if I can't find it in the Bible, I'm not interested.

If it's not *in* the Word, it is not of the Lord. We should always be able to say, with Peter, "This is what was spoken of," and have a scriptural basis for what we are doing.

Someone will come along periodically and say, "I am a prophet of God, and have a new revelation for the Church. What I'm about to say has never been revealed before." If you hear someone talk like this, walk (very quickly) in the opposite direction. If you're in a meeting where this is proclaimed, it's time to get up and leave. The fact is, if it is "new," then it isn't true, and if it is true, then it isn't new.

Frankly, I'm not looking for a new revelation. I have more than enough revelation to deal with in the Word of God itself. There are people who run here and there, always looking for new words from the Lord, and they have never even read THE Word from cover to cover.

There is plenty to occupy yourself with in the pages of the Bible—more than you can begin to deal with in a lifetime. There is no need for "new revelations."

The Prototype Message

When Peter stood to preach in the second chapter of Acts, he delivered the very first message of the early Church. Though it is over 2,000 years old, it remains a classic prototype of how to bring the gospel to our generation.

We live now in a time described as the "postmodern generation." In some church circles you'll hear talk about "how to reach postmodern people," with special instruction on what works and what doesn't work, what believers ought to say and what they ought not to say.

Here's what I think about that: *The gospel doesn't change*. It doesn't matter if you're addressing an ancient culture—pre-modern, modern, post-modern, or post-post-modern. Whatever you want to call the age in which you live, the Good News about Jesus Christ is essentially the same. So when we look at the message Peter delivered on the Day of Pentecost, we're not viewing it like kind of interesting historical relic, but rather as a living message, every bit as relevant today as it was on the day when it was delivered.

Peter's message not only contains principles for preachers giving sermons, it also has something for any of us who want to be more effective communicators as we tell others about the Lord. I see seven helpful principles in his message.

#1: Peter Knew His Audience

"People of Israel, listen! God publicly endorsed Jesus the Nazarene by doing powerful miracles, wonders, and signs through him, as you well know. But God knew what would happen, and his prearranged plan was carried out when Jesus was betrayed. With the help of lawless Gentiles, you nailed him to a cross and killed him. But God released him from the horrors of death and raised him back to life, for death could not keep him in its grip. King David said this about him:

'I see that the Lord is always with me. I will not be shaken, for he is right beside me. No wonder my heart is glad, and my tongue shouts his praises! My body rests in hope. For you will not leave my soul among the dead or allow your Holy One to rot in the grave. You have shown me the way of life, and you will fill me with the joy of your presence.'

"Dear brothers, think about this! You can be sure that the patriarch David wasn't referring to himself, for he died and was buried, and his tomb is still here among us. But he was a prophet, and he knew God had promised with an oath that one of David's own descendants would sit on his throne. David was looking into the future and speaking of the Messiah's resurrection. He was saying that God would not leave him among the dead or allow his body to rot in the grave.

"God raised Jesus from the dead, and we are all witnesses of this. Now he is exalted to the place of highest honor in heaven, at God's right hand. And the Father, as he had promised, gave him the Holy Spirit to pour out upon us, just as you see and hear today. For David himself never ascended into heaven, yet he said, 'The Lord said to my Lord, "Sit in the place of honor at my right hand until I humble your enemies, making them a footstool under your feet."'

"So let everyone in Israel know for certain that God has made this Jesus, whom you crucified, to be both Lord and Messiah!"

Peter's words pierced their hearts, and they said to him and to the other apostles, "Brothers, what should we do?" Peter replied, "Each of you must repent of your sins, turn to God, and be baptized in the name of Jesus Christ to show that you have received forgiveness for your sins. Then you will receive the gift of the Holy Spirit. This promise is to you, and to your children, and even to the Gentiles—all who have been called by the Lord our God." Then Peter continued preaching for a long time, strongly urging all his listeners, "Save yourselves from this crooked generation!"

Those who believed what Peter said were baptized and added to the Church that day—about 3,000 in all. (Acts 2:22-41, NLT)

Peter said, "*People of Israel, listen…!*" He knew his audience. Peter knew very well that some of the people he addressed that morning had literally been involved with the crucifixion of Jesus. This was only weeks after the Lord had died and risen again. Certainly some of these same people, standing before Pilate, had screamed, "Crucify Him, crucify Him!"

Peter was aware of that.

He knew his audience.

He also knew that they would have a working familiarity with the Old Testament Scriptures, and his goal was to convince them that Jesus Christ was the long-awaited Messiah of Israel.

Peter's message was quite different from the one Paul delivered on Mars Hill, in Athens. Yes, it was still the essential gospel message, but Paul knew he had a very different set of listeners from the ones he'd been accustomed to speaking to. These philosophers, poets, and intellectuals had little to no knowledge of Jewish culture or the Old Testament Scripture. As a result, Paul took time to assess their culture and build appropriate bridges to make the gospel understandable to them.

To effectively communicate the gospel to someone, it helps to know a little bit about him or her. And guess what? Everybody's favorite subject is himself or herself! That is why, if I have the luxury of time, I will take a few minutes to converse with a person before I share the Gospel. (Witnessing is more effective as a dialog than a monolog!)

I will ask them questions, and then listen to their answers—whether I agree with them or not. The idea here is to engage the person, not blow them out of the water with your "gospel gun."

One of the challenges we face today as we seek to spread the gospel is scaling the language barrier. We can no longer assume that our hearers or listeners understand what we're talking about. There was a time when you could reference a story from the Bible—talking, perhaps, about Adam and Eve or Moses or Noah's ark—and people would understand. But with biblical illiteracy rate at an all time high, there are many young people today who simply have no idea who or what you're talking about.

They've never heard of Adam and Eve. They have no idea who Moses or Joshua or David was. So what does that mean? That we don't quote the Bible anymore?

No, we certainly quote it. But we don't automatically assume that the listener knows what we're referring to. So now when I use a biblical reference—especially when I am presenting the Gospel—I take time explain it and tell the story. And when I use certain phrases familiar to most Christians, I don't assume a person who is not yet a believer necessarily knows what I'm saying.

When you speak to a non-believer today and say, "You need to repent, invite Christ into your life, and follow Him as His disciple" you might as well be speaking in Croatian…. "*Bog je toliko volio svijet da je dao svojega jedinorođenog Sina da nijedan koji u njega vjeruje ne pogine, nego da ima vječni život.*"

Say what?

We need a translation here!

It means nothing to them. "I need to do what? Repent? What does repent mean? What do you mean 'follow Jesus'? Who was Jesus? What's a disciple? What are you talking about?"

So we need to break down the terms, as Paul did for audience of philosophers and intellectuals in Acts 17. These guys weren't lacking in intelligence or education; they just didn't know a Bible from the Athens phone book.

On the day of Pentecost, Peter knew his audience tracked with Old Testament Scriptures, and knew that as loyal Jews they were deeply interested in the subject of the Messiah and His coming. So he targeted the message directly at their hearts. Which brings me to a second principle.

#2: Peter Adapted to the Situation

Knowing his audience as he did, Peter adapted to the situation in which he found himself. In other words, he knew where he was, and he knew whom he was speaking to. It reminds us that as we share Jesus with people, we must become, as Paul said, "All things to all men."

One size does not fit all, and when you deal with people, everyone is different. Have you ever noticed that Jesus, the master communicator, never dealt with any two people in exactly the same way? For instance, His conversation with Nicodemus was not the same as His conversation with the woman at the well. And both of those were different from His conversation with the rich young ruler.

Yes, He invited all three of them into relationship with Himself, but He emphasized different things with each person, tailored to the individual needs and life situation.

In 1 Corinthians 9, Paul lays out his own methodology:

Even though I am a free man with no master, I have become a slave to all people to bring many to Christ. When I was with the Jews, I lived like a Jew to bring the Jews to Christ. When I was with those who follow the Jewish law, I too lived under that law. Even though I am not subject to the law, I did this so I could bring to Christ those who are under the law. When I am with the Gentiles who do not follow the Jewish law, I too live apart from that law so I can bring them to Christ. But I do not ignore the law of God; I obey the law of Christ.

When I am with those who are weak, I share their weakness, for I want to bring the weak to Christ.

Paul's bottom line?

Yes, I try to find common ground with everyone, doing everything I can to save some. I do everything to spread the Good News and share in its blessings (vv. 19-23).

The objective is building bridges with non-Christians, not burning them. Too often we unnecessarily alienate our listeners by things we say—or don't say.

So Paul basically says, "Listen, as an ambassador of Jesus Christ, I've learned to adapt to whatever situation in which I find myself." He says, "I fit in with the Gentles as much as I can."

I think we ought to be able to say the same thing about the nonbelievers in our lives. We ought to be able to say, "When I'm around a nonbeliever, I fit in with them as much as I can."

Yes, we must draw a line when we're with those who are outside of the faith. Later on, in the book of Ephesians, Paul writes: "Try to find out what is pleasing to the Lord. Take no part in the worthless deeds of evil and darkness; instead, rebuke and expose them. It is shameful even to talk about the things that ungodly people do in secret" (5:10-12, NLT).

Sometimes I will hear people say, "Well, I want to reach my nonbelieving friends, so you know, I just need to hang with them and be like them, and not be too holier-than-thou."

I agree; we should never come off looking sanctimonious, or like we don't really care about people and their needs. But be very careful. The Bible also says, "Do not be misled: 'Bad company corrupts good character.'"[6]

Don't cross the line. Sometimes in our attempt to "build bridges," in our efforts to relate, we end up becoming more like them than they become like us.

#3: Peter's Message was Scriptural

Standing up in front of that vast crowd with no notes, no Bible, no pulpit, and no teleprompter, Peter quoted Joel 2:28 to 32 from memory. He also quoted David, drawing from Psalms 16 and 110.

It's obvious that Peter had committed great portions of Scripture to memory, and he made good use of it as he declared the Good News for the very first time.

The truth is, any Christian worth his or her salt should be able to stand up at a moment's notice and clearly articulate the gospel message without notes. Every one of us should be able to share the Gospel in three minutes or less.

What if you were on an airplane that was plunging toward a crash, and you only had three minutes to until impact? Could you tell the person sitting next to you how to come to Christ? Could you break it down fast and cut to the chase in an understandable way? "*Here's how you can get right with God and put your faith in Jesus Christ.*"

We need to know the Scripture. I can't emphasize enough how important the Bible is when you are sharing your faith. The book of Isaiah puts it like this:

> "For as the rain comes down, and the snow from heaven,
> And do not return there,
> But water the earth,
> And make it bring forth and bud,
> That it may give seed to the sower
> And bread to the eater,
> So shall My word be that goes forth from My mouth;
> It shall not return to Me void,
> But it shall accomplish what I please,
> And it shall prosper in the thing for which I sent it."
> (55:10-11)

When I think of Billy Graham preaching all those years, what immediately comes to mind is his generous and constant use of Scripture. How many times have we heard him say, "The Bible says…."? I love that about him; he always acknowledges the authority of Scripture, and we who desire to be effective in sharing the gospel of Christ must do the same. As an artist uses his pens and brushes (and nowadays his computer program) to create works of art, as a chef uses his knives and cookware to prepare sumptuous meals, as a master mechanic makes use of his wide array of tools to restore an engine to peak proficiency, so you and I need to know how to use the Word of God to declare the Person of God and the work of Christ. As Paul told his young associate Timothy, "The scriptures are the comprehensive equipment of the man of God and fit him fully for all branches of his work."[7]

The devil will do everything he can to keep you from reading—and sharing—your Bible. How familiar are you with Scripture? It has been said, "A Bible that is falling apart usually belongs to someone who isn't."

Is your Bible falling apart…or your life? Maybe if you invested more time reading and heeding what the Bible says, you'd find your life in better shape. God's Word will prosper in the place where He sends it.[8]

#4: Peter's Message was Christ-Centered

In verse 22 he says, "Jesus of Nazareth." In verse 32, referring to Jesus, he speaks of "this Man." And in verse 36, he boldly declares, "God has made this Jesus, whom you crucified, both Lord and Christ."

When you are sharing the gospel, tell the story of Jesus. That's the bottom line. There is *power* in the story of the life, death, and resurrection of Jesus Christ. That's why Paul told the Corinthians, "For I resolved to know nothing while I was with you except Jesus Christ and him crucified."[9]

When you tell *your* story, it is always a bridge to *His* story, which is the greatest story ever told. That is the message we want people to hear.

But the problem today is that many people deliberately leave out the cross of Christ in their preaching and witnessing. In their attempts to "crossover," they are not bringing the *cross over*—thereby missing the point.

Peter's message was great because it was Christ centered.

Maybe you have thought, "Oh man, if I could just perform a few miracles, I know my friends would believe."

Do you really think so?

"Oh yeah," you say. "I'd have them over for a barbecue, throw the meat down on the grill, and say, 'Check this out!' Then I'd pray, 'Lord, let Your fire fall from heaven and consume these meat patties.' Then the Lord would send the fire—whoosh!—and everyone would be blown away. They'd all say, 'The Lord, He is God! The Lord, He is God!' And they'd all become believers."

No, miracles won't necessarily bring people to faith.

In Jesus' parable of the rich man and the beggar in the gospel of Luke, the rich man finds himself in hell, and begs Abraham to send someone from the dead back to earth to warn his still living brothers about that place of torment.

"But Abraham said, 'The Scriptures have warned them again and again. Your brothers can read them any time they want to.'

"The rich man replied, 'No, Father Abraham, they won't bother to read them. But if someone is sent to them from the dead, then they will turn from their sins.'

"But Abraham said, 'If they won't listen to Moses and the prophets, they won't listen even though someone rises from the dead.'" (Luke 16:29-31, TLB)

As much as we might like to think so, we will not reach a lost world through so-called "signs and wonders." If God *wants* to do them, then, glory to His name, He can do them where and when He chooses. But the primary way we will reach a lost world is through simply declaring the gospel message—that Jesus died on the cross and rose again from the dead, and that He will come into their life if they will put their faith in Him.

#5: Peter's Message Called Sin, Sin

In verse 38, Peter declares, "Each of you must repent of your sins, turn to God, and be baptized in the name of Jesus Christ to show that you have received forgiveness for your sins" (NLT).

This is very important, because the essential message of the gospel is that you can be forgiven of your sins. What is the literal definition of the gospel? *Good news.* Yes, but before I can fully appreciate the good news, I have to know the bad news.

We've all heard those good-news bad-news jokes. (Why do they always seem to be about doctors?)

The gospel certainly has great good news: Jesus will come into your life, He will fill the void inside of you, you'll be happier, you'll find peace, you'll have eternal life in heaven after you die.

But it has to begin with where people are. People outside of Christ are lost. Spiritually dead. Bound for eternal judgment. And they are *sinners*.

That's not a popular word these days, even in Christian circles. People don't like to hear that. "I'm not a sinner," they will say, "I'm basically a good person." So you have to define what you mean, by quoting the Scripture that says, "For all have sinned and fall short of the glory of God" (Romans 3:23).

But many people don't want to hear that...or *say* that.

One of the most popular preachers in America won't even use the term from the pulpit. In an interview with Larry King recently, Larry asked this pastor if he ever used the word "sinner." The pastor replied, "No. I don't use it. I never thought about it, but I probably don't. But most people know they are doing wrong."

Do they? Do most people really understand that they're doing wrong? I don't think that's necessarily true. I think a lot of people imagine they're doing just fine—that everything is rosy as long as they're sincere, try to live a good life, or have a certain religious idea in their head. Somehow, they imagine, everything will turn out all right.

But the Bible assures that everything *won't* turn out all right for those outside of faith in Christ. Romans 6:23 says, "the wages of sin is death, but the gift of God is eternal life in Christ Jesus our Lord." So God calls us to break the bad news to them: "I'm sorry to tell you this, friend, but you *are* a sinner. You have broken God's commands. You have fallen short of His eternal standards, and there is nothing you can do to tilt the scales or make this right. But God loved you so much He sent Jesus to die on the cross for you, and if you will turn from that sin and put your faith in Christ you can be forgiven."

The bad news helps them to fully appreciate the good news. And I would go so far as to say anything less than this is a false gospel that will give false assurance. That is why Paul writes words like these in Galatians chapter 1:

> I am astonished that you are so quickly deserting the one who called you by the grace of Christ and are turning to a different gospel—which is really no gospel at all. (vv. 6-7, NIV)

The Bible makes it clear: We must be careful to preach the *real* gospel.

#6: Peter's Message was Incredibly Bold

Peter looked right into the eyes of his audience and said, "Therefore let all the house of Israel know assuredly that God has made this Jesus, *whom you crucified*, both Lord and Christ" (v. 36).

Talk about taking a risk! They could have killed him for saying that. But at that point, Peter was going for broke. He probably thought, "Okay, maybe I cowered before the opinion of some woman I didn't even know by the fire in the courtyard of Caiaphas, but those days are gone. I have new power now. I have the wind filling my sail. I have the Holy Spirit permeating my life. And I am going to tell you the truth. If you don't like it what I'm saying, then so be it. But here it is. You killed Him. You crucified the Messiah. You are responsible."

Was he out of line? Over the top? Judge for yourself by the reaction of that large audience.

> Now when they heard this, they were cut to the heart, and said to Peter and the rest of the apostles, "Men and brethren, what shall we do?" (v. 37)

Cut to the heart! Literally, *pierced* to the heart. This phrase appears only here in the New Testament. It means to pierce or stab, depicting an action that is both sudden and unexpected. And who was wielding the knife? It was the Holy Spirit.

Stabbed in the heart! Has that ever happened to you?

To be stabbed in the heart, the person stabbing has to be facing you. Looking you in the eyes. We've probably all been stabbed in the back at one time or another. People have said things about us behind our backs, when we weren't around to defend ourselves.

But if someone really loves you and has something hard to say to you, something that isn't easy for you to hear, he or she won't do that behind your back. No, it will be right to your face.

Does it hurt? You bet it hurts! And sometimes the reason it hurts so much is that you know that person is right. They're taking a risk and speaking truth to you that no one else is willing to speak. And something inside you—even though you may have all the natural, defensive reactions—says, "He's right, and I need to face up to it."

Being pierced to the heart by the Holy Spirit is a *good* thing. Don't think of it as a sword that is killing you, think of it as a scalpel in the hand of a surgeon bent on saving your life. Cutting out the cancer. Putting a new heart in the place of the old diseased one. Extending your life.

And so it was in this instance. These Jews from all over the world were pierced by the scalpel of the Holy Spirit, and suddenly realized, "He's right. That's just what we did. We murdered the Messiah. We have sinned. We have blown it. What shall we do?"

#7: Peter's Preached Repentance

And Peter replied, "Each one of you must turn from sin, return to God, and be baptized in the name of Jesus Christ for the forgiveness of your sins; then you also shall receive this gift, the Holy Spirit." (Acts 2:38, TLB)

This is something lacking in many gospel presentations today. We may say to someone, "Just believe in Jesus. Ask Him into your life and everything will change."

Yes, but…what does it mean to believe in Jesus? To believe and repent are like two sides of the same coin. To repent is to let go of something, and to believe is to take hold of something. And when I take of hold of Jesus and believe in Him, I am letting go of my sin and turning my back on my old life.

Some people think they don't have to let go of anything. They say, "Oh, I believe in Jesus"—but they go on breaking God's commandments left and right. They're still living an immoral lifestyle, still doing things they shouldn't be doing. They've never repented! And if you have never repented, you are not converted.

The Bible says, "Repent therefore and be converted, that your sins may be blotted out, so that times of refreshing may come from the presence of the Lord" (Acts 3:19).

My concern is that there are people walking around today who think they are Christians, but may not be Christians at all, because they have never met God's criteria. Instead, they've just brought Jesus into their life like a "helpful additive."

If you want the salvation offered by Christ, you need to repent—change your mind about the direction in which you're headed. Deliberately turn from your sin.

Have you done that?

THREE
Secrets of the Early Church: Part 1

Stella, my little granddaughter, loves secrets.

Even when she's in a bad mood or maybe fussing about something, I can kneel down in front of her and say, "Stella…want to hear a secret?"

She will say, "Yeah!" and eagerly lean over for me to whisper into her little ear.

Now at this point in her life, the secret doesn't have to be particularly profound. She's not all that particular about it. Not long ago, for instance, I gave her the secret, "*Chicken before bread.*"

Maybe I should explain. Stella loves bread, and when we go out to eat, she wants to eat all the bread on the table, just filling up on it. Then of course, when it comes time to eat her main course, she's too full. So my secret to her was "chicken before bread."

She got it.

The next time I said, "Stella, want to know a secret?"

"Yeah," she said, leaning again.

I whispered, "*This happy feeling comes from Jesus.*" And she smiled, because that's a little song we like to sing together.

Stella is not alone in loving secrets. Most of us do. If you're in a restaurant and someone in the booth next to you says to someone else, "Hey, I want to tell you a secret. Make sure you don't share this with anyone else," what do you do? Do you keep listening?

Of course you do. You'll do your best to tune in, without being too obvious about it. Because we all like to hear a secret or two.

In the next two chapters, we will consider some secrets of the early Church.

But it's not as though these truths are hidden. In fact, they're plain as day to anyone reading the Scriptures. But we still might refer to these points as "secrets," because they seem to be unknown—or ignored—by so many people today.

Hypocrites in the Church?

So often in contemporary church circles we hear people say, "We need to re-envision the way that we do church."

No, we don't.

There is no need to recast or redefine what God has already clearly defined in the pages of Scripture. What we need to do is get back to the Church that Jesus Himself set up.

Granted, it's all-too-easy to be critical of the Church these days—and some of that criticism has been well earned. But don't forget this: In the years Jesus Christ walked this earth, He started only one organization, and it is called the Church. And He said, "The gates of hell shall not prevail against it."[10]

Some might dismiss the Church with a wave of the hand and say, "Aw, the Church is full of hypocrites."

But so what? There's certainly nothing new in that comment. *Any* organization made up of human beings will be laced with hypocrites. There are hypocrites in Congress, in the White House, in Buckingham Palace, and in your own city council. That's just the human condition. There were plenty of hypocrites to go around in the First century Church as well. In fact, one of our Lord's handpicked disciples turned out to be a notorious hypocrite. Hypocrisy is nothing new. It's been around since there were two fallen human beings to rub shoulders. (I'm not excusing hypocrisy, just explaining it. I have heard people say

"If I find the hypocrite-free church, I'll join it!"

(Please don't, because you would only spoil it!)

Jesus once told a story we have come to know as the parable of the wheat and tares.[11] In this story He talks about a farmer who plants wheat in his field, and then one night an enemy comes in and sows the seeds of tares or weeds among the wheat. The particular weed Jesus described, also known as darnel seed, is virtually indistinguishable from wheat as both sprout from the soil. In fact, it continues to look just like wheat through most of its growth process. But in the end, along toward harvest, the darnel uproots and destroys the wheat.

Jesus was saying to them, "Do you see how this works? In the kingdom of God here on this earth, you'll find the fake right next to the real. The counterfeit side-by-side with the genuine."

And so it is in the Church today. The tares and the wheat will grow together, and we won't necessarily know who is who and what is what till that final day. But God knows.

I have often said there will be three surprises when we get to heaven. The first surprise will be the people there who we never thought would be there. The second surprise will be the people who won't be there that we thought for sure would be there. And the third surprise? We will be there! But really, that's not true, I fully expect to be in heaven, because I have placed my faith in the Lord Jesus Christ.

So yes, there are certainly hypocrites among us, destructive tares growing alongside the genuine wheat. And only God knows which is which. As the Holy Spirit told the prophet Samuel in the early days of David, "The LORD does not see as man sees; for man looks at the outward appearance, but the LORD looks at the heart."[12]

Each one of us, of course, has our own moments of hypocrisy. (We would be hypocritical to deny it!) So don't worry too much about the hypocrites in the Church, because there's always room for one more. Come on in and join the family!

Jesus was committed to the Church, and we should be, too. There is nothing this world offers that's even close to it. The Church may have many critics but it has no rivals!

When I travel around the world, the special bond between followers of Jesus Christ transcends all others—even the bonds of race and nationality. Yes, I am certainly proud to be an American, and believe the United States of America to be the greatest country on the face of the earth.

But I am a Christian first, and an American second. I will sit down with people from different countries, and though we might see the world a little bit differently and might not agree on every political fine point, we can agree on the fact that Jesus Christ is the Savior of the world, and that He has changed our lives.

The Bible calls us fellow members of the body of Christ, and that's just what we are. We are His Church.

Everyone Doing Their Part

In the book of Acts, we encounter the Church that changed the world. The Church that turned the world upside down. What was their secret?

It is the simple fact that every Christian believed they were called to do his or her part. Every person mattered.

A Spartan king once boasted to a visiting monarch about the superb, impenetrable walls of Sparta. The visiting king, however, was somewhat confused by these claims; as he looked around, he could see no city walls at all. "Where are these walls you speak of?" he asked.

For a reply, the Spartan king gestured around him at his bodyguard of magnificent troops. "Just look around you," he said. "Here are the walls of Sparta. Every man is a brick."

In the same way, in the Church every man and every woman is a brick—or as the Bible terms it, *a living stone.*[13] It's easy for someone to stand on the sidelines and be critical of the Church—pointing out all the areas where it's falling short. But God never called us to stand on the sidelines. He called us to be involved in His Church, fighting the battles, standing toe to toe with enemies in the arena. Perhaps those who are so critical would have a different perspective if they were a living part of the living church.

President Theodore Roosevelt made this statement: "It is not the critic who counts. Not the man who points out how the strong man stumbles or where the doer of deeds could have done them better. The credit belongs to the man who is actually in the arena, whose face is marred by dust and sweat and blood who strives valiantly who errs and comes up again and again, because there is no effort without error and shortcomings."

So yes, we in the Church have our shortcomings. But we are in the arena, attempting to do the work of God in a Christ-rejecting world.

Over in Ephesians 4:15 we read that we should hold to the truth in love, because the whole body is perfectly fitted together as each part does its special work. Each part helps the other parts grow, so that the whole body is healthy and growing and full of love.

We are living in a time, however, when people are saying, "We need to reinvent the Church."

Again I say, *No we don't*. I agree that we need to be relevant to the culture we're living in, adapting to changing styles or design or music or peripheral things. We want to make sense to the people we're seeking to speak to. But our core beliefs and our mission must not change one iota. At Harvest Christian Fellowship, where I pastor, we're essentially still doing today what we were doing thirty-five years ago, and by God's grace, we *will* be doing thirty years from today if the Lord doesn't return for us first. Styles change, terms change, approaches change, and music changes, but undergirding all that, we hold to core principles that must never change.

There is no better place to find such core principles than in the pages of Scripture. For here in Acts chapter 2 are the secrets of the effective and successful or—better yet—the *biblical* church.

Is Bigger Better?

The Church described in Acts chapter 2 was a very large church. Today we might call it a megachurch.

We usually think of successful as "big," don't we? Especially here in America. That's been our philosophy: Make it bigger and it will be better.

I love the way that mentality affected our car design back in the 50s. Many feel that the golden era of car design was between 1955 and 1957. (I would have to agree with that). Detroit built some really cool cars in those years, and everything kept getting bigger. (Especially the fins on the Cadillacs!) Now you see some of those cars on the road and they look like the Millennium Falcon!

When people from other countries come to visit, that is often their impression of America: That everything is bigger here—and especially our food portions. In many countries where I have traveled overseas, the portion sizes served in restaurants seem uniform—and uniformly small! Then you go to some of the more popular restaurants here in Southern California, and one entrée could feed a whole family!

And if it's not big enough, you can always "super-size" it.

So it's not surprising that we would take some of that bigger-is-better mentality and apply it to the Church, assuming that the larger a church is, the more successful it is.

But that's not necessarily true. You can have a big church, and yet not have a *strong* one. The fact is, there are many things you can do to draw a crowd. You could go out and start a fight and draw a crowd! So it's not about just being big, it's about being *strong*. And it is about being biblical.

On the other hand, some people are automatically critical of a church just because it happens to be well attended. You'll hear people say, "I hate these megachurches. You drive in there and you have to wait for parking! They have parking lot attendants! Can you imagine that?

Let's think about that for a moment.

It would be like someone saying, "There are two restaurants I can choose between. One restaurant has a line around the block, and the other never has anybody in it, except the people that work there. Where do you think we should go eat?"

Can you hear someone replying like this? "Well, let's go to the place with no line, because we won't have to wait." Probably not! Did you ever stop and think that there might be a *reason* there is no line? Maybe the food in the other place is better than the place with no people inside of it.

So sometimes a large church is that way because a large number of people are finding their souls fed, love the worship, and love the fellowship they find there.

Even so, it's never been my objective to have a large church. But it has always been my desire to pastor a biblical church and a strong church. As to the size, we've always felt that we should just leave the growth up to God. There is no virtue in being small in and of itself.

Not every church is going to be a large church, but every church should be a *growing* church. And the fact is, if you don't have new people coming into your church, it will begin to stagnate. In the book of Acts, we read that "the Lord added to the Church daily those who were being saved" (2:40).

That First century church recorded daily growth, as a constant flow of new converts were coming in. New converts are the lifeblood of the Church! And if a church doesn't have *that* kind of growth, I have to say to you right now that there's something wrong with it.

So why is the Church here? To just be big? No. The objective of the Church is to be as *faithful* as we can be to what God has called us to be. Because on that final day, Jesus is *not* going to say, "Well done good and *successful* servant. Oh, and by the way, how many numbers were you running on Sunday mornings?"

So what is the purpose of the Church? I believe the Church exists for three reasons. The exaltation of God, the edification of believers, and the evangelization of the world. Or to put it another way, our directions are to be upward, inward, and outward.

Reason #1: Upward: To Exalt God

The Church of Jesus Christ exists to honor and glorify God. That is why we at our church we give great place to singing, praise, prayer, and worship. The New Testament tells us that "we, who were the first to hope in Christ, might be for the praise of his glory."[14] We are here to praise our glorious God.

This idea may come as a revelation to some people. Why? Because they actually think their purpose on earth is to find personal happiness.

"Isn't that why I exist?"

No, that is not why you exist. And if you chase after personal happiness, you will never really find it.

"Wait a minute. What about finding that right person, getting married, and raising a family? Isn't that what I live for?"

Marriage and family are both very good—priceless blessings from the Lord Himself. But even as wonderful as they are, these are not the primary reasons why you draw breath. You have been put on earth to honor and glorify and praise God.

A poll was taken among young people recently where they were asked what their primary goal in life was. The number one response was "to be rich and famous."

For a few people, that may happen. (And then after it happens, they really don't like it very much.) But that's not why you're here. That's not why you open your eyes each morning to a new day. You are here to glorify and exalt and honor God. That is why every one of us has been placed on this earth: To bring glory to the God who made us. Jesus said, "By this My Father is glorified, that you bear much fruit."[15] In his first letter to the Corinthians, the apostle Paul tells us, "You do not belong to yourself, for God bought you with a high price. So you must honor God with your body" (1 Corinthians 6:19-20, NLT).

I spoke with a man the other day who had just gone through major, life-threatening surgery. Coming through that experience has caused him to reevaluate his life. He has a good career in sales, but he said to me, "You know, I'm beginning to wonder if this what I should be doing with my life."

Knowing that God graciously spared his life and kept him on earth for a reason has prompted this man to think deeply about why he is here, and what his life is supposed to mean.

I told him, "God put you here to glorify Him. That is why you exist." He was already beginning to realize that life was more about significance than success.

Significance. What am I doing with my life? What impact is my life making on others? Sometimes people will go through a near-death experience like that and think, "Maybe I need to quit my job and go out on the mission field or be in full time ministry."

That may indeed be what the Lord is saying to you. Then again, maybe He would have you stay exactly right where you are and honor Him there. Wherever you are, whatever you are doing, make sure you can glorify God while you are doing it.

> And whatever you do [no matter what it is] in word or deed, do everything in the name of the Lord Jesus and in [dependence upon] His Person, giving praise to God the Father through Him. (Colossians 3:17, AMPLIFIED)

Reason #2: To Edify Believers

The apostle Paul said his goal was not merely to evangelize but, according to Colossians 1:28, "Warning everyone and teaching everyone with all the wisdom God has given us. We want to present them to God, perfect in their relationship to Christ. That's why I work and struggle so hard, depending on Christ's mighty power that works within me" (NLT).

That is why we are here as the Church of Jesus Christ.

We don't exist to just pop into church on Sunday morning, sing a few songs, hear a (hopefully) quick message, and then go on our merry way. We are here as the Church to exalt and worship the Lord, to be taught and equipped, and to equip one another. Yes, we want people to come forward and receive Christ. But we also want those people to go forward and follow Christ for the rest of their lives.

The Great Commission begins with the Lord's command to go into all the world and preach the gospel. Then Jesus continues on and says, "…Teaching them to observe all things that I have commanded you."[16]

So His commission involves both an element of proclamation *and* the element of teaching and discipleship. We are here to build up one another.

Reason #3: To Evangelize the World

This is the natural outgrowth of the first two reasons. If we are glorifying God and building up one another, we will naturally want to share the hope of salvation with others through our loving actions and words. As Pastor Chuck Smith has often said, "Healthy sheep will reproduce themselves."

It is essential that we keep these three principles in their proper balance. The Church is not to emphasize one of these things at the expense of the other or take them out of their order. For instance, you might have one church that says, "We're called to evangelize. We don't care about teaching Christians or making well-fed believers even fatter."

I heard it said once by a pastor "We are not called to be keepers of the aquarium but fishers of men!"

Well, that is a clever saying, but no, that is not your *whole* mission. The purpose of the Church is to glorify God, to build up believers, *and* to preach the gospel.

Another church will say, "We're not called to evangelism. We are called to in-depth Bible study. We are called to study deeply and learn more."

Yes, that is part of your calling. You are truly called to Bible study. But you are also called to edify one another and evangelize the world. You see, it's not part of our calling to *customize* the Church. Our objective is to follow the original template in the book of Acts, and ask ourselves, "How can we get as close to *that* church as possible?" That is our objective. Why? Because *that* is the Church that changed the world. *That* is the Church that turned the world upside down.

First Steps of the Baby Church

Gathered together in an upper room, the believers waited together for that which Jesus had promised just before He ascended into heaven.

> "Behold, I send the Promise of My Father upon you; but tarry in the city of Jerusalem until you are endued with power from on high." (Luke 24:49)

They knew the Holy Spirit would come, but they had no idea what to expect or what to look for. When the Spirit suddenly arrived, no one had to wonder whether He had come or not! His entrance was dramatic: A mighty, rushing wind; divided tongues of fire resting above each head; and an outpouring of languages they had never learned before, declaring the wonderful works of God.

Stunned by all of this, a huge crowd formed. Looking at each other in sheer amazement, they were saying, "What in the world does all this mean?" That's when Simon Peter, who once cowered before a stranger when asked if was one of Jesus' disciples stood up and gave a very bold and brilliant presentation of the gospel, resulting in the salvation of 3,000 people.

And what did they do *then*? Let's read about it.

> And they continued steadfastly in the apostles' doctrine and fellowship, in the breaking of bread, and in prayers. Then fear came upon every soul, and many wonders and signs were done through the apostles. Now all who believed were together, and had all things in common, and sold their possessions and goods, and divided them among all, as anyone had need.

> So continuing daily with one accord in the temple, and breaking bread from house to house, they ate their food with gladness and simplicity of heart, praising God and having favor with all the people. And the Lord added to the church daily those who were being saved. (Acts 2:42-47)

The Church that turned the world upside down was alive, healthy, and vibrant.

And here's why….

They Were a Learning Church

They continued steadfastly in the apostles' doctrine…. (Acts 2:42)

This is a consistent trend we see throughout the book of Acts: the Spirit of God working through the Word of God in the hearts of the people of God.

Were these believers filled with the Holy Spirit? You'd better believe it! They had experienced the Day of Pentecost together. So what is the sign of a Spirit-filled church? Check out the very first thing that Dr. Luke brings to our attention: *They were studying the Word of God.*

When you think about it, it could have been a real temptation for these believers to say, "Wow! What an experience we had on the day of Pentecost! The wind! The fire! Speaking in tongues! Lord, give us more supernatural phenomena. Let us experience that all over again!"

But that's not what we read. Instead, we find them just reveling in the Word of God. And what is true of a church is also true of individuals, because the Church is made up of people. If you are really Spirit-filled, you will love the Word of God. If you have no interest in the Bible, if you find Scripture boring and uninteresting and don't really care about reading and studying it, I have to wonder if you've been filled with the Holy Spirit at all—or if you even know the Lord Jesus as your Savior.

It's a trend in many contemporary churches today to disregard the study of Scripture—to no longer have Bible study as the centerpiece of a service. For some groups—including the so-called emergent church—you might say that questions are the new answers. They will say, "Let's not have a sermon. Let's instead have a discussion, a dialogue. We're on a journey together, and isn't it rather arrogant for anyone to say that he or she actually understands what the Bible teaches? No, let's instead discuss our doubts together as we travel through life together. We can talk about the latest books and movies and our own spiritual journey. Better still, we can sit around and criticize the evangelical church! In fact, let's not even go to church on Sunday. Let's just go down to the local coffee place, order some espresso, and talk about the ups and downs of our spiritual journeys."

Those First century believers loved to assemble, loved to worship, and loved to study the Word of God.

Another trend in the Church today is to simply marginalize Scripture. The Bible is there, yes, but it's off to one side, half out of sight. You attend a service, and there's a lot going on…songs, drama, film clips, testimonies, maybe even a dance or two. There might be a brief sermon, usually topical in nature, with very little Scripture involved. Instead of a meaty message from God's Word, we have a "sermonette." (The only problem with this is that "sermonettes" often produce "Christianettes.")

That not the template of the book of Acts church. They valued preaching and the apostles' doctrine.

Acts chapter 20 gives us a revealing instance of this that took place in the city of Troas, where Paul had come to preach one evening.

> On Sunday we gathered for a Communion service, with Paul preaching. And since he was leaving the next day, he talked until midnight! The upstairs room where we met was lighted with many flickering lamps; and as Paul spoke on and on, a young man named Eutychus, sitting on the windowsill, went fast asleep and fell three stories to his death below. (Acts 20:7-9, TLB)

Paul rushed out with the rest of the crowd, prayed for this young man, and raised him up from the dead. Now you'd think that after a traumatic incident like that the preacher might have called it a night and sent everyone home. Not Paul! The Bible says, "They all went back upstairs and ate the Lord's Supper together; then Paul preached another long sermon—so it was dawn when he finally left them!" (v. 10, TLB).

The Word of God was their focus, and they loved it.

Something wonderful happens when believers study the Bible together. It's great to study it individually, and we need to do that daily. But when we all come together for Bible study and we turn together to a passage in our Bibles, reading the words and making discoveries together, that is a special thing.

God has ordained preaching as a primary function of the Church. In some of the last words Paul would ever write, he told his young disciple Timothy, "Preach the word of God. Be prepared, whether the time is favorable or not. Patiently correct, rebuke, and encourage your people with good teaching. For a time is coming when people will no longer listen to sound and wholesome teaching. They will follow their own desires and will look for teachers who will tell them whatever their itching ears want to hear. They will reject the truth and chase after myths" (2 Timothy 4:2-4, NLT).

I like that phrase "itching ears." Another way to say it might be, "An itch for novelty." That certainly sounds a lot like today, doesn't it? "*Hey, what's new? What's cool? What's different?*"

We need to get back to reading, study, teaching, and preaching of the Word of God. And what is preaching? Martin Lloyd Jones defined it as "logic on fire." I like that. We've all encountered sermons that were all logic and no fire—the kind that will put you to sleep.

The teaching may be sound, solid, and theologically correct, but it's also B-O-R-I-N-G. Then you have other sermons that are all fire and no logic. The message gets you excited, but afterwards, when someone asks you, "What was the sermon about?", you really have no idea!

We need passion and content, logic and fire. The world certainly needs to hear it. Why? Because preaching is God's primary way of reaching lost people. Don't ask me why. It was God's choice. We're told in 1 Corinthians 1:21: "For since, in the wisdom of God, the world through wisdom did not know God, it pleased God through the foolishness of the message preached to save those who believe."

According to some leaders of the "emergent church," we shouldn't even be using the term "Word of God." One such leader recently stated: "To say Scripture is the Word of God is to employ a metaphor. God cannot be thought of as literally speaking words, since they are an entirely human phenomenon, that could never prove adequate as a medium for the speech of an infinite God."

Yet the Bible itself says God chose the medium of preaching the Word to reach and save lost men and women. We are to declare a known God to a world that does not know Him. *God can be known.* That should be the message of His Church today.

Paul wrote: "I want to know Christ and experience the mighty power that raised him from the dead" (Philippians 3:10, NLT). Don't tell me God is a mystery and can't be known. God can be known. God should be known. God *must* be known. And it will happen as His Word is proclaimed with passion and authority.

That's not to say that each of us doesn't wrestle with our personal struggles and doubts from time to time. But it's not our job to indulge and wallow in our doubts with a lost world on their way to hell. Our job is to point them in the right direction. To point them to Christ.

Paul didn't get up at Mars Hill in front of the Athenian intellectuals, and say to them, "I see you worship an unknown god. So do I! We're all on a journey together. So pour me an espresso, and let's talk about it!" No. Paul said, "I see you worship an unknown God, and this is the God I want to proclaim Him to you. You can know Him just as I do!" (See Acts 17:22-32.)

Martin Lloyd Jones said it this way: "Come to the Word of God. Stop asking questions. Start with the promises in their right order. Say, 'I want the truth, whatever it costs me,' and bind yourself to it. We are not meant to be left in a state of doubt and misgiving, of uncertainty and unhappiness."

Steadfast

While it is true that we need preaching and teaching that has been anointed by the Spirit of God, we also need anointed listening!

Acts 2:42 says that the people "*continued steadfastly* in the apostles' doctrine."

Those are two important words, speaking of both *attention* and *intention*. They had a hunger and a desire for the Word of God, and an openness to receive it.

In later years, perhaps the apostle Peter was remembering that hunger for the Word of God in the book of Acts church, when he wrote: "Like newborn infants, long for the pure spiritual milk, that by it you may grow up into salvation" (1 Peter 2:2, ESV). Peter is saying, "Just like a little baby craves his mother's milk, so you should crave and desire the Word of God." Healthy believers are hungry believers.

We should come to the Word of God with a desire to not only hear its truths, but to apply them to our lives. Get yourself a notebook, and jot down the thoughts that God brings to your heart as you read. Then review them again later in the day, or maybe at night before bedtime.

Come to the Bible with a wide-open heart, saying, "Holy Spirit, what do You want to say to me today?"

If you want to be a strong Christian you need to be someone who loves the Word of God.

FOUR
Secrets of the Early Church: Part 2

The Church portrayed in the pages of the book of Acts was strong, vibrant, and healthy.

That is our model, and I'm so glad that it is.

Why? Because I don't much like dead churches or dead services or dead preachers. And we have far too many of all three out there today, where people sit in pews like expressionless mannequins—or preachers get up and somehow manage to take the dynamic, life-changing, power-packed message of the Word of God and make it as dull as watching hubcaps rust.

I heard a story about a pastor that spoke to his congregation one Sunday, and really had to wonder how the message went over, because he had so little feedback. Standing in his traditional place at the back of the auditorium after the service was over, he smiled and shook hands with people, waiting for someone to say something.

People were polite and smiled, but no one said a word about the message.

Finally, he found himself shaking hands with a lady who could usually be counted on to say something thoughtful. So he said to her, "Tell me, Martha, what did you think of my sermon today? How was it?"

"Oh pastor," she said, "your sermon reminded me of the peace and love of God."

He was pretty relieved to hear that. "Wow," he said, "I've never had anyone actually say that to me before. Tell me, how did my message remind of you of the peace and love of God?"

She said, "Well, like the peace of God, it passed all understanding, and like the love of God, it endured forever!"

Sometimes you're better off just receiving the compliment, and not asking for specifics!

The book of Acts church, however, had passion and excitement to spare, blended with a strong commitment to love and serve one another. Acts 2:42 tells us that "They continued steadfastly in the apostles' doctrine, in fellowship, the breaking of bread, and prayers."

I like that word *steadfastly*. These men and women were living in a first-love relationship with Jesus Christ, and their hearts burned with love for Him. This was no casual attitude, like you might find at a social club, sales meeting, or political rally—it was a spiritual excitement that went right to the core. As a result, they diligently applied themselves to what was taught from the Word of God.

As we noted in the previous chapter, they were a *learning church*, a group of people who believed in the teaching and preaching of the Bible. That's the way it is with genuine believers who have been filled by the Spirit of God: They will love the Word of God. As John Stott said, "The Spirit of God leads the people of God to submit to the Word of God."

But beyond being a well-instructed church, they were deeply committed to one another as well.

They Were a Loving Church

Verse 42 says they continued steadfastly in fellowship.

What does this word "fellowship" mean? It's a word Christians like to throw around a lot.

"We'll meet in the fellowship hall."

"Let's have some fellowship."

"Come for food, fun, and fellowship."

But what does that really mean? What is fellowship, anyway?

It comes from the Greek word *koinonia*, and that's the term used here. They continued in *koinonia*.

In fact, it's not the easiest term in the world to translate. It could be translated "fellowship" or "partnership" or "communion." It is also carries the sense of being *generous*.

Koinonia is far more than socializing, for more than cookies and coffee. Anyone can socialize. People can get together and rally around their passions, be it sports or cars, quilting or kung fu. This is different altogether. This is where people get together to talk about their shared life in Christ. And how the Lord loves that!

Have you ever been in a room and heard your name mentioned in some conversation by someone who didn't know you were there? Have you ever noticed how your ears perk up? "What? Did someone just say my name?" Or maybe you've been someplace and you heard a conversation going on, and heard the name of Jesus Christ mentioned. And you're immediately interested to know what they are saying about your Lord.

Listen to what God said in the Old Testament about a small group of believers who met together to seek the Lord and talk about Him during a time of national cynicism and decay:

> Then those who feared the LORD spoke to one another,
> And the LORD listened and heard them;
> So a book of remembrance was written before Him
> For those who fear the LORD
> And who meditate on His name.
>
> "They shall be Mine," says the LORD of hosts,
> "On the day that I make them My jewels."
> (Malachi 3:16-17)

The text says that "*the LORD listened and heard them*." That phrase could be translated "to prick the ear, to bend down, so as not to miss a single word."

When we say the name Jesus, He listens.

Sometimes I will hear people use His name as profanity, and I will say, "Be careful. He listens when you say His name."

People may think you're crazy when you tell them that, but it's completely true. God listens with special attention when someone speaks His name. The Bible says, that "Whoever will call upon the name of the Lord will be saved." Why? Because He is paying attention.

When those who love Him, then, call His name, when His own sons and daughters speak His name in honor and love, having fellowship around His name, He loves that. It isn't just socializing; it's in a whole different category than that. It's *koinonia*.

At two and a half years, my little granddaughter Stella calls me "Papa," because she can't say "Grandpa." And I'll tell you this, whenever I hear "Papa," I'm all ears. I pay complete attention to her. Am I busy? Sure I'm busy. But I make time for her. Papa always has time for Stella.

And so it is with the Lord. "Busy" as He might be running the universe and answering the prayers of billions, He makes time for you. He listens when you speak His name.

In Numbers chapter 6, God gave the priests a blessing to pronounce upon God's people. It's a beautiful piece of Hebrew poetry, and most of us have probably heard it at one time or another.

"The LORD bless you and keep you;
The LORD make His face shine upon you,
And be gracious to you;
The LORD lift up His countenance upon you,
And give you peace."
(Numbers 6:24-26)

Notice the phrase, "*The LORD lift up His countenance upon you.*" What does that mean? It means to lift up one's face, or literally, to look, to see, to be interested, to have one's full attention. God is saying, "I am watching you. I am looking at you. I am listening to you, and I like it. I love it when you sing My praises, when you speak of My name, when you gather together for fellowship."

Fellowship is praying together…serving together…sometimes weeping together…aging together. These are the strong fibers of fellowship. And fellowship with God and with His people go hand in hand. The apostle John tells us: "We proclaim to you what we ourselves have actually seen and heard so that you may have fellowship with us. And our fellowship is with the Father and with his Son, Jesus Christ. We are writing these things so that you may fully share our joy" (1 John 1:3-4, NLT).

In other words, as I get to know God through His Word, I will long for fellowship with other believers. That's just the way it works in the kingdom of God: the stronger your vertical fellowship, the stronger your horizontal fellowship will be. And conversely, if you find yourself out of fellowship with God, you will soon find yourself out of fellowship with other believers as well.

If your motive, when you step through the doors of a church, is to be critical and find things that are wrong and out of balance (as you see it), then you'll probably find exactly what you're looking for. The Church of Jesus Christ is comprised of imperfect people, led by imperfect leaders, who imperfectly seek to love and serve God and follow His Word.

If that's what you're looking for, that's what you'll find. Imperfection everywhere!

It's a funny thing: Sometimes the people who are most critical of sin in the lives of others struggle with those same sins themselves. A person with covered sin in his own life will always try to uncover sin in others' lives. Sometimes the reason you are so quick to find fault in others is because you see so much of it in the mirror! Maybe we shouldn't be so picky, judgmental, and critical, and put on a little humility instead as we come to fellowship with God's people.

Peter said it like this: "All of you serve each other with humble spirits, for God gives special blessings to those who are humble, but sets himself against those who are proud."[17]

Caring for one another in practical ways is another part of true *koinonia*. The book of James says: "Suppose you see a brother or sister who has no food or clothing, and you say, 'Good-bye and have a good day; stay warm and eat well'—but then you don't give that person any food or clothing. What good does that do?" (James 2:15-17, NLT).

These believers in the early Church shared their resources.

> And all the believers met together in one place and shared everything they had. They sold their property and possessions and shared the money with those in need. (Acts 2:44-45, NLT)

Let's not misunderstand this verse. The Bible isn't advocating communism or socialism here, because this sharing was strictly *voluntary*. It's simply saying that the believers who had the resources were willingly helping those who did not. Not everyone participated in this. Not everyone sold homes or possessions. The verb forms in verses 45-46 indicate that the selling and giving were occasional, in response to particular needs, not something once-and-for-all. Be that as it may, these people loved and cared for each other in a way that caught the attention of the watching world, and we should do the same.

They Were a Worshiping Church

> So continuing daily with one accord in the temple, and breaking bread from house to house, they ate their food with gladness and simplicity of heart, praising God and having favor with all the people. (Acts 2:46-47)

This phrase "gladness and simplicity of heart" simply means that these believers worshiped God and met together with open and unaffected joy. But it was a joy mixed with awe and reverence, as we read in verse 43:

> Then fear came upon every soul, and many wonders and signs were done through the apostles.

Fear and joy. Both are important elements of worship. The Spirit-filled church will be a worshipping church, and the Spirit-filled

Christian will be a worshipping Christian. Something very unique happens when believers come together with one heart and one desire in corporate worship. Yes, of course God loves it when you sing to Him in the shower, when you lift a chorus of praise to Him while you're walking on the beach, or when you're having your own private devotional times. That's all part of the "sacrifice of praise" that Hebrews 13:15 speaks of, and God is honored when you do that. But God manifests His presence in a wonderful way when His people approach Him to honor His name *together*. Jesus said, "For where two or three are gathered together in My name, I am there in the midst of them."[18]

The Bible also says that—in some mysterious way beyond our full understanding—the Lord actually inhabits the praises of His people.[19] Our God, of course, is *omnipresent*, which means that He is everywhere at all times. But on the other hand, when you gather together with other believers and lift up His name in praise, God blesses that action with a special sense of His presence, and even His glory.

There is nothing in the world like worship.

You and I were truly created to worship the Lord and glorify Him. And when we do, we discover a sense of fulfillment that's like nothing else in life.

The Christian faith is a singing faith—and that's not necessarily true of other religions. Yes, they may chant. They may recite their petitions. They may have their various forms of music. But there is no faith that is as full of vibrant, joyful singing like Christianity. We have the best and most joyous songs of any religion on earth. And the Lord keeps giving us more and more of them! Why? Because we have more to sing about than anyone else!

So start singing, my friend. And find someone to sing with you. The fact is, you'll be getting a head start on heaven. In the book of Revelation, the apostle John gives this eyewitness account:

"I saw in heaven…what looked like a sea of glass mixed with fire and, standing beside the sea, those who had been victorious over the beast and his image and over the number of his name. They held harps given them by God and sang the song of Moses the servant of God and the song of the Lamb" (Revelation 15:1-3, NIV).

For sure, we're going to be learning some great new songs, probably playing instruments we've never played, and singing with all our hearts when we reach our eternal Home. So we may as well get started now!

"Well," you say. "I don't know about that. I really don't have a very good voice."

There's nowhere in the Bible that says you could or should have a professional quality set of pipes when you praise God. The truth is, you are God's own child, He made you exactly the way you are, and He loves to hear you make a joyful noise unto Him.

"But sometimes," you say, "I just don't feel like worshiping."

I understand that. There are certainly times when we're not in the mood to sing or express our hearts in thanks and praise. But let me ask you this: Do you think those first century believers always *felt* like praising God? They were harassed. They were beaten. They were threatened. They were mocked, mimicked, and minimized. And that was all before breakfast! But they worshipped the Lord nonetheless.

Earlier I mentioned Hebrews 13:15. The passage urges us with these words: "Through Jesus, therefore, let us continually offer to God a sacrifice of praise—the fruit of lips that confess his name."[20]

Yes, praise and worship can sometimes be a sacrifice, because we don't feel like engaging in it. Our flesh resists it, it doesn't seem convenient. Or perhaps we feel a bit down and depressed, and things aren't going well for us. Maybe we've experienced a real tragedy in your life, and just don't want to thank God.

Worship is not about you, it's about God. It's not about how you feel in any given moment, it's about the worthiness of the One we honor.

Do you think Job felt like praising God when he lost everything in a matter of moments? He lost his family…his home…his possessions…his health. But what does the Bible say about how this stunned, grieving man responded? Did he complain? Did he curse God? No, here's what the record tell us:

> Then Job arose, tore his robe, and shaved his head; and he fell to the ground and worshiped. And he said:
>
> "Naked I came from my mother's womb,
> And naked shall I return there.
> The Lord gave, and the LORD has taken away;
> Blessed be the name of the LORD."
> (Job 1:29)

Uttering those words wasn't easy for Job. It *cost* him something, and it was a sacrifice that pleased the Lord. And notice that the Hebrews passage says we should offer the sacrifice of praise giving thanks with our lips. In other words, this is something we need to verbalize—just as a wife needs to hear her husband say, "I love you," or a husband needs to hear that he is loved and valued by his wife.

We need to verbalize our love one to another, and in the same way, we need to speak forth our love for God our Father, and Jesus our Lord.

I'm not saying God *needs* praise from us, because He doesn't need anything. If He needed anything, He would no longer be God. But He *wants* our praise, He delights in our heartfelt expressions of thanks, and He tells us specifically to verbalize those expressions. When you're in church with God's people, then, lift your voice and really sing out loud—to Him and for Him. Don't worry about what the people around you are doing or thinking. In those moments, you truly have an audience of One…God Himself.

The Bible doesn't say to give thanks to the Lord because you feel good or because you're experiencing some kind of emotional high. The Word of God tells us to "Give thanks to the LORD, for *He is good*! For His mercy endures forever" (Psalm 107:1).

Your worship is also a witness to others. Did you know that?

Acts 2:47 says of these First century believers that they were "praising God and having favor with all the people. And the Lord added to the church daily those who were being saved."

There is a direct connection between worship and witness. We *are* being watched by the outside world. And when a Christian can praise God through his or her tears, when a believer can hold high the name of the Lord even in a time of hardship or tragedy, it is a powerful testimony to those who observe.

Sometimes that "outside world" comes into our church building and sits beside us in a chair or pew. And that person (whether you're aware of it or not) takes note what kind of worshiper you are.

"Well," you say, "does that really matter?"

Actually, it does.

It could be that they've never been to church before, and this may be the first time they've worked up the nerve to walk through the door and check things out. And that person—though you would never know that he or she is paying attention to you at all—notices how you're chatting with a friend or texting someone when others are worshiping the Lord. Someone looking on can tell if you are really engaged, if this is actually something that means something more to you than an empty habit or ritual.

So what do they conclude by observing you? Maybe that worship isn't very important to you at it all—that it's just another way of playing at church, but doesn't really touch your heart and soul.

This is an important point to me, because I came to faith because of worshipping Christians. No one invited me to their meeting. No one broke the gospel down to me and said, "Here's how to come to Jesus Christ." But I saw a group of Christians sitting on the front lawn of my high school campus singing songs to Jesus, and I stood there watching them for a while. I wanted to walk away, but something (or Someone) wouldn't let me go.

I thought to myself, *Something's different here. These kids mean what they're singing here. They have something I don't have.* Somehow, that created an opening in my heart to hear the message that followed.

There is a connection between our worship and our witnessing. By simply having our heart in the right place with God as we worship, others will be drawn to the Lord.

They Were an Evangelistic Church

"...And the Lord added to the church daily those who were being saved." (Acts 2:47)

What an attractive band of people this was to a lost and watching world! Truly, this was something new; here were people who did everything together—learning, loving, caring, worshiping, praying, and helping each other out in a thousand practical ways. They looked out for each other, and as those around them watched and paid attention, people came to faith.

Witnessing isn't just something we say or do or practice. It is something we *are*. Acts 1:8 says, "But when the Holy Spirit has come upon you, you will receive power to testify about me with great effect…" (TLB).

Evangelism for the early Church wasn't some occasional, sporadic thing; it was happening all the time. Acts 2:47 says that people were coming to the Lord *daily*.

That's the way it ought to be for every church. Every week we should be giving people an opportunity to respond to the gospel message, and come to Christ. Show me a church that doesn't have a constant flow of new believers coming into it and I will show you a church that is stagnating. The Church needs new believers to remind us of what our life here on earth is all about. And new believers need the Church to stabilize them, love them, teach them, and be there for them in times of need.

We enjoy taking our grandchildren to Disneyland just as we enjoyed taking our sons. It is so fun to enter the Magic Kingdom with a little one. I think they should just make a rule that you can't go to

Disneyland without having a child along! When you enter Disneyland as an adult in the company of other adults, it's a completely different experience. You can even talk yourself into being miserable.

As adults we start whining right away about how hot it is, how long the lines are, how much the food costs, and on and on. But when you go with a child, you get to see it all through their eyes, and some of that wonder and fun and delight comes back. You begin to remember what it felt like before you became bored and cynical and ho-hum about life.

It's the same when you're around a young believer, and watching them encounter so many wonderful truths and experiences for the first time—things you might have perhaps been taking for granted for years.

The early Church had new believers constantly coming in. And we need that. At Harvest Christian Fellowship, I make no apology for the fact while we emphasize Bible exposition, discipleship, prayer, worship, and helping the needy, we will never get away preaching the gospel, and inviting people to come to Christ.

Outreach was a vital part of the early Church's DNA, and we move away from that strong biblical priority at our spiritual peril.

Potlucks and Communion

They worshiped together at the Temple each day, met in homes for the Lord's Supper, and shared their meals with great joy and generosity…..
(Acts 2:46, NLT)

When the believers in Jerusalem parted company on Sunday, they didn't say, "See you next Sunday."

What they shared together wasn't just a Sunday-morning-go-to-meeting kind of Christianity. It was their very lives, and they met all the time. Something was always going on. They had home Bible studies. They had meals together. In fact, they "*shared their meals with great joy and generosity….*"

In other words, they ate together often with plenty for all, and there was lots of laughter.

I love that. I love that the Bible's template for the Church included *eating*. At some point, they began to be called "love feasts." Like a modern potluck—or, in some parts of the country, a "covered dish supper"—people would bring food to eat and food to share. For some who were impoverished, this might be the one good meal you would get in a day.

So the believers would gather in different homes, break bread together, have some laughter and fun, maybe do a little singing, and talk about the things of God with one another. Then, before everyone went home, they would often end with communion, or "the Lord's supper," where they would receive the broken bread and the cup, and remember their Lord's broken body and shed blood.

Why do we have communion? Why does the Church celebrate the Lord's Supper?

Bottom line…so that we will remember Jesus.

Why do we need to do that?

Because we so easily forget.

"Well," you say, "I would never forget Jesus."

Perhaps not, in the broad sense. But there is something specific that He wants us to always bear in mind. He wants us to remember His suffering, His death, and His resurrection.

Sometimes after we have been a believer for a period of time, we might forget about how we came to receive our salvation. We might forget our roots.

Perhaps you can't imagine such a thing happening. You love the Lord, you've memorized Bible verses, you're serving in your church, and you're even leading others into the faith. That is all as it should be. But just remember there was a day when you realized you were a poor, helpless sinner, and an offense to a righteous, holy God. But you heard that Jesus Christ the Son of God died on the cross and shed His blood for you, and you turned from your sin and put your faith in Him, and you were forgiven.

So it is that Jesus, who knows us so much better than we know ourselves, says, "I want to give you something that will jog your memory. I want to place something into your life that will remind you again and again of how you came to be where you are. I want you to remember Me with broken bread, and with the fruit of the vine. Broken bread because My body was broken for you. The fruit of the vine because My blood was shed for you."

The Lord's supper is a very brief time in our busy lives when we can completely focus on these precious things that literally transformed our lives, changing our eternal destinations from hell to heaven.

Use those times carefully. Don't let other thoughts crowd these truths out. Think about Jesus, and what He has done for you. Revisit His cross, in your imagination again. Remember the suffering, the sacrifice. Remember the nails in His hands and His feet.

Reread the four gospel accounts, and as much as you can, imagine yourself standing at the foot of that crude Roman cross, with our beaten, bloodied Lord hanging there in front of you.

Remember what He did.

Remember that He did it for you.

In the original language of the New Testament, however, it's more than just remembering. It is remembering with affection, remembering with love. So Jesus is saying, "Come with an affectionate remembrance of Me."

Sometimes we make communion just a little too somber, a little too much like a funeral. Yes, there is certainly a place for feeling sorrow over what Jesus endured for us, and for some serious introspection. In 1 Corinthians 11, Paul cautions us with the reminder that "a man ought to examine himself before he eats of the bread and drinks of the cup. For anyone who eats and drinks without recognizing the body of the Lord eats and drinks judgment on himself."[21]

So we never want to approach the Lord's Supper in a careless, flippant, or cavalier way.

But on the other hand…this is a time for affection and even joy.

For as much as He had to suffer for us—enduring things beyond what we can begin to imagine in our finite minds—this was something Jesus *wanted* to do for us, because of His great love for us. Hebrews 12:2 tells us that it was "for the joy that was set before Him" that Jesus "endured the cross, despising the shame, and has sat down at the right hand of the throne of God."

Isaiah 53, an Old Testament passage that looks forward through the centuries at the suffering of Christ, declares, "And when he sees all that is accomplished by the anguish of his soul, he shall be satisfied; and because of what he has experienced, my righteous Servant shall make many to be counted righteous before God, for he shall bear all their sins."[22]

At this very moment, there is joy and satisfaction in the heart of God's Son, because of what He has accomplished on the cross for each one of us. He anticipates the day when will be with Him, and He will show us all the wonders of His Father's house (see John 14:1-3; 17:24).

Because of the cross, because of Calvary, there is joy in my heart, too. I have a relationship with God because of Christ's sacrifice for me. My sins have been forgiven, I have a strong purpose for living, and I have the hope of being with Jesus and loved ones in Him who have gone on before me after I die. So I rejoice in these things. Yes, I have great reverence in my heart at the communion table, but my heart also wells up with affection and praise.

The early Church, in all their daily activities, meetings, meals, and shared joys and sorrows, made sure that they would never forget the most basic truth and the most important fact of all:

They were alive because Jesus had died for them.

FIVE
They Had Been with Jesus

> When they saw the courage of Peter and John and realized that they were unschooled, ordinary men, they were astonished and they took note that these men had been with Jesus. (Acts 4:13, NIV)

Our contemporary culture today contains a number of people you might call would-be-Christians, could-be-Christians, and may-be-Christians.

But what we need are no-doubt Christians.

What we need are men and women who walk and talk with Jesus Christ. People who—before they even open their mouths or speak a single word—show forth a quality that sets them apart from those around them. People who through their godly lifestyles have earned the right to be heard.

I'm talking about people who have been with Jesus.

Where's the Evidence?

Let's imagine you bumped into a friend at the mall, and his face was bright red. You might say to him, "Uh-oh, looks like you're getting a little too much sun," or maybe, "Did you fall asleep in the tanning booth?"

You don't have to be a prophet to know that your friend's skin has been burned under the sun or a ultra-violet light. The evidence is right there before you: beet-red skin!

In the same way, people need to see the *evidence* of our Christian faith. They should be able to tell that we have been with Jesus. That we've been walking with Him and talking to Him. That we've allowed His Holy Spirit to saturate and fill us.

Could that be said of you? Could someone just look at you and your lifestyle and say, "You've been with Jesus, haven't you?"

Is it really that obvious?

Yes, it is.

In his second letter to the Corinthians, Paul makes this statement: "But thank God! He has made us his captives and continues to lead us along in Christ's triumphal procession. Now he uses us to spread the knowledge of Christ everywhere, like a sweet perfume. Our lives are a Christ-like fragrance rising up to God" (2 Corinthians 2:14-15, NLT).

It's a spiritual fragrance that clings to our lives. If you worked in a pizza parlor all day, you'd come home at night smelling like pizza. If you worked in a garage doing car repair, you would come home at night smelling like gas and oil. If you worked in some factory bottling perfume all day, you'd come home with the aroma of that perfume wrapped all around you. And when someone who has been walking with Jesus Christ for weeks, months, and years walks into the room, you catch the fragrance of heaven.

You may not say it out loud, but you find yourself thinking, *That person has been with Jesus.*

To put it another way, if you were arrested for being a Christian would there be enough evidence to convict you? Could people tell you have been with Jesus…by the way you treat others…by your outlook… by the way you act around your family…even by your countenance?

In the early chapters of the book of Acts we read about two men, Peter and John, who had been radically impacted by their relationship with Jesus Christ. And when they were hauled before the religious authorities—the same authorities that had condemned the Lord Jesus to death—the officials who confronted Peter and John "realized that they had been with Jesus."[23]

In this chapter, I will identify a few traits that are true of a man or woman who "has been with Jesus." But first, a little background as to what led to this statement….

On an Ordinary Day....

Pentecost was over. The little tongues of flame that had appeared over the heads of the disciples were no longer visible.

But that doesn't mean they weren't on fire!

The little flames had been replaced by burning hearts.

With their own hearts aflame, Peter and John headed over to the temple one afternoon to take part in a prayer meeting. It was 3:00 p.m. on an ordinary day. We don't read of an angel instructing them to go to the temple because a miracle was about to be performed, nor do we read about a pillar of fire going before them and leading them to their destination.

It was a day like any other day. But when you are filled with the Holy Spirit and walking in the will of God to the best of your understanding, you just never know what opportunities will open up to you on any given day. If you are a Christian, you need to be ready at all times to respond to the leading of the Lord. In fact we are told in Scripture, "Be ready in season and out of season." Or as another translation puts it, "Be on duty at all times."[24]

This story in Acts, among other things, shows how God can use ordinary people in extraordinary ways. Now we have to understand as we read through the book of Acts together that although we see some marvelous miracles, they didn't necessarily happen every day. Yes, there were visions, angelic appearances, healings, and even a resurrection from the dead. But these things didn't happen on a daily basis. We sometimes forget that the book of Acts was compiled over a period of some thirty years.

So even though we read about some amazing happenings in the pages of this book, most days for Christians in that era were pretty much like your days. They would just get up in the morning, and as best they knew how, they would walk by faith and allow the Lord to lead them.

In Acts 3, as Peter and John walked into the temple for prayer, they had no idea that a miracle awaited them around the corner. They didn't know it was coming, didn't know what God was about to do.

One of the problems I have with contemporary "miracle ministries" is the way they claim to announce miracles in advance. They'll put out a poster that will say, "Miracle Service Today." Or maybe, "Miracle Crusade. Signs and Wonders, 7:00 to 9:00 pm." And people go to these meetings expecting to see miracles on demand.

Why do I have a problem with that? Because that's not the way miracles take place in the Bible—unless God announced it Himself. You never read about a miracle being announced ahead of time in the book of Acts.

If there was a miracle, it occurred because God sovereignly chose to work one. Peter and John didn't print up posters proclaiming "Miracle service at the Beautiful Gate at 3:00. Watch the man lame from birth get miraculously healed!"

No, they didn't have "miracle ministries" in the book of Acts. They had gospel preaching ministries, Bible teaching ministries, and they served the Lord with the gifts that He gave them. And every now and then, the Lord sovereignly performed miracles—and He did so when and where He wanted to.

So on a day like any other day, Peter and John made their way to the temple.

As they approached the Temple, a man lame from birth was being carried in. Each day he was put beside the Temple gate, the one called the Beautiful Gate, so he could beg from the people going into the Temple. When he saw Peter and John about to enter, he asked them for some money.

Peter and John looked at him intently, and Peter said, "Look at us!" The lame man looked at them eagerly, expecting some money. But Peter said, "I don't have any silver or gold for you. But I'll give you what I have. In the name of Jesus Christ the Nazarene, get up and walk!"

Then Peter took the lame man by the right hand and helped him up. And as he did, the man's feet and ankles were instantly healed and strengthened. He jumped up, stood on his feet, and began to walk! Then, walking, leaping, and praising God, he went into the Temple with them.

All the people saw him walking and heard him praising God. When they realized he was the lame beggar they had seen so often at the Beautiful Gate, they were absolutely astounded! They all rushed out in amazement to Solomon's Colonnade, where the man was holding tightly to Peter and John. (Acts 3:1-10, NLT)

This disabled man had probably been a fixture outside of the temple for years. Every day, through the kindness of friends, he was carried and put in position there at the Beautiful Gate, where he would hope for some compassion and a little money from the people coming out from a prayer service.

After many months of this, perhaps years, I imagine people stopped even noticing him. Maybe they even stepped over him as they talked amongst themselves and made their way into the temple.

Sometimes we can do the same thing. We can become so wrapped up in our own lives that we're oblivious and indifferent to the needs all around us. You know how it is. There's so much pain in the world that we don't even notice someone suffering right in front of us. We're rushing to and fro or talking on our cell phones, and we walk right by people in need, missing opportunities right on our doorstep.

Here's what's so ironic: We might be on our way to a conference on evangelism, when God suddenly puts a person in our path who needs to hear the gospel. But we're late for our meeting, and our tendency is to hurry on by and miss that opportunity so near at hand.

On this particular day, however, the supernatural was about to invade the natural, as God decided to shake things up a bit. Let me make an important point here: Simon Peter did *not*—in and of himself—have the faith to do what he was about to do. This was a miracle. And in that moment when Peter's eyes met the crippled man's eyes, God sovereignly gave Peter a special measure of faith. It was the faith to not only say to the man, "Rise up and walk," but the faith to reach down, grip him by the hand, and help him to his feet.

That's what you call a sink or swim moment.

Peter's words and actions in that moment were either going to be a great victory, or a horrible disaster. Imagine Peter yanking on this guy's arm, only to have him collapse in a heap on the pavement.

"Oh…sorry about that."

But Peter was going for broke, and you've got to give him credit. He was willing to take a step of faith. Are you?

Sometimes we're willing enough to take a step of faith—if there's an adequate backup plan or safety net. Yes, there is certainly a place for caution and prudence and seeking godly counsel. But there is also a time and a place for acting out your faith and taking a few risks. And the older people get, the less willing they are to take such risks.

Most of us want everything neatly laid out for us before we make a move. We want all our "what-ifs" answered, and some advance word about what's going to happen after this and after that. Sometimes, however, the Lord will whisper to us, "Just trust Me. Step out now and obey Me."

The truth is, I would rather try something for the Lord and fail at it rather than never try anything at all. If I fail I will learn from my failure. God Himself will pick me up, dust me off, and set me back on His chosen pathway for my life. It has been said that the doorway of success is often entered through the hallway of failure. So if at first you don't succeed, relax… you're just like the rest of us!

Take a chance and do something for the Lord!

"Well, Greg, I was thinking about starting a little Bible study at work—but I don't know if anyone would come."

Go for it!

"I was thinking of sharing the gospel with that person. But I don't how they'll respond."

Step out and do it!

Pray about it, yes. Ask the Lord for direction, yes, and seek some counsel where it's appropriate. But we can't always see more than one intersection ahead of us at a time. If you see a green light, move on ahead. Take a risk here and there and watch what the Lord will do.

That's what Peter did when he grabbed the crippled man's hand and pulled him to his feet. Here are a few things I notice from this incident.

#1: Peter saw an opportunity for the gospel and ran with it.

Peter saw his opportunity and addressed the crowd. "People of Israel," he said, "what is so surprising about this? And why stare at us as though we had made this man walk by our own power or godliness? For it is the God of Abraham, Isaac, and Jacob—the God of all our ancestors—who has brought glory to his servant Jesus by doing this." (Acts 3:12-13, NLT)

"Peter saw his opportunity...."

I really like that.

As Peter approached the temple that afternoon, he had no idea that God would hand him a custom-made, wide-open opportunity to address the people and tell them about Christ. But when such an occasion suddenly opened up in front of him, he stepped into the gap.

Look for those opportunities!

Sometimes someone will say to me, "Greg, I really want to be in ministry."

I will say, "Really? What do you mean by 'being in ministry'?"

"Well, you know...I want to serve the Lord. Share the gospel. I want to teach God's Word or help others know the Lord."

"Wonderful."

"So...I'm thinking about quitting my job and going overseas."

"Okay. The Lord might lead you to do just that. But let me ask you a question. Have you ever shared the gospel with your neighbors?"

"No. I haven't done that. But I want to cross the seas for Christ."

"Maybe you should cross the street first."

Here's my point: Ministry is everywhere. Opportunities are everywhere. Jesus said, "I tell you, open your eyes and look at the fields! They are ripe for harvest."[25]

There are ministry opportunities wherever you go—in your neighborhood, at your workplace, on your campus, or in the laundry room at your apartment. You need to open your eyes, as Jesus said, and look for those opportunities.

#2: Peter preached Christ and Him crucified.

Peter always made a beeline to the cross, pointing people to the sacrifice and death of Jesus.

In verses 13-15, Peter gives it to them with both barrels.

> "This is the same Jesus whom you handed over and rejected before Pilate, despite Pilate's decision to release him. You rejected this holy, righteous one and instead demanded the release of a murderer. You killed the author of life, but God raised him from the dead. And we are witnesses of this fact!" (NLT)

Within just a few seconds of conversation, Peter had already come back to the death and resurrection of Jesus Christ.

#3: Peter told them, "To be forgiven, you must first repent."

In verse 19, Peter declared: "Repent therefore and be converted, that your sins may be blotted out, so times of refreshing may come from the presence of the Lord."

The only way to find forgiveness of sins is by confessing and turning from them—not by justifying and hiding them. Some people are unwilling to do that, and as a result, sin must run its terrible course in their lives. After the initial euphoria, sin will sooner or later bring the bitter taste of its bitter fruit.

Is dabbling with sin exciting? Yes, there can be that little bit of a thrill or euphoria that comes with doing something forbidden. But that pleasure will be short-lived, and what comes in its wake will be brutal. Sometimes the repercussions of that sin can literally last for a lifetime. The Bible itself acknowledges there can be pleasure in sin for a season. But then payday comes, and it is a hard, hard payday. And you don't want to go down that road.

But here's the good news. If you have been living a life of sin and hate where that life has taken you, the Lord will forgive you if you repent and call on His name. You need to say, "Lord I admit this sin in my life, and I'm tired of justifying it and blaming it on other people. I'm really to call it what You call it, and turn away from it. I'm so sorry for what I've done and ask that You would forgive me."

If you do that, God promises here in Acts 3:19 that "times of refreshing will come from the Lord." He will forgive you and refresh you and give you a fresh opportunity to live for Him.

I love that word "refreshing." It's like we have been in a self–imposed, blazing desert of pursuing sinful things. Then we happen to glance up toward the horizon, and see an oasis—replete with shady palm trees, a gushing fountain, and a pool of aqua-blue water.

What do we do? We plunge ourselves in the cool water and find immediate refreshment! That is what happens when we repent and turn to Christ from our sin. "Times of refreshing" come from the Lord. It's really up to us: Do we want to stay in the desert or beat a quick path to the oasis?

So Peter delivered his impromptu message, and as the old saying goes, it did not play well in Peoria. The Sadducees, the religious leaders of the time who refused to believe in the resurrection of the dead, had the temple police apprehend the apostles and brought them before the rulers.

Here, then, is what happened as Peter and John stood before these angry, hostile authorities.

> They brought in the two disciples and demanded, "By what power, or in whose name, have you done this?"

Then Peter, filled with the Holy Spirit, said to them, "Rulers and elders of our people, are we being questioned today because we've done a good deed for a crippled man? Do you want to know how he was healed? Let me clearly state to all of you and to all the people of Israel that he was healed by the powerful name of Jesus Christ the Nazarene, the man you crucified but whom God raised from the dead. For Jesus is the one referred to in the Scriptures, where it says, 'The stone that you builders rejected has now become the cornerstone.'

"There is salvation in no one else! God has given no other name under heaven by which we must be saved."

The members of the council were amazed when they saw the boldness of Peter and John, for they could see that they were ordinary men with no special training in the Scriptures. They also recognized them as men who had been with Jesus. But since they could see the man who had been healed standing right there among them, there was nothing the council could say. (Acts 4:7-14, NLT)

Verse 13 says, "They had no special training." Another translation says, "They were untrained laymen." It was a source of amazement to these religious leaders that these ordinary blue-collar guys were so well versed in the Scriptures—and more importantly in the *understanding* of them. They appeared to have a greater grasp on the Word of God than even the rabbis, the trained professionals. And how was this so?

Even though these authorities didn't want to admit it, they already had their answer. These men "*had been with Jesus.*" Or as another translation puts it, "The religious leaders realized what being with Jesus had done for them."

It's no different today. You can tell if someone has been with Jesus… or not. I saw a minister on Larry King the other night. And as Larry so often does, he asked this pastor, "Why is there suffering in the world?"

Suddenly, the pastor got that deer-in-the-headlights look. He stuttered, stammered, and didn't know what to say. It was like he'd never heard the question before! But this is Apologetics 101! Every pastor—every believer should know how to answer this question. We have students in our church who would have knocked that question right out of the park. I've seen these kids out sharing their faith, giving wise and thoughtful answers to hard questions that nonbelievers throw at them. And I have seen them do a better job of it than some of the so-called professional ministers that are in pulpits today.

And do you know how they do it? It really isn't rocket science.

They spend time with Jesus and in His Word.

God delights to use ordinary people who spend time in His presence. As a corollary to that, I would add: God deliver us from the so-called professional ministers out there who have been ordained by man, but not by God. Yes, they give us religiosity, they give us politics, they give us philosophy, and even psychology—but they don't give us the Word of God.

As a pastor, that's really *all* I have to offer. I wrote my autobiography, *Lost Boy*, for one principle reason. I wanted people who read about my life and all that God has brought me through to say to themselves, "Wow, if God could use a guy like this, then I guess there's hope for me!"

And my story pales in comparison to the wild résumés of people that God used in the Bible. These are people most churches would never hire! Yes, Noah was a great man of faith who built the ark. But he also became drunk and disorderly. Abraham was a liar on more than one occasion. Jacob was a conniver and a schemer. Rahab was a prostitute. Jeremiah and Timothy were considered too young. David had an affair. Moses was a murderer. Elijah was suicidal at one point. Jonah ran from God. Peter denied Christ. The disciples fell asleep when praying. The Samaritan woman was divorced more than once. Timothy had an ulcer. And Lazarus? He was *dead*.

So what's your excuse? Don't imagine that God can't use you. Give Him a chance!

How Can You Tell?

How can you tell if a person has been with Jesus? I would like to put forward four traits for your consideration.

#1: A person who has been with Jesus will boldly share their faith.

The same Peter who just months earlier had crumpled under pressure and denied his Lord was now speaking with the same boldness of Jesus Himself. Yes, He was filled with the Holy Spirit, but there's an additional reason for this new courage under fire. The more you spend time with Jesus, the more you are going to resemble Him.

When people have been married for a long time, they start looking like each other. Did you ever see those couples with matching shirts? They'll even start finishing each other's sentences. As the years go by, you know just how your spouse will react to this or that. When you're around someone day after day, year after year, you become more and more like each other. God's principle objective in the life of the believer is to shape us into the image of His Son, Jesus Christ. He wants you to become more and more like Him each and every day. Romans 8:29 says, "Whom He foreknew, He also predestined to be conformed into the likeness of His own Son."

Can you imagine the frustration of Annas and Caiaphas and the other Jewish leaders in Acts 4? After the crucifixion, they thought to themselves, "Well, we've finally put this issue to rest. This Jesus is in His grave, and that's the end of that."

But then came the stories of the resurrection.

And then came Pentecost.

And now here are two disciples before them, bold and fearless, who look and sound very strangely like the Galilean they just put to death. And over there is James…and over there is Thomas…and over there is Mary Magdalene, and…where were all these people coming from?

They were everywhere! The leaders thought they had destroyed the

Christian faith by killing Christ, but that's not the way it worked out at all. Instead, they played right into the plan and purpose of God, and Jesus was living in a dozen others…a hundred others…ten thousand others! And they realized there was no stopping this, because these men, these women, had been with Jesus. Can people tell that about you?

#2: A person who has been with Jesus will know Scripture.

One thing that immediately gets your attention in Peter's sermons is his grasp and knowledge of the written Word. Read through his messages in Acts 2, 3, and 4 and take note of all the Scripture quotations. This simply shows that when you have been with Jesus, you will spend time in His Word.

What is the Bible? It's the autobiography of God, telling you all that you need to know about Him. It also tells you everything you need to know about life, yourself, how to live, what to do, what not to do, how to think, how to act, how to react. It's all between the covers of this incomparable Book God has given us. If you want to get closer to God, you have to give priority to reading and studying and meditating on the Scriptures.

In Hebrews 10:7, Jesus is quoted as saying:

"Behold, I have come—
In the volume of the book it is written of Me."

That may be the best reason of all to spend time in the Book…because you will encounter Jesus Himself in its pages.

I read recently of an online auction taking place to benefit the Robert F. Kennedy Memorial, with various things you can bid on. For instance, for $11,000 you can have tea with Alan Greenspan. For $32,000 you can have a walk-on role in a film starring Johnny Depp. And for $70,000 you can receive a tennis lesson from Andre Agassi.

I probably won't be doing any bidding for those opportunities, but I can see how people might enjoy spending an hour with a famous movie star or tennis pro. But how much better to invest an hour with the Creator of the universe, who has made Himself available to spend time with you whenever you like, for as long as you like! And it won't cost you any money at all. It's free! Just open up the Word of God and spend time with Him.

#3: A person who has been with Jesus will be a person of prayer.

After being released by the authorities after stern warnings to cease and desist preaching the message of Jesus, Peter and John went back and joined the other disciples. And what did they do? They had a prayer meeting. And what a prayer meeting it was!

You might have expected that young church to hunker down and pray for protection from the authorities, or favor from the government, or maybe a little comfort after the intimidation and attacks.

But no, that's not what these Christians prayed for. They said:

> "Now, Lord, look on their threats, and grant to Your servants that with all boldness they may speak Your word, by stretching out Your hand to heal, and that signs and wonders may be done through the name of Your holy Servant Jesus."
>
> And when they had prayed, the place where they were assembled together was shaken; and they were all filled with the Holy Spirit, and they spoke the word of God with boldness. (Acts 4:29-31)

I like that. They were saying, "Lord, don't let us be intimidated by these threats. Give us even more boldness and courage to speak Your Word and do wonders in Your name." And as we can read, God immediately answered that request.

There is one last indicator that a man or woman has been with Jesus. And this is one you might not like.

#3: A person who has been with Jesus will be persecuted.

> Now as they spoke to the people, the priests, the captain of the temple, and the Sadducees came upon them, being greatly disturbed that they taught the people and preached in Jesus the resurrection from the dead. (Acts 4:1-2)

Because we have been with Jesus and have become like Jesus, it only follows that we will be treated as Jesus was treated.

Remember what Jesus warned in the gospel of John?

> "If the world hates you, remember that it hated me first. The world would love you as one of its own if you belonged to it, but you are no longer part of the world. I chose you to come out of the world, so it hates you. Do you remember what I told you? 'A slave is not greater than the master.' Since they persecuted me, naturally they will persecute you. And if they had listened to me, they would listen to you. They will do all this to you because of me, for they have rejected the One who sent me." (John 15:18-21, NLT)

It's nice to be liked. It's pleasant to be popular. It makes us feel good when everyone compliments us and says nice things about us. But listen…if everyone thinks you are wonderful and if you don't have an enemy anywhere, something is wrong with your life.

Maybe you expected me to say the opposite. Possibly you thought to yourself, "If I am a Christian, I should just be sweetness and light and everyone should love me."

Yes, it's true that a loving, sweet, kind person won't make too many waves. But the Bible also calls you to be a godly person—a truthful and righteous person. And when your stand for Jesus Christ and His Word puts you in direct opposition to the whole trend and current of our contemporary culture, well, some people are bound to take issue with that. Your speaking out for righteousness is going to bother some people, perhaps even making them very angry.

Jesus said, "Woe to you when all men speak well of you, for that is how their fathers treated the false prophets."[26]

You can tell a great deal about someone by whom their friends are… *and their enemies.* And if you are really walking with Jesus, you will face some persecution in this life. Jesus said you would. What form will that persecution take? Rejection? Slander? Mockery? Actual physical attacks? I can't say. I only know that the Bible promised that at least in some measure, the true follower of Jesus Christ would be treated like his or her Master.

If you're not a true believer, then persecution will cause you to quickly abandon what little faith you thought you had, and you'll decide that it makes more sense to "go with the flow." But if you are a real Christian, then persecution will not weaken you, it will only make you stronger.

Why are we persecuted? It's not always for the reasons we may imagine. Sometimes people push back at us simply because we are obnoxious and unnecessarily offensive. We behave like self-righteous, insensitive fools, and wonder why people don't like us. And then we console ourselves with the passage, "Blessed are they that are persecuted."

That kind of persecution—getting hassled for being a jerk—doesn't win you any credit at all in heaven. There's no value for you or anyone else when you are unloving, or arrogant, or just plain foolish. The gospel already has offense built into it—don't make it worse by being offensive yourself! Deliver the Good News with some compassion… some humility…even with a touch of humor whenever possible.

Jesus said, "Blessed are those who are persecuted for righteousness' sake, for theirs is the kingdom of heaven."[27]

If we're going to face persecution, let's face it for the right reason: Because we are a true representative of Christ. Because we are *like* Christ.

Frankly, that just comes with the turf of being a Christian. Jesus promised many wonderful things to those who follow Him, but one thing He never promised was an easy life.

Being a Christian is the most joyful and exciting life there is, and it's also the most challenging. It's a life the world doesn't really understand, because you have yielded control of all that you are to someone besides yourself. As a result, you do what He tells you to do, go where He wants you to go, and say what He wants you to say. If you don't want to live that way, if it all has to be about you, and you want the world to revolve around you, then you will not make it as a Christian.

To quickly summarize, if you want to be recognized as a person who has been with Jesus, you will be bold in your witness, a student of the Scriptures, a person of prayer…and at times you will be rejected, scorned, or outright persecuted just as Jesus Himself faced these things.

These four elements working in the lives of these early disciples caused them to turn their world upside down.

Have you been with Jesus?

SIX
Honest to God

Believe it or not, there was a time in my life when I actually wore a hairpiece. No bald person that I know really likes being bald, and for one brief season in my life, I tried to hide the evidence with a hairpiece stuck on the top of my head.

It came in the mail as a gift from a friend, and as far as hairpieces go, it wasn't bad—maybe a "7" on a scale of 10. But when I tried it on and looked in the mirror, I wasn't so sure. I couldn't get over the feeling that I had a bird's nest sitting on top of my cranium. But since my friend had gone to all that trouble to have it made for me and sent to me, I thought I at least ought to give it a try.

(Here's a news flash for you. If you wear a hairpiece *everyone knows*. You may think—wish, hope, pray—they don't, but they really do.)

While I couldn't bring myself to wear the thing in the pulpit, I thought, *Maybe I'll just take it out for a little test drive*. So when my wife and I went out to Costco one evening, I actually put it on my head and wore it out of the house.

As it turned out, there was a pretty stiff wind blowing that night, and the back of the hairpiece started coming up. *Good grief*, I thought to myself, *this thing is going to launch*. As nonchalantly as I could, I tried to hold it down while we walked from the parking lot into the store. I knew it would be terrible to have the hairpiece blow away, because my friend had actually inscribed the thing on the underneath side. It said:

"For Pastor Greg Laurie." And then, "Praise the Lord!"

I could just imagine some poor guy having that thing land on him, flailing his arms, and saying, "What is *that*?" And then he would have to return it to me, saying, "Here you go, Pastor Laurie. I found your rug."

That was the last time I ever tried such a thing. From that time on, I've been bald and liberated!

Author Peggy Noonan once described a hairpiece as "a lie on your head." She has a point there, and I don't think any of us want to have a lie on our head—or in other area of our lives. As followers of Jesus Christ, we want to be honest and true, and don't want to be found to be hypocrites. Why? Because as everyone knows, the number one reason (or at least the one most commonly stated) people who aren't believers in Christ use for staying away from church is that "the Church is full of hypocrites." People outside of Christ throw around the word "hypocrite" whenever they see (or think they see) any inconsistency in a Christian's life.

But let's take a closer look at that timeworn word. What is a hypocrite? Or perhaps more to the point, what *isn't* a hypocrite?

Portrait of a Hypocrite?

A hypocrite is *not* someone who believes something, and then falls short of that belief. If that were true, we'd all have to wear that label. All of us fall short of our beliefs and ideals at one time or another. We have standards that we seek to live by, and we fail to meet those marks time after time.

But as I said, that doesn't make us hypocrites, that makes us *human*. We are imperfect people trying to serve a perfect God, but as James expressed it, "We all stumble in many ways."[28] Even the great apostle Paul made a candid admission of his many failures in his letter to the church in Rome.

"I don't really understand myself, for I want to do what is right, but I don't do it. Instead, I do what I hate. But if I know that what I am doing is wrong, this shows that I agree that the law is good. So I am not the one doing wrong; it is sin living in me that does it. And I know that nothing good lives in me, that is, in my sinful nature. I want to do what is right, but I can't. I want to do what is good, but I don't. I don't want to do what is wrong, but I do it anyway."[29]

Now that wasn't necessarily an everyday experience in Paul's life, but it was certainly an honest admission from his heart.

Having said that, and having acknowledged it as our true condition, that doesn't mean we should just shrug our shoulders, say, "Oh well," and settle for spiritual mediocrity. We should always reach for the goal of pleasing our Lord and becoming more godly men and women. As Paul also wrote in the book of Philippians, "No, dear brothers, I am still not all I should be, but I am bringing all my energies to bear on this one thing: Forgetting the past and looking forward to what lies ahead, I strain to reach the end of the race and receive the prize for which God is calling us up to heaven because of what Christ Jesus did for us" (3:13–14, NLT).

Listen, the further we go in the Christian life, the further we realize we must go. The more I grow spiritually, the more I discover I must grow spiritually.

So a hypocrite isn't someone who simply fails to live up to everything that he or she believes. A hypocrite is something different altogether. The word *hypocrite* comes from a Greek term that means "to wear a mask." Paul's readers would have been familiar with Greek theater, where all the actors wore masks. A hypocrite, then, is an actor—someone pretending to be someone or something they're not. Someone who believes an ideal or truth, tries to live up to that ideal, but fails, isn't the one we're talking about here. It is rather someone who doesn't believe at all, but slips on a mask and pretends to be a believer.

In Acts chapter 5, we're given the story of two hypocrites who found out the hard way that you can't pull the wool over God's eyes. And the Lord dealt with them harshly.

Satan's Inside Job

God truly hates the sin of hypocrisy. When our Lord walked this earth He reserved His most scathing words for the religious elite of the day, the Pharisees and the Sadducees. These were men who claimed to have dedicated their lives to the keeping of the Law, men who would pray dutifully three times a day at the sound of the trumpet, and put on a great religious performance for every eye to see. But on the inside, their hearts were full of envy and greed. In the end, these religious leaders conspired together with the Roman government to bring about the execution of the Messiah.

As we have seen, the Book of Acts is the record of the Holy Spirit and His activities in the early Church—the believers who turned their world upside down.

But don't imagine that this great tsunami of light breaking across the Roman world somehow went unnoticed by Satan and his dark legions. The one who is known as "the adversary" wanted to stop the new movement in its tracks. And that's the way it will be until Jesus returns: Wherever God is at work in this world, the devil will rise up to oppose that work.

It was Spurgeon who said, "Satan never kicks a dead horse." In other words, the devil isn't going to waste his energy on areas that are no threat to his kingdom. But if he perceives a threat to his plans and his long-held turf, he will attack.

If you would say to me, "Greg, I can't remember the last time I was hassled for being a Christian or experienced any kind of spiritual attack," then I would be inclined to check and see if there is a pulse. Because, quite frankly, if you are walking with the Lord you should be facing some measure of persecution, some form of attack.

The Bible says, "Yes, and all who desire to live godly in Christ Jesus will suffer persecution" (2 Timothy 3:12).

Did you notice that little word A-L-L? Some form of persecution is a reality for believers who seek to follow Jesus ever day. It's a reality.

Whenever God is working, the devil will be opposing.

Satan has two primary ways that He attacks the work of God: outwardly and inwardly. Sometimes he comes like a roaring lion in a bold frontal attack, but more often he comes slithering in the back door like a serpent. You can have all your defenses up, and tell yourself, "I'm ready! The devil will never penetrate this fortress." And then he slinks through some little crevice or opening you didn't even know about.

In Acts 5, we find the devil operating by that old adage, "If you can't beat 'em, join 'em." He had tried a savage outward attack—a direct assault against the apostles that included arrests, threats, and official intimidation. Instead of weakening the believers, however, it strengthened them. The adversary would return to those intimidation attacks in subsequent chapters in the book of Acts, bringing imprisonment, beatings, murder, and mayhem to the Church. But in Acts 5, for the moment at least, he tries a different tack.

Infiltration.

Here's the account from the text itself.

> But there was a certain man named Ananias who, with his wife, Sapphira, sold some property. He brought part of the money to the apostles, claiming it was the full amount. With his wife's consent, he kept the rest.

> Then Peter said, "Ananias, why have you let Satan fill your heart? You lied to the Holy Spirit, and you kept some of the money for yourself. The property was yours to sell or not sell, as you wished. And after selling it, the money was also yours to give away. How could you do a thing like this? You weren't lying to us but to God!"

> As soon as Ananias heard these words, he fell to the floor and died. Everyone who heard about it was terrified. Then some young men got up, wrapped him in a sheet, and took him out and buried him.

> About three hours later his wife came in, not knowing what had happened. Peter asked her, "Was this the price you and your husband received for your land?"

> "Yes," she replied, "that was the price."

> And Peter said, "How could the two of you even think of conspiring to test the Spirit of the Lord like this? The young men who buried your husband are just outside the door, and they will carry you out, too."
>
> Instantly, she fell to the floor and died. When the young men came in and saw that she was dead, they carried her out and buried her beside her husband. Great fear gripped the entire church and everyone else who heard what had happened.
> (vv. 1-11, NLT)

Sometimes we'll hear people say, "I wish we could see more miracles today like we see in the book of Acts."

Really? How about *this* miracle? If God dealt with believers today as He did with Ananias and Sapphira, every church would have to have a fulltime undertaker on staff and a morgue in the basement. People would be dropping like flies in the pews and even the pulpits. Who could stand?

Why did God deal so severely with these two—and what exactly did they do? The sobering truth is, Ananias and Sapphira committed a specific sin against the Holy Spirit that can still be committed today. In verse 4 we read: "You have not lied to men, but to God." The sin of Ananias and Sapphira is that they lied to the Holy Spirit.

When Peter said, "You have not lied unto men, but unto God," he was underlining the fact that the Holy Spirit is part of the Trinity. He is God, just as God the Father is God, and God the Son is God. Sometimes we may think of the Holy Spirit as being more of an "it" than a Him. We imagine Him as some sort of impersonal force.

The Bible makes it clear, however, that He is a real Person, with a personality. As such, He can be specifically sinned against. In fact, the Bible identifies six sins that we can specifically commit against the Holy Spirit. Some of these sins are committed by believers, and others by nonbelievers.

Sins Against the Holy Spirit

#1: Lying to the Holy Spirit

That's what we see in this chapter. More on that in a moment.

#2: Grieving the Holy Spirit

Ephesians 4:30 (NIV) says, "And do not grieve the Holy Spirit of God, with whom you were sealed for the day of redemption. Get rid of all bitterness, rage and anger, brawling and slander, along with every form of malice."

The word "grieve" means to make sad or sorrowful. So the Bible is saying, don't bring sorrow to the Holy Spirit. When you, as a redeemed child of God, allow bitterness, rage, anger, harsh words, or slander to be a part of your life, you are bringing sadness to the Holy Spirit.

Let's take a little snapshot of that area of our lives right now. Are you harboring a grudge against someone? Have you been slandering someone or even passing on information that you've heard and yet don't know if it's really true? Have you been snapping at people, or flying into fits of rage? According to Scripture, this sort of behavior brings grief to the Holy Spirit's heart.

#3: Quenching the Holy Spirit

This too, applies to believers. Writing to the Christians in Thessalonica, Paul said, "Do not quench the Spirit."[30]

What does that mean? The word Paul uses for "quench" in this passage conveys the idea of extinguishing a fire. It's no different than being on a camping trip, and pouring a bucket of water on the campfire before you get ready to go.

In a similar way, it's possible for us to seek to extinguish or quench the work that the Holy Spirit seeks to accomplish in our lives. Maybe you would say, "Well, obviously God could never use a person like me." And because of your blatant unbelief, He doesn't. Or you might say, "God would never answer *my* prayers." And again, because of your unbelief, He doesn't. Concerning our Lord's own hometown of Caper-naum, we read in Matthew 13:58: "Now He did not do many mighty works there because of their unbelief."

He *could* have done such works. He was *available* to do those miracles. He *desired* to have a mighty work among them. But none of that happened, because of their stubborn unwillingness to believe. When God wants to work in your life and He encounters unyielding, obstinate unbelief, it hinders His good plans for you. Why? Because God works through faith in our lives, as we place our trust and belief in Him. Maybe you've heard the Lord saying, "I want you to share My Gospel with that person."

But you say back to Him, "No, I can't do that. I'm afraid they would reject me." That refusal to follow the clear prompting of the Holy Spirit is quenching His work in your life. Are you doing that?

Sometimes a church can quench the Spirit by clinging to sterile traditions, and refusing to allow the Spirit to do a fresh, innovative work in their midst. The Church leaders or key members will say, "No, we don't want to do that. We've never done it that way before." So they reject an idea or a fresh moving of God's Spirit—not because it's unbiblical—but simply because it's "different." As a result, the work of God's Spirit is quenched in that place.

#4: Resisting the Holy Spirit

This sin applies more to an unbeliever. When Stephen, who ended up being the first martyr of the early Church, was preaching to the Sanhe-drin he said, "You stubborn people! You are heathen at heart and deaf to the truth. Must you forever resist the Holy Spirit?" (Acts 7:52, NLT).

The work and the mission of the Holy Spirit in the life of an unbe-liever are to lead him or her to God. In that process, the Spirit is incred-ibly patient and persistent, but it is possible to resist His pleadings. And as God says in Genesis 6:3, there can come a point where God says, "My Spirit will not always strive with man."

Apparently the crowd that Stephen was addressing that day had resisted the Spirit over and over again. It would appear from the text that these people actually accepted what Stephen was saying as true, but stopped their ears in a rage and refused to believe it. In doing so, they resisted the Spirit's gracious work in their lives, and became guilty of murder.

When God is trying to bring a person to faith, and that man or woman pushes back and continues to resist Him, that can lead to yet another sin against the Spirit.

#5: Insulting the Holy Spirit

This is a sin that only a nonbeliever could commit. In John 16, Jesus says that the work of the Holy Spirit in the world is to convince and convict the world of sin, of righteousness, and of judgment. And when someone refuses to accept Christ, insisting that they don't want or need salvation, they are denying the very mission of God's Spirit on earth.

By rejecting the God who loves them and the Savior who died for them, they are in effect saying, "Not only am I saying no to receiving Jesus, but I really don't care if Jesus died. And if He did die it was a waste. I don't care if He shed His blood. It means nothing to me."

That is an insult to the Holy Spirit, and those are grave words to say. In Hebrews 10:29 we read, "Just think how much worse the punishment will be for those who have trampled on the Son of God, and have treated the blood of the covenant, which made us holy, as if it were common and unholy, and have insulted and disdained the Holy Spirit who brings God's mercy to us" (NLT).

To steadfastly resist the Holy Spirit's appeal is to insult God, and effectively cut off all hope of salvation. Which brings us to that verse that says, "How shall we escape if we ignore such a great salvation?"[31]

#5: Blaspheming the Holy Spirit

I am asked about this from time to time what Jesus meant when He spoke of an "unpardonable sin." He told us in Matthew 12:31, "Every sin and blasphemy will be forgiven men, but the blasphemy against the

Spirit will not be forgiven them."

What does that mean? Let me reiterate the point I made earlier. The very mission and work of the Holy Spirit in the life of a nonbeliever is to show them their need for Jesus and bring them to faith. But if you continue to say no, continue to resist, continue to turn your back on God's gracious offer of forgiveness, you ultimately insult and even blaspheme Him, and go beyond a point of no return.

Acts 5 tells us that Ananias and Sapphira lied to the Holy Spirit. How did they do that? They did it by pretending to be something they were not. Here was a couple that wanted others to think they were more devoted to God than they really were. Ironically, the name Ananias means "God is gracious." But he also found out that God is holy! Sapphira means "beautiful." But she found out how ugly sin can be.

To read this story in context, we have to bear in mind that at this point, the young church was living together communally. Because of the persecution in those days, believers had lost their homes and their jobs, so other believers who had resources and means were helping out. Everybody had the option of doing whatever the Lord led them to do. Some were taking properties, selling them, and giving the money to the Church, but not everyone was doing that. It was up to the individual before God.

It was a very unique and precious time in the life of the infant church, and the world looked on in amazement as these believers poured out their lives for one another. In the midst of this season of beautiful, sacrificial love, Satan slithered into the scene in an attempt to spoil that whole picture of Christ-like love.

Ananias and Sapphira sold a property and laid the proceeds at the apostles' feet, but decided together that they would keep back a portion of the money for themselves. So the issue here is not about giving or not giving. The issue here is about lying—saying you did one thing when you really did another.

This is precisely what Jesus caught the Pharisees doing, as they went about performing their "good deeds." One contemporary translation renders the Lord's words like this:

> "Be especially careful when you are trying to be good so that you don't make a performance out of it. It might be good theater, but the God who made you won't be applauding.

> "When you do something for someone else, don't call attention to yourself. You've seen them in action, I'm sure—'playactors' I call them—treating prayer meeting and street corner alike as a stage, acting compassionate as long as someone is watching, playing to the crowds. They get applause, true, but that's all they get. When you help someone out, don't think about how it looks. Just do it—quietly and unobtrusively." (Matthew 6:1-4, THE MESSAGE)

We've all done this, haven't we? There have been times when every one us has tried to appear more godly or spiritual than we truly are. Have you ever been praying with a group of people and opened your eyes to look around a little? Everyone else is praying, but you're peeking. Then someone else looks up, and you catch each other. Immediately your close your eyes again. You think to yourself, *I didn't look very spiritual just then. I'd better close my eyes and look real sincere.*

We want to appear so pious, when in reality, we're not praying at all.

That is why I love kids. They're just so honest. A kid will tell you where he's at. There is no pretense. They just are what they are.

My little granddaughter Stella burped the other day. Most of us adults would say, "Oh sorry, excuse me," if we burped out loud. But Stella simply smiled and said, "Stella burped." She was proud of it. It was cute because she just is what she is and says what she thinks. She doesn't try to put any spin on it or appear to be something she's really not.

I'm not suggesting that people throw manners overboard and belch out loud here. Courtesy is a good thing. But it's interesting how, as we grow up and the years go by, we learn how to play act more and more; we learn how to smile when our hearts are frowning, to act sympathetic or caring when we don't feel that way at all, or to say one thing to a person's face, but something entirely different when his or her back is turned.

In Romans 12:9, Paul said, "Let love be without hypocrisy." Another translation says, "Let us have no imitation Christian love."[32] In other words, Paul understood our tendency to *fake* love toward one another when in reality our hearts are cold and apathetic. What was he saying, then? Stop expressing love because you don't really mean it? No, he was saying, *really mean it*. Get your heart made right, let the love of Jesus flow through you, so that the love you show will be real and genuine, not forced or plastic.

It would have been better, so very much better, if Ananias and Sapphira had simply said, "That's not where our hearts are right now. Maybe we could do something later, but for now, we'll just pass." Instead, they wanted to look like Jesus without paying the price to really be like Jesus.

Actors and hypocrites, their "compassion" was an outward thing, that really didn't express their hearts. And at that particular time and season in the Church, God wasn't willing to put up with that.

Earlier in this book, I made reference to Jesus' parable of the wheat and tares—the story of the enemy who had sown destructive weeds in the farmer's wheat fields, weeds that looked just like the wheat as they grew together. Jesus gave us this story to point out that His Church has people, to this very day, who have infiltrated its ranks. There is wheat and there are tears, side by side, in the Church of Jesus Christ. And you and I don't know which is which and who is who. We stand in the same sunshine, sit in the same pew, sing the same songs, read the same Bible, and breathe the same air. And one may be a believer and the other may be a full-blown nonbeliever.

That's the way it will always be. There will be people like Ananias, Sapphira, Judas Iscariot, Demas, and Alexander, smiling sweetly, in our pictorial church directories. These are the satanic plants that undermine the Word of God and seek to weaken the people of God.

But here's the bottom line on hypocrites. It's not our job to identify them and weed them out. We can't discern a person's true heart and we can't determine a person's true motives. That's a job that belongs to God. Remember, it wasn't Peter or the apostles who called out this hypocritical couple in Acts 5, it was the Holy Spirit.

Your concern shouldn't be with pointing out hypocrites, your concern should be not to become one yourself! Your job isn't to identify the look-alike weeds, but to make sure that you are really the genuine article.

Speaking of His return, Jesus said, "But take heed to yourselves, lest your hearts be weighed down with carousing, drunkenness, and cares of this life, and that Day come on you unexpectedly. For it will come as a snare on all those who dwell on the face of the whole earth. Watch therefore, and pray always that you may be counted worthy to escape all these things that will come to pass, and to stand before the Son of Man" (Luke 21:34-36).

Our job is to take care of ourselves. To take heed to ourselves and make sure that we are true believers. Because there is coming a day when we will all have to face the music.

Face the Music?

Have you ever wondered where that expression came from? I read about that recently. It seems that the phrase originated in Imperial Japan. There was a man who was part of the Imperial Orchestra, but in reality couldn't play a note. Because he was a man of great influence and wealth, however, he had demanded to be given a place in the prestigious group, because he wanted to "perform" before the emperor. So the conductor gave him a seat in the second row of the orchestra, even though this man could not read or play any music whatsoever. He was given a little flute, and when the concert would begin, he would raise his instrument, pucker his lips, and move his fingers as though he were playing. But he never made a sound.

This deception went on for two years. And then a new conductor took over, and told the orchestra he wanted to personally audition every member of the orchestra. One by one they performed in his presence, and then came the flautist's turn. Terrified because he didn't want to be discovered, he feigned an illness and was sent to the doctor. The doctor, however, said there was nothing wrong with the would-be musician. So he finally had to face the conductor and admit he was a fake.

He couldn't face the music, and that's where the expression came from.

Ananias and Sapphira had to face the music. And although they had done a brilliant job of deceiving others, they never even for a moment deceived God. It has been said you can fool all of the people some of the time, and you can fool some of the people all of the time. But you can't fool God any of the time. Yes, you might be a skilled actor. Maybe you deserve an Oscar or an Emmy because everyone believes you are what you claim to be. But you know in your heart of hearts that you aren't. You know that you are another person altogether.

Don't let that condition go any further! Don't play the hypocrite and don't play the fool. We should all be thankful God doesn't deal with the Church today as he dealt with Ananias and Sapphira. But at the same time we should also recognize that we are truly going to have to face the music one day and give an account for our actions.

By the way…*none* of us can live this life perfectly and flawlessly. All of us are going to fall short of God's glory time and time again. But having said that, there is a difference between a person seeking to live a godly life and tripping, stumbling, fumbling, and failing now and then, and a person who isn't even trying, but just putting on an act.

Better to face the music now, and get on the road to recovery with the rest of us recovering hypocrites, than to face the music later, when it's too late to change…forever.

SEVEN
A Life Well-Lived

I'm at a point in my life that is sometimes called "middle-aged."

I wouldn't mind that so much, if I only knew a few more one-hundred-year-old people! The truth is, I think I'm a bit further along than "middle-aged."

I've heard it said that you know when you're middle-aged when you begin to wonder who put the quicksand in the hourglass of time. Because the days seem to fly by at a blur. Months go by quickly. Years go by quickly. *It is Christmas so soon? Is it summer already? Is it our anniversary already?*

Middle age is that point of life when you have met so many people that every new person you meet reminds you of someone else. It's when you know all the answers, and no one ever asks you the questions! You begin to understand the truth of the Scripture that says, "Our life is like a story that has already been told."

What story is your life telling? As for me, I am living proof that God can take a mess of a life with the deck stacked against it and completely redeem it. He can take an unplanned, illegitimate child who could have been an abortion statistic, and intervene in that life for His glory.

That's my story. What's yours? We all have a story to tell. And we all need to take stock of your life and ask, "What is my life all about? What is the legacy that I will leave? How will I be remembered?"

Charting a Course

You may be a person who is relatively young, and you think to yourself, *Legacy? That's something you think about when you're getting old.*

The truth is, it's an even more important question when you're young. Why? Because right now you are charting the course your life will take. You are developing habits, setting direction, and making decisions that will affect you the rest of your days.

Your habits. Your career. Your life partner. It's so very important to make the right decisions now because as you grow older, you will become more and more set in your ways. You'll only want to listen to the oldies stations. Your favorite part of the newspaper will come under the heading, "25 Years Ago Today." You'll start eating at the same restaurants, wanting to sit at the same table, and ordering the same things.

In other words, you'll find yourself settling into a routine.

That's not all bad…depending on the routine. Because if you establish good habit patterns, you'll follow those as well—like a daily time reading the Word, having a prayer life, and being a faithful participant in a local church.

So I'm not saying habits and routines are all bad, I'm simply saying that the evening of your life will be determined by the morning of your life. The stand you make today will determine what stand you will make tomorrow.

As you scan the magazine headlines in a supermarket line, you can see that many people are preoccupied with prolonging their lives. If it isn't stem cell research or cryonics, it's the newest potion or lotion, pill, or miracle food.

It always makes me laugh.

Listen, you can eat all the tofu and wheat germ you want, but your life is going to end when it's going to end.

In a counterpoint, one magazine did a cover story a while ago about aging that asked the question: Would we really *want* to stop aging—even if we could? In other words, do we really want to live forever?

I guess it really comes down to what kind of life you are living right now. Medical science can seek to add years to your life, but only God can add life to your years, giving you a life that's worth living.

Our objective as Christians shouldn't be a long life as much as a full and meaningful one. A life with purpose.

Maybe you've heard the name Jim Elliot. He was a young husband and father when he was called by God to take the gospel to the Auca tribe in Ecuador. Tragically, Jim and his fellow missionaries were martyred, slain in their attempts to share Jesus Christ. In the months and years that followed, however, many members of that very tribe ended up coming to Christ—including the man who took the life of Jim Elliot with his spear.

In his journal, Elliot had written these words: "I seek not a long life but a full one, like You, Lord Jesus." Life, then, really doesn't boil down to the number of years that we live. It's a matter of what we do with those years.

In Acts chapters 6 and 7, we encounter the story of a young man who died at an early age—"well before his time," as some might say. Because of his bold stand for Jesus Christ, he became the first martyr of the Christian church. And His name was Stephen.

The Person God Uses

Some might look at the way Stephen's life ended and say, "What a tragic waste!" But to quote Jim Elliot once again: "He is no fool who gives up what he cannot keep, to gain what he cannot lose."

As we look at Stephen's life we see a life that is well lived. And we also discover the kind of man or woman God is looking for to use for His glory.

Who is the person God uses? What qualifications does a person need to be selected by the Lord as an instrument He will use for His purposes on earth?

A towering intellect?

Musical gifting?

Multiple college degrees?

A physically attractive body?

A bold, outgoing personality?

How about the person who struggles with timidity? What about the individual who's kind of a regular Joe, or a plain Jane? Is there a place for people like these in God's scheme of things?

Yes, especially for them. We see over and over in Scripture—and in life—that God seems to go out of His way to use people the world disdains, overlooks, or has written off altogether. If my life is an evidence of anything, it is an evidence of that.

And why does the Lord do this? We are given the answer in Paul's letter to the 1 Corinthians 1:26, where he writes,

> Take a good look, friends, at who you were when you got called into this life. I don't see many of "the brightest and the best" among you, not many influential, not many from high-society families. Isn't it obvious that God deliberately chose men and women that the culture overlooks and exploits and abuses, chose these "nobodies" to expose the hollow pretensions of the "somebodies"? That makes it quite clear that none of you can get by with blowing your own horn before God. Everything that we have—right thinking and right living, a clean slate and a fresh start—comes from God by way of Jesus Christ.
> (1 Corinthians 1:26-30, THE MESSAGE)

That's exactly what is happening to this very day; the Lord is still looking for the unexpected person to use in His kingdom. Why? So that all the glory can go to Him, where it rightly belongs.

The Threat of Division

No, sadly Stephen didn't live a long life, but he certainly lived a worthwhile one. He left his mark in a profound and significant way. Let's pick up the story in Acts 6.

But as the believers rapidly multiplied, there were rumblings of discontent. The Greek-speaking believers complained about the Hebrew-speaking believers, saying that their widows were being discriminated against in the daily distribution of food.

So the Twelve called a meeting of all the believers. They said, "We apostles should spend our time teaching the word of God, not running a food program. And so, brothers, select seven men who are well respected and are full of the Spirit and wisdom. We will give them this responsibility. Then we apostles can spend our time in prayer and teaching the word."

Everyone liked this idea, and they chose the following: Stephen (a man full of faith and the Holy Spirit), Philip, Procorus, Nicanor, Timon, Parmenas, and Nicolas of Antioch (an earlier convert to the Jewish faith). These seven were presented to the apostles, who prayed for them as they laid their hands on them.

So God's message continued to spread. The number of believers greatly increased in Jerusalem, and many of the Jewish priests were converted, too.

Stephen, a man full of God's grace and power, performed amazing miracles and signs among the people. (Acts 6:1-8, NLT)

Look at verse 1 again. "As the believers rapidly multiplied, there were rumblings of discontent." Or as the King James Version puts it, "There arose a murmuring."

Isn't that interesting? In the days when so many were being saved, so many miracles were being performed, and the Church was growing exponentially, there were unhappy people who started complaining.

Satan is a very clever adversary. He had tried to stop the Church through persecution, but instead of arresting their development, he actually helped them get on with the job of being what the Lord had called them to be. And instead of cowering in fear, the Church became a lean, mean, preaching machine.

So then Satan tried to infiltrate or join the Church through Ananias and Sapphira, two blatant hypocrites. But the Lord put a stop to that right away, as we read in the last chapter. So what was the devil's next battle tactic?

Divide and conquer.

He sought to pit one group of believers against another, and create a rift and division in the ranks of the young church. He must have felt he got some mileage out of that technique, because he has used it to devastating effect in the Church of Jesus Christ ever since.

People begin to complain and murmur, whisper and grumble, and the bitterness in their hearts starts to poison whatever the Lord is seeking to do in a given place.

This time, it was a struggle between the Greeks and Hebrews in the Jerusalem church. The Greek culture was prevalent in much of the world at this time, because of the conquests of Alexander the Great. However, after the Romans conquered the Greeks and effectively bludgeoned the world into submission, they went on to adopt much of the culture, language, and even religion of the former world masters.

Greek influence, then, was very prominent in the world of the New Testament. In Acts 6, we encounter two groups of Jewish widows in the Church, those who spoke Hebrew and those who spoke Greek. The Greek-speakers had probably been raised outside of Jerusalem, and then moved back to the Holy Land. As a result, they daily rubbed shoulders with those we might describe as old-school Hebrews— those who had always lived in Judea, and still observed the language and customs of that area.

This was not a spiritual clash, but a cultural one.

We still have such clashes today, don't we? Each generation has a style of music they prefer, a way of dressing, and certain cultural morays they believe to be important. Sometimes these preferences are built on a biblical concept, but many times they are simply that…preferences.

We in the body of Christ should never, never divide ourselves because of personal preferences. It's okay to have opinions and favor one style or practice over another. But it is wrong when you would divide from a fellow Christian over something of that nature.

I heard a story about a guy who was finally rescued after being stranded on a desert island. As the rescuers surveyed this desolate place where the man had been a castaway for so many years, they came across three buildings.

"Well, this is interesting," they said. "You've built three buildings. What are they?"

"The first building is my house," he said. "And that building over there is my church."

"Okay," they replied, "that's two of the buildings. What's the third one?"

"Oh—that's the church I used to go to."

People will leave churches over the silliest things, getting hung up on the most minor of issues—things that should never, never divide believers one from another.

There is a statement I like that says, "In essentials unity; in nonessentials liberty; in all things charity."

In essentials unity. We must not and cannot deviate from the essential doctrines of our faith—foundation stones like the deity of Christ or the authority of Scripture. But in the lesser teachings—matters that boil down to one person seeing things a little bit differently from another? In these things there ought to be liberty…and love.

The apostles, filled as they were with the Holy Spirit, must have sensed Satan's tactic to divide the body and distract the leadership. So they said, in effect, "Look, we can't hassle with this. We've got to get on with the work of ministry. Let's get some guys in charge of this who can handle these kinds of details, and work out some godly plans."

So they found these seven men who were full of the Holy Spirit (who became what we might call "deacons" today), and delegated to them many of the details and "people issues" that kept popping up in this Jerusalem mega-church.

Stephen emerged from the ranks of these men who had stepped forward to serve others in the body of Christ. Let's identify a few principles about his life.

Qualities of a Well-Lived Life

Stephen was filled with the Holy Spirit.

The apostles' instructions had been: "Seek out from among you seven men of good reputation, full of the Holy Spirit and wisdom" (Acts 6:3), and Stephen was one of those men.

This quality is the most important of all. If you had all the other qualities I will mention, but lacked this one, then you would be of little use to the Lord.

The Bible tells us in Ephesians 5 to "be filled with the Holy Spirit." As we've noted already, that could be translated "controlled" by the Spirit, or more literally, *permeated* by the Spirit. The Holy Spirit wants to guide us in all that we think and do in life—a practical power that will help us to change our world and our culture.

Stephen was filled with wisdom.

Again, the passage speaks of Stephen as one who was "full of the Holy Spirit and wisdom." As we will note in Acts 7, he was obviously a student of the Scriptures. Knowing the Bible as he did made him a powerful instrument in the Lord's hands, but it was his God-given wisdom that instructed him on how to use and apply that knowledge. Here's the sad truth: You can have a vast amount of knowledge—even Bible knowledge—but if you aren't guided by the Holy Spirit and godly wisdom, that learning will be of little help to you or those in your life.

We know that Stephen was wise beyond his years, because we read later that his opponents simply could not stand against the wisdom and spirit by which he spoke.

Stephen was faithful in the little things.

As a deacon, a servant of the Church, this young man diligently pursued the tasks that God had set before him. Initially, that involved waiting on tables and helping to care for widows (and settle their squabbles). In other words, he pitched in and did what needed to be done in the family of God.

I have found that if you want to be used by God, you have to be willing to do the little things first. The truth is, you can never be too small for God to use…but you can be too big.

I remember, at the age of nineteen, when I first walked in the door at Calvary Chapel in Costa Mesa and volunteered my services to Pastor Chuck Smith.

"Pastor Chuck," I said, "I want to be used by God. I'll do whatever you want me to do around here."

Who knows? I thought to myself. *Maybe he'll want me to take one of the midweek services and start preaching.* Instead, Chuck said, "That's wonderful, Greg. I have a man I want you to talk to. Come meet Pastor Romaine."

Now I didn't know who Pastor Romaine was at that point. As it turned out, he used to be a drill sergeant in the Marine Corps, and took a special delight in whipping young bucks like me into shape. My first job, as it turned out, was to do janitorial work, basically for free. They never paid me for it.

So I found myself pushing a broom.

Wait a second, I thought. *I thought they were going to let me serve the Lord.* But that was just what they were doing. Though they never said it in so many words, they were telling me, "Show faithfulness in the little things, if you want to do bigger things." So I faithfully went about what was set before me, and in time they sent me out to do a Bible study in a place no one else wanted to go to. I ended up teaching in some pretty interesting places—even doing a couple of services in a mental institution.

So it wasn't all janitorial work. I also made hospital calls, visited convalescent centers, and went basically wherever they would allow me to go. Sometimes, when all of the pastors would go out to lunch, I would tell the Church secretary, "Route all the calls over into this office, and I'll counsel the people while the pastors are gone." Little did people realize that when they called Calvary Chapel Costa Mesa for counsel, they ended up talking to a nineteen-year-old ex-hippie.

The truth is, I was anxious to do whatever I could to serve the Lord. And I still am.

Jesus said, "He who is faithful in what is least is faithful also in much; and he who is unjust in what is least is unjust also in much" (Luke 16:10). So Stephen faithfully served the Lord in whatever opportunity was placed before him, whether large or small.

To this day I love serving the Lord. Yes, there are times when that service is difficult, challenging, and depleting. But even when the work is hard, I derive great joy from doing what I know to be the will of God. I don't mean just preparing and delivering a message to God's people, I mean being used by God in any way that He sees fit. I count it a great privilege to be called by God, and to have the opportunity to represent Him. If you have discovered this, too, then you'll know exactly what I'm talking about. You sense God's blessing on you, and there's nothing else like it.

One of my favorite movies of all time is *Chariots of Fire*, which deals in part with the life of Eric Liddell of Scotland. He was an Olympic champion runner in his time, and went on to be a career missionary. As a committed Christian, Liddell struggled for quite awhile as to whether he should compete, or leave immediately for the mission field.

In one scene, his sister presses him to abandon his career in running, and being his missionary work immediately. Liddell replies (in that classic Scottish brogue), "I believe God made me for a purpose. But he also made me *fast*. And when I run I feel His pleasure."

I've always loved that line.

Could you say the same thing? Do you feel God's pleasure in what you are doing? Is your life being lived well? Are you doing what God has called you to do? Or do you find yourself squandering and wasting your life?

Stephen was faithful in the little things as he went about his Father's business. And soon the Lord was using him to preach the gospel and work mighty miracles.

A Savage Attack

Here is how one contemporary translation sets the stage for Satan's brutal assault on this vibrant young disciple:

> Stephen, brimming with God's grace and energy, was doing wonderful things among the people, unmistakable signs that God was among them. But then some men from the meeting place whose membership was made up of freed slaves, Cyrenians, Alexandrians, and some others from Cilicia and Asia, went up against him trying to argue him down. But they were no match for his wisdom and spirit when he spoke. (Acts 6:8-10, THE MESSAGE)

You can almost imagine what Satan was thinking. "This has to stop!" The devil hates evangelism, and was furious at seeing the name of Jesus spreading further and further among Jews of many nations.

This time, Satan's attack went beyond intimidation or even a beating. This time, he wanted one of these guys taken out. And because the Lord allowed it, Stephen was about to become the first martyr of the Church.

The actual incident fell into a pattern that we see again and again in Scripture and history, right up to the days in which we live. Because Stephen's enemies couldn't find anything wrong to hang on him, they made up lies. Acts 6:11 says that "they secretly induced men to say, 'We have heard him speak blasphemous words against Moses and God.'"

So Stephen was brought up on false charges before the Sanhedrin, the Jewish ruling body of that day—something like our Supreme Court. Obviously, in a situation like that, you had to be very careful what you said. These guys had the power to let someone go, or to simply kill them.

Stephen, however, didn't look at the Sanhedrin as a group to cower before. He saw it as a group of people to reach—one more audience for the gospel he loved to preach. And so he seized the opportunity and went for it with all his heart.

We read about it in this Acts account:

> At this point everyone in the high council stared at Stephen, because his

face became as bright as an angel's.

Then the high priest asked Stephen, "Are these accusations true?" (Acts 6:15; 7:1, NLT)

I'm not sure what the Sanhedrin was expecting from this young man. An apology, perhaps? An attempt to clear up an unfortunate misunderstanding? Maybe a servile groveling for mercy?

Whatever they may have expected, what they received was a brilliant overview of Israel's history. One thing is clear: Stephen knew his Bible! What's that expression movie critics like to use? A *tour de force*? That's what he gave those guys that day, sweeping them through their own history from Joseph, to Moses, to David and Solomon. The Sanhedrin may have actually liked hearing the history part, but it was all leading to a conclusion that they would *not* like. In fact, it would send them into a murderous fury.

Looking around the room into the smug faces of these rulers, Stephen wrapped up with this amazing denunciation:

"You stubborn people! You are heathen at heart and deaf to the truth. Must you forever resist the Holy Spirit? That's what your ancestors did, and so do you! Name one prophet your ancestors didn't persecute! They even killed the ones who predicted the coming of the Righteous One—the Messiah whom you betrayed and murdered. You deliberately disobeyed God's law, even though you received it from the hands of angels." (vv. 51-53, NLT)

The Sanhedrin had thought they were sitting in judgment of Stephen, but it was the other way around. And the words that came from this young man's mouth weren't mere human words; Stephen was filled with the Holy Spirit, speaking the words of God Himself to them.

Why was His face glowing like that of an angel? For one reason, he knew he was in the center of God's will, doing the very thing God had put him on earth to do. There is great joy in that.

"Well Greg," you say, "I wish I felt the joy of the Lord in my life. I feel like I've become dried up, spiritually."

Let me ask you this: How long has it been since you've shared your faith with someone? The Christian life isn't meant to be hoarded, it's meant to be shared. We're told in Proverbs 11:25, "The one who blesses others is abundantly blessed; those who help others are helped."[33]

You have been blessed to be a blessing to others.

See here's what it comes down to. As you start declaring what God has done for you, *it will become more real for you as you make it real to them.* In other words, as truth passes through you from the Holy Spirit to someone else's heart, it doesn't just pass through, it enriches your life in transit!

Every one of us needs to look for opportunities to tell others about Jesus. I can't tell you how many times that I have been depleted and drained and felt like I had nothing to offer. But as I begin to speak about the Lord, He gives me the right words to say—and then I can't seem to say enough. I start off on empty and end up on full.

Jesus said, "Give, and it will be given to you. A good measure, pressed down, shaken together and running over, will be poured into your lap. For with the measure you use, it will be measured to you" (Luke 6:38, NIV).

So on that day when so much was at stake for a young man just getting started in the Christian life, Stephen may have said to himself, "I may not ever have an opportunity like this again. I'm going for it!" And as he preached, his face just lit up, shining like the face of an angel. I don't know exactly what that last expression means, but I know there must have been something about his life right then that just radiated the presence and love of God. Unbeknownst to Stephen, death waited right around the corner for him. But in that moment, he was never more alive.

You might say, "I'll be honest, Greg, I'm just not experiencing much joy in my life right now. Things have been pretty tough." I can well understand those feelings, but I'll tell you this: If you begin ministering in the name of Jesus and in the power of the Holy Spirit, if you begin helping someone who is hurting even worse than you, you too will be changed by the power of God.

That's what Stephen was experiencing. And God was blessing him as he boldly proclaimed the gospel without hesitation or fear.

And how were these religious leaders responding?

They were *seething* with hatred. Without even consulting with one another, they had already decided, "We're going to execute this young man today." Look at the blind bias of their hatred for Stephen and his message in verse 57.

"At this they covered their ears and, yelling at the top of their voices, they all rushed at him."[34]

Shut up! Stop! Stop glowing! Stop radiating truth! Shut your mouth—we don't want to hear it. We can't take it!

Amazing. Here were cultured, affluent, well-educated, powerful religious leaders, yet they can't even allow a young Christian with an angelic face to speak truth in their presence.

Isn't it interesting how angry and completely irrational people can become when the subject of Jesus Christ comes up? You can have a discussion with them about any topic under the sun, and even find yourself agreeing on a number of issues and even disagreeing in a civil way. But the moment the subject turns to religion—and more specifically to Jesus Christ—things change. Suddenly that rational, intelligent, even intellectual individual turns to emotional, irrational, heated arguments. Red-faced and angry, he or she begins screaming at you.

You say to yourself, "What's going on here?"

I'll tell you what's going on. It is the conviction of the Holy Spirit. In the words of the book of Acts, they have been "cut to the heart" by what you have shared. Very possibly, they have been fighting a long battle with God in their lives already, running from Him and resisting His Spirit. And then you come along with your simple word of testimony and they can't handle it.

In John 3:20 (NLT) Jesus put it like this: "All who do evil hate the light and refuse to go near it for fear their sins will be exposed."

UPSIDE DOWN LIVING **127**

Verse 48 tells us that "they rushed at him and dragged him out of the city and began to stone him."

Now understand that this did not happen in a few seconds; death by stoning took awhile. When you were going to stone a person you would generally strip down to the waist, because it was a long, arduous workout. And Stephen, being a young, able-bodied man, did not die as quickly as others might have. What then did Stephen do as those stones were hurled against his body? Did he call a curse on those who were doing this to him? Did he cry out in anger against God for allowing this?

No. He prayed.

> As they stoned him, Stephen prayed, "Lord Jesus, receive my spirit." He fell to his knees, shouting, "Lord, don't charge them with this sin!" And with that, he died. (vv. 59-60, NLT)

Jesus heard the prayer of his brave son and soldier Stephen, and gave him grace. The words "Lord Jesus, receive my spirit," indicate that Stephen knew full well that the moment he left earth he would pass immediately into the presence of God in heaven. The Bible does not teach that there is a lull or a gap between our death on earth and our arrival in the presence of God. Scripture knows nothing of holding places, purgatories, or soul sleep. No, when a believer dies he or she immediately enters the presence of God. The Bible clearly teaches that "to be absent from the body is to be present with the Lord."[35] Jesus Himself told the thief on the cross beside Him, "I tell you the truth, today you will be with me in paradise" (Luke 23:43, NIV).

Today. Not tomorrow or a month later or after a millennium or so in the grave.

John Bunyan wrote, "Death is but a passage out of a prison into a palace." In other words, when death strikes the Christian down, they fall into heaven.

Stephen's prayer was answered, and he was ushered into the

presence of the Lord. I love his amazing statement in verse 56:

"*Look! I see the heavens opened and the Son of Man standing at the right hand of God!*" Why is that an amazing statement? Because normally when we read of Jesus in heaven, He is *seated* at the right hand of the Father. But here we read He is standing. Why?

Jesus said, "Whoever acknowledges me before men, I will also acknowledge him before my Father in heaven."[36] As Stephen stood for Jesus on earth, Jesus stood for Stephen in heaven. When you stand for God here, He will stand for you there. It's almost as though the Lord is standing in honor of the first martyr. "Come home, son. I am proud of you. Well done. I love you."

And who could help but notice how Stephen's last words on earth echo the words of Jesus as He hung on the cross? "Father forgive them, for they know not what they do." Stephen says, "Lord, do not lay this sin against their charge."

What Do We Learn from Stephen?

What take-away truths are there for us in this brief, powerful biography from the pages of Acts? Many…but I will conclude this chapter with two.

Live life to the full for Christ...right now

One thing that occurs to me is simply this: God knows when death will come, so don't stress over it. The Bible says that there is "a time to be born, and a time to die,"[37] and "it is appointed unto men once to die, but after this the judgment."[38]

So you can take every precaution and do whatever you can to try to prolong your life, but when your time comes, it comes. God allowed Stephen's life to be taken because it was this man's hour—young as he was—to depart earth and enter heaven. As with his forefather David, he had fulfilled his purpose in his generation (see Acts 13:36).

This is why we want to make the most of our lives, because none of us knows when that hour might be for our own homegoing.

So do you want to serve the Lord? Then what are you waiting for? Don't wait for some mythical "later" or "ideal" time in your life to start living for Jesus with all your heart.

Jim Elliot wrote: "Wherever you are, be all there. Live to the hilt every situation you believe to be the will of God."

God has purposes beyond our understanding.

Tragedies like the murder of Stephen can be difficult to handle. Why would God allow such a thing to happen to His loyal servant? Why would God permit such a promising life of ministry to be cut short like that?

We'll have to wait for heaven to receive answers to many of the troubling questions we have on earth. But in Stephen's case, the Bible makes it clear that his martyrdom made an indelible mark on the soul of at least one of those powerful members of the Sanhedrin: Saul of Tarsus.

The Bible says that Stephen's executioners laid their coats at Saul's feet, indicating that he was in probably in charge of this bloody operation. I wonder if Stephen looked right into his eyes as he called on the Lord to forgive his murderers. I wonder if he was thinking, "*Oh Lord, if You would save a man like Saul—what a change You could bring to the world through Him!*"

Saul of Tarsus, of course, did come to faith in Jesus Christ, and became the man we now know as the apostle Paul. Later in his ministry, as he looked back on the Lord's commissioning him to preach, he recalled praying, "Lord…when the blood of Your martyr Stephen was shed, I also was standing by consenting to his death, and guarding the clothes of those who were killing him" (Acts 22:19).

He would never forget that terrible day, and I believe it was a turning point in his life. A man who was driven by hate became a man motivated for the rest of his life by love, and I believe that Stephen was the one who reached him more than any other. So Stephen may not have had many converts, but he had one in the apostle Paul that would lead to the conversion of untold millions—make that, *billions*—of others.

I have done many, many funerals as a pastor, and over the years I have noted this one significant fact: Sometimes when a believer leaves for heaven, the people he or she has been praying for and trying to reach through many long years come to Christ at the funeral!

It sometimes takes the death of the one who has faithfully witnessed and prayed for that non-believing relative or prodigal to wake them up. No, the individual who did the witnessing doesn't know about that conversion…or do they? Jesus said that the angels in heaven celebrate when a lost soul comes to faith—and who's to say that the redeemed believers on the other side don't join in that happy celebration?

My point is, your testimony and the legacy of your life continue on after you have died. And that is why you want to be diligent to make all the impact you can make for Jesus right now—even though you may not know the full implications of what you accomplished until you're in eternity.

Maybe you are investing in the life of someone right now that no one really knows or cares about. But who knows? This person could become the next Billy Graham.

No, Stephen wasn't granted time to gather a large number of converts, but even if he'd only had one—Saul of Tarsus—it was enough for a lifetime.

In subsequent chapters, we'll see how Saul threw himself into a relentless persecution against the Church, hunting down believers and having them imprisoned or executed. Ultimately, however, he gave his life to Jesus. This gives us hope as we think about the people in our lives who seem especially hardened to the gospel or give us a hard time about our beliefs. You know whom I'm talking about…that coworker who is always on your case about your faith…that family member who peppers you with hard questions whenever you're together…that kid at school who mocks you more loudly than all the others put together. You say to yourself, *There is no hope for that person.*

But once again, you never know. He or she might be closer to the kingdom of God than you think. In fact, the very reason for their increased hostility may be because they are under the Holy Spirit, and are striking out at the one who dares to tell them the truth.

We all want to live a life that is full and meaningful. Knowing that life is short and that death will come, we don't want to waste those few years God gives us on earth.

Because death *will* come, as it came for Stephen and as it will come for us all. Will you be ready to meet God when that moment arrives?

EIGHT
Leading Others to Christ

I had been up early, my body clock thrown into confusion by a trip to Israel and the resulting jet lag.

Instead of sitting around for an hour drinking coffee, however, I decided to maximize the moment and take an early morning walk. The air was fresh and cool and, much to my surprise and delight, a magnificent rainbow arched across the sky in front of me.

We don't see all that many rainbows in Southern California, so the sight truly thrilled me. On an impulse, I pulled out my little iPhone with its two-megapixel camera and snapped a quick shot.

The resulting picture, however, wasn't anything to talk about; you really couldn't even tell there was a rainbow. *Oh well*, I told myself, *I'll just enjoy the journey. That's the best I can do.*

But was it? I wasn't that far from home, and I could run back and get my good camera. What a shot that would be! And even as I hesitated, the rainbow grew more beautiful, the colors more vivid. On a 1-to-10 scale, it had started at a 5, and had now soared to a 6.

Then—even as I stared at it—it became a 7!

That made my decision for me. I had to run home and get my camera and try to capture this. Breathless and back at the house, I remembered that I'd left the camera in the car. Perfect! I jumped behind the wheel, driving back to the spot where I'd been walking. Was the rainbow still there? Yes, it was. By now it was an 8, a fiery swath of colors across the morning sky.

Then I thought of an even better place that would give me a perfect angle for the shot. As I drove, the rainbow burned even brighter. Now it was a 9 or 10. I could have just pulled off the road right then (if only I had!), rolled down my window, and snapped a picture of it. But I wanted to get to that "perfect" place.

Arriving at the place I had envisioned, I jumped out of the car with my camera and…it was gone. The rarest and most perfect of rainbows had burned itself right out of the sky, and there was no bringing it back. Getting back into the car, I thought, *This is why people should not chase rainbows*.

Trying to be Ansel Adams, trying to get the shot of the century, I ended up missing the whole thing. How frustrating! It would have been far better to just continue with my early morning walk, worshiping and praising the Creator for the beauty He had brought across my path.

Later it occurred to me that my experience had been a pretty good metaphor for life—especially our tendency to chase after things always just out of reach.

You know how it goes. When you're really young you think to yourself, "When I finally get into high school, that will be really cool. I can't wait."

And then…"When I graduate from high school, I'll be on my way."

And then…"When I get through college, life will really begin for me."

And then…"When I get into my career, it's going to be great."

And then…"When I move up the ladder in this company and make a little more money, I'll be ready to roll."

And then…"When I own my own business, I'll be set."

And then…"When I get married, I'll be happier."

And then…"I was happier single, I think I'll get a divorce."

And then…"But I'm lonely now. I'll get married again."

And then…"Maybe what I needed was some kids to raise. That will make me happy."

And then…"How can I get away from these kids? They're driving me crazy."

On it goes. Life flies by, and you find yourself chasing rainbows, never quite catching up to them. Then one day you wake up and realize there is more life behind you than there is in front of you. And you ask yourself the question, "What happened to my life? Where did it go?"

Hole in His Heart

When I read the story of the Ethiopian official in Acts chapter 8, I have to wonder if he had been a man who had chased a few rainbows. Here was a man with influence, power, and wealth. In his own nation, he was probably a renowned and well-respected man.

Here is how Scripture introduces him.

> And behold, a man of Ethiopia, a eunuch of great authority under Candace the queen of the Ethiopians, who had charge of all her treasury, and had come to Jerusalem to worship, was returning. (Acts 8:27-28)

He was secretary of the treasury of a powerful nation, second only to the queen in his power and influence. Yet for all of that, he had an emptiness in his heart that had sent him on a long journey in search of the true and living God.

His search led him to Jerusalem, the spiritual capital of the world at that time. Yet even there, though he had the opportunity to learn more about Judaism and marvel at the great Temple, he did not find what he had been looking for.

But he had come away with a very precious possession—a scroll of the book of Isaiah. It's evident from the story that he was committed to search that scroll from one end to the other, seeking clues and knowledge about this great God of the Hebrews.

God will always respond—someway, somehow—to a seeking heart. And unbeknownst to this African official as he rode along in his chariot on a bright, sunny day in the desert, he was about to meet his heart's desire.

It's always a great story when a person gives his or her heart to

Christ. And we can see quite clearly from this story that when a person really believes in Jesus Christ, their life changes—because this man went from emptiness and misery to overflowing joy. In fact, the story ends by saying, "He went on his way rejoicing."

The Bible says that when we believe in Jesus Christ we pass from darkness to light, from the power of Satan to the power of God. God's Word is describing what takes place in an individual's life.

But here's what we need to recognize: No two people will come to faith in the same way—different individuals, possessing different temperaments, will experience conversion in different ways. Some have an intense emotional response when they come to put their faith in Jesus. Others don't. But the emotions of the moment have little to do with the *reality* of that transforming moment. As we all know, feelings come and go; tears and goose-bumps are no guarantee that an individual's decision for Christ will stand the test of time.

In His parable of the sower and the soils, Jesus spoke about seed sown in rocky soil that sprouted and shot up quickly. But it withered just as quickly in the hot sun, because it had no root. As the Lord explained, "These likewise are the ones sown on stony ground who, when they hear the word, immediately receive it with gladness; and they have no root in themselves, and so endure only for a time. Afterward, when tribulation or persecution arises for the word's sake, immediately they stumble" (Mark 4:16-17).

An emotional experience, then, does not guarantee you have really met God. When I prayed and asked Christ to come in my life, I felt nothing at all. Because of that lack of a defining experience, I falsely concluded God had rejected me. It was only later that I discovered the Christian life is a walk of faith, not of feeling.

Even though emotions and experiences may vary for those who come to Christ, certain things remain true about every genuine conversion. As we look more closely at how this Ethiopian official found salvation out on a desert road, we will consider five principles common to every genuine conversion.

Phillip's Surprise Assignment

In Acts 8, we see how Philip led an influential foreign official to faith in Christ. Have you ever had the privilege of leading someone to the Lord?

"Well, Greg," you might say, "I just can't see God using me in that way. I don't have that gift."

Perhaps you've believed that leading someone to Jesus is an experience reserved for a few specially anointed people with the spiritual gift of evangelism.

But if that were the case, why is the Great Commission given to every Christian? The fact is, all believers in Christ are called to go into all of the world and preach the gospel. We are all called. We all have a part to play.

The primary way God has chosen to reach people who are not yet believers is through verbal communication. I have always found that a little bit amazing.

In a recent interview, the writer said to me, "You seem to be very natural when you speak. It must come easily to you."

"Nothing could be further from the truth," I told him. "Before I was a Christian, I wasn't a public speaker at all. Far from it!" After I came to faith in Jesus Christ, however, I realized the best way to help people believe was through verbal communication. So as I began to speak a little bit, here and there, in front of people, I came to realize it wasn't about *me* anyway. It was all about the message.

What if you had somehow come across a sure-fire cure for cancer—a remedy so effective that it reversed and eventually eliminated every form of the disease in every patient. Beyond any shadow of a doubt, you knew that this cure would work for every cancer patient everywhere.

Now imagine that you meet an individual with Stage 4 cancer—someone with only weeks, perhaps even days, to live. And in your heart you knew very well that if that individual would only accept your cure, he or she would be instantly healed.

What would you do?

"That's a dilemma," you say, "because I'm really not comfortable talking to strangers. And I don't know if I want to leave my comfort zone, engage this person in conversation, and actually say, 'I have found a cure for cancer.' They might think I was being forward. Or maybe I wouldn't word it right, and they wouldn't like the way I said it. Or maybe they would reject me and send me away. Besides, the whole thing is a little bit embarrassing."

Obviously, you would have to get over such feelings, because that individual's life would be infinitely more important than your temporary discomfort.

You already know where I'm going with this! The message we have as Christians is even more important than a cure for cancer. For this is the cure for *sin*. This is the only way to get right with God, and determines the destiny of an eternal soul. There has to come a moment where we say to ourselves, "You know what? It's not about me. It's not about whether I feel comfortable or don't feel comfortable. It's about me obeying the Lord."

No matter what we might think about it, the primary way that God reaches people who do not yet know Him is through verbal communication—God's children talking to people who aren't yet His children. Romans 10:14 (NLT) says, "But how can they call on him to save them unless they believe in him? And how can they believe in him if they have never heard about him? And how can they hear about him unless someone tells them?"

Who is that "someone"?

It might very well be you…or me.

God chooses to reach people through people. And that brings us to our first principle.

#1: God is the One Who Saves People…Not Us

No matter how many times we may have heard this, I'm not sure it really sinks in. We still find ourselves thinking that somehow everything depends on our performance or technique or Bible knowledge or winning personality. But it just isn't true. Of course, God can use any or all of those things, but He is in no way limited by their presence or absence. In the final analysis, He must be the One that touches a heart, prepares a heart, and draws a heart to Himself.

In John 6:65 Jesus reminds us, "No man can come to Me unless the Father has enabled him."

So just for good measure, let's say it again.

It isn't something I do.

It isn't something I bring about.

It isn't dependent on my clever arguments or power of persuasion.

Sometimes all I will be able to do is sow the tiniest little seed of truth about Jesus. At other times, maybe I'll have a quick opportunity to add just a little water to a seed someone else sowed already—perhaps a long time ago. At another time—who knows?—I may be in the right place at the right time to simply help someone take that final step into the kingdom.

Remember Paul's words to the Corinthians?

"Each of us did the work the Lord gave us. I planted the seed in your hearts, and Apollos watered it, but it was God who made it grow. It's not important who does the planting, or who does the watering. What's important is that God makes the seed grow. The one who plants and the one who waters work together with the same purpose. And both will be rewarded for their own hard work" (1 Corinthians 3:5-9, NLT).

Believe me, I know that it can be discouraging when you talk to people or when you try to reach family members and they won't listen or respond. And sometimes you feel like saying, "Oh just forget about it. No one wants to hear this anyway. I'll just keep my mouth shut."

It's like a farmer who invests his resources and plants a crop, only to see his little seedlings destroyed by a storm or drought. But when he replants and then enjoys a bumper crop, it becomes worth it all, and his discouragement is forgotten.

In the same way, we can maintain a faithful witness for the Lord, and nothing ever seems to happen. And then one day, the seed takes root. One person gets it, gives his or her life to Jesus, experiences the joy of salvation, and all the angels of heaven cheer from the celestial grandstands.

Jesus affirmed that there is "joy in heaven over one sinner who repents."[39] The psalmist agrees, saying, "Those who sow tears shall reap joy. Yes, they go out weeping, carrying seed for sowing, and return singing, carrying their sheaves."[40]

#2: We Need to Have a Heart for Nonbelievers.

Then Philip went down to the city of Samaria and preached Christ to them. And the multitudes with one accord heeded the things spoken by Philip, hearing and seeing the miracles that he did. For unclean spirits, crying with a loud voice, came out of many who were possessed; and many who were paralyzed and lame were healed. And there was great joy in that city. (Acts 8:5-8)

Before the incident with the Ethiopian royal official ever takes place, we already know from Scripture that Philip had a heart for nonbelievers.

Remember that Philip, along with Stephen and five other Spirit-filled men, had been called to be deacons in the Jerusalem church, backing up the apostles by taking care of day-to-day church operations.

But you never know where the wind of the Spirit will blow a Spirit-filled man or woman, do you? When a storm of persecution broke out after the death of Stephen, Philip grabbed his suitcase and headed for Samaria with the gospel.

Samaria? That's a name that may not mean a lot to you and me, but when you understand the culture of that day, it was something of a shocking destination for Philip. To begin with, he was a Jew, and Jews and Samaritans *hated* each other. With a generational enmity that had persisted for centuries, Jews were taught from their youth to hate the Samaritan people, regarding them as illegitimate before the Lord.

After all, the Jews reasoned, the Samaritans worshiped God in the wrong way and in the wrong place. Besides all that, their ancestors had intermarried with Gentiles, so they weren't true Jews anyway.

But Philip had deliberately set his eyes on the city of Samaria, and God had placed the desire in his heart to reach them with the Good News.

It makes a simple point: If you want to be an effective communicator, you need a willingness to approach people who are different than you. Most of us prefer to hang around people who are most like us, don't we? We feel naturally inclined toward people who look like us, talk like us, and have the same interests as us. We're uncomfortable when we find ourselves in a group that holds different values than we do, and speaks or dresses in ways so very different from our own circle of friends and acquaintances.

But what if God calls you to such a group or such an individual? Would you be willing to make yourself uncomfortable for His sake? Would you be willing to acknowledge that all prejudice is wrong, and that everybody needs Jesus? Are you prepared to represent your Lord without embarrassment in front of people who may not accept you or cheer you on?

Philip was. And that's just what he did.

The truth is, we can talk all day about the latest evangelism techniques and methodologies. I was listening to a Christian radio broadcast the other day, and some guy announced he'd come up with a set of clever new conversation starters—designed to steer everyday encounters toward sharing the gospel. That's fine. I applaud his efforts. But the fact is, none of that will matter if you really don't care much about people.

Don't kid yourself, a person can tell right away if you care about them or not. My goodness, even a dog can tell that! A person knows within seconds if you are sharing with them out of sincerity or if you're doing it out of a mere sense of duty.

The Samaritans must have sensed Philip's heart for them right away—or he would have never got to first base with them when he went to preach Christ.

#3: We Need to be Open and Obedient to the Holy Spirit

An angel came to Philip in Acts 8:26, and said, "Arise and go toward the south."

Angels are fascinating creatures working behind the scenes, doing the work of God in this world. The book of Hebrews calls them "ministering spirits sent to serve those who will inherit salvation."[41] In the psalms, we learn that "the angel of the Lord encamps all around those who fear Him, and delivers them."[42]

So that means that every one of us have angels that have been involved in our lives. The Bible says it's even possible that you have met an angel without knowing it.[43]

But here's the thing about angels. They're very careful about not drawing attention to themselves; they are instantly obedient to God, and do His work quietly and effectively. Billy Graham once described them as "God's secret agents."

So we read that an angel came to Philip and said, "Here's your assignment….Get up and go toward the south." And that was the end of it.

But there is another way Acts 8:26 could be translated. Instead of reading (as it does in the NIV) "Go south to the road—the desert road—that goes down from Jerusalem to Gaza…", the passage could just as easily read "Go to the desert at noon."

So the angel's instructions to Philip might have been, "I want you to go to this desolate part of the wilderness, and I want you to do so during the hottest part of the day."

The angel specifically directed him onto the desert road, a seldom-used route between Jerusalem and Gaza. It would be like God coming to you and saying, "Go out into the Mojave Desert in July at twelve noon, and I'll tell you what to do next."

How easily Philip could have argued with the angel. "You want me go where and do what? Preach to lizards? Hey, that place is too hot even for them! You want me to leave this place of revival, blessing, joy, and miracles to head off by myself into the middle of nowhere? Really, does that even make sense?"

Notice that the angel did not tell him what was going to happen when he got there. There was no blueprint, no itinerary, no vision statement or set of objectives. He was being led one step at a time.

Philip discovered what you and I may also discover: *God's way becomes plain when we start walking in it*. Obedience to revealed truth guarantees guidance in matters unrevealed.

Has the Lord shown you something He wants you to do? Then just do it. Because there is a time to sit and there is a time to move. There is a time to sow and there is a time to reap.

So Philip, the one-time-deacon of the First Jerusalem Church, simply salutes, straps on his sandals, and obeys. It would have been totally understandable if he had run in the other direction, as the prophet Jonah had done (the original chicken of the sea) when he received baffling directions from the Lord.

But to Philip's credit, he left everything and headed south.

"Sorry guys, I've got to leave the revival now."

"What? Are you kidding? This thing is about to explode! Where are you going?"

"To the desert."

"Why the desert?"

"Because an angel told me to."

"By yourself?"

"Yes, by myself."

"Why? What will you do there?"

"I have no idea. But God said to go, so I'm going. See you down the road."

Sometime later Philip stood on that deserted wilderness road in the blazing sun, probably thinking to himself, "Okay, Lord. What's next?"

Suddenly he saw a cloud of dust in the distance—a caravan

lumbering south from Jerusalem. As the procession drew nearer, he saw mounted men and bodyguards surrounding a man in an ornate chariot. Evidently, the man was reading something.

Suddenly it dawned on Philip. "Oh! I think I get it, Lord. This must be what You want me to do."

Who was this man from Ethiopia? In New Testament days, Ethiopia was a large kingdom located south of Egypt. To the Greeks and Romans, it represented the outer limits of the known world. And this particular Ethiopian, identified as the eunuch, was very possibly second only to Candace the queen. (Candace, by the way, wasn't the queen's name, it was her title—like "Caesar" or "Pharaoh.")

This African official had gone to Jerusalem looking for answers, and had apparently found none. But as we mentioned, he had somehow come away with a copy of the scroll of Isaiah. Back in those days, people didn't have shelves full of Bibles like many of us do today. They read from scrolls that had been meticulously copied by hand.

As Philip approached, the Ethiopian "just happened" to be reading from the passage we know today as Isaiah 53—which contains a vivid prophetic description of the death of Jesus, written hundreds of years before our Lord walked this earth.

So the traveler read, re-read, and pondered.

This was Philip's moment of opportunity. And just in case he might have missed it, the Spirit nudged him and said, "Go near and overtake this chariot."

In verse 30 we read:

> So Philip ran to him, and heard him reading the prophet Isaiah, and said, "Do you understand what you are reading?"

In that moment, Philip utilized something that is often lacking in many presentations of the gospel.

That something is called *tact*.

Tact has been defined as the intuitive knowledge of saying the right thing at the right time. Some Christians don't seem to have much of this quality at all—or even see its importance.

Jesus was so tactful. Think back to His encounter with the woman at the well in Sychar, Samaria, described in John 4. Here was a woman who had been married and divorced five times, and was currently cohabiting with yet another man. And this was back in the day when a lifestyle like that was considered scandalous. (Today we celebrate it.) So this social outcast went at noon to draw water from the community well, because that was the time when she least expected to meet anyone.

As she approached the well, however, she saw a Man sitting there. And not just a man from the village, but also a Jewish man. I can just imagine how she must have braced herself for a confrontation. She probably thought, *Oh no, this is going to be trouble. He's going to say something mean to me or treat me like dirt. For sure He's going to insult me.*

Trying her best to ignore this Stranger, she lowered her bucket into the well and began to fill her water pot. That's when the Man at the well shocked her to the core by looking right into her eyes and asking her a question.

"Would you give Me a drink of water?"

Surprised as she was, she answered, "Why would a Jew ask for a drink of water from a Samaritan? Don't you know that Jews have no dealings with Samaritans?"

Jesus replied, "If you knew who I was, you would ask Me and I would give you living water."

"Living water? What are you talking about?"

Just that quickly, a conversation developed, as Jesus had tactfully built a bridge of communication to this woman. Far too often we burn our bridges when we ought to be building them, and establishing a dialogue.

I used that word "dialogue" deliberately. Many of us have imagined sharing our faith to be more of a monologue—a one-way information dump. In a real conversation, however, you ask questions, you listen, and you respond appropriately, seeking to build a bridge of communication so that you might bring a word of witness to that individual.

That's what Jesus did, and that's what Philip was doing when he said, "Excuse me sir. Do you understand what you're reading?"

The official said, "How can I, unless someone guides me?" And he asked Philip to come up into the chariot and sit with him. That was all the introduction Philip needed. He knew the man's heart had already been prepared and made ready by the Holy Spirit.

#4: Give the Gospel Accurately

We've all heard about quack doctors who attempt surgeries they've never been properly trained to perform. Sadly, there are some quack preachers out there, too, offering false assurances to people seeking spiritual help.

Some of these ministers are guilty of spiritual malpractice. Why do I say that? Because they give a gospel message that lacks the true essentials. They tell a person, "Just believe," but don't warn them of a hell or impress on them the need to repent. Some don't even give much weight to the death of Jesus on the cross.

They offer Jesus as though He were just a product you could buy off a shelf, a commodity that will make your life just a little bit better. They don't make it clear that Jesus is the only way to God, and that there is "no other name given under heaven whereby a man could be saved." People who listen to such teachers may embrace an incomplete, watered-down version of the gospel, and thus have a false hope based on a false premise.

That is why God says of the false prophets in Jeremiah 6:14: "They offer superficial treatments for my people's mortal wound. They give assurances of peace when there is no peace."[44]

In the Message paraphrase, the words are rendered, "My people are broken—shattered!—and they put on band-aids, saying, 'It's not so bad. You'll be just fine.' But things are not 'just fine'!"

Why was Philip's message accurate?

First, because *it was centered in Scripture*. In verse 35 we read: "Philip opened his mouth, and beginning at the Scripture, preached Jesus to him."

Any effective presentation of the gospel must be biblical. Why? Because God's Word says of itself that it will not return void.[45]

Second, *it was centered on Jesus*. Philip preached Jesus to him. He didn't preach prosperity or positive self-image or the dangers of global warming or politics or world peace, he opened the Scripture and zeroed in like a laser on Jesus Christ.

It's all about Jesus. The gospel *is* Jesus. It's Jesus prophesied, born, crucified, resurrected from the dead, and coming again. It is Jesus who can change a life, not philosophy, not religion, not even "Christianity." The gospel message is about a relationship with God through Jesus Christ, the only way to the Father.

That's what Philip preached to the official in his chariot as they bounced down that desert road under the hot desert sun.

And the man believed.

In 1 Corinthians 15:1 Paul says, "Let me now remind you, dear brothers and sisters, of the Good News I preached to you before. You welcomed it then, and you still stand firm in it. It is this Good News that saves you if you continue to believe the message I told you—unless, of course, you believed something that was never true in the first place. I passed on to you what was most important and what had also been passed on to me. Christ died for our sins, just as the Scriptures said. He was buried, and he was raised from the dead on the third day, just as the Scriptures said" (1 Corinthians 15:1-4, NLT).

Embed that thought deeply into your mind. The gospel in a nutshell is this: Christ died for our sins and was raised again on the third day.

Someone once asked C. H. Spurgeon, the great British preacher, if he could put his Christian faith into just a few words. Spurgeon said, "Yes. It is in four words. *Jesus died for me*."

#5: The Gospel Must be Responded to Appropriately

It's important to have a heart for people outside of the faith, to be led by the Holy Spirit, to know Scripture, and to focus on Jesus.

But no heavenly transaction is actually completed unless and until the listener *responds* to the gospel message. And we need to ask people if they want to respond.

Here's an example that's pretty typical. A young man came up to me after one of our services a few weeks ago. He had some questions about Christianity, and we talked a little bit. My impression was that he was open to the gospel, and that he might like to receive the Lord.

So I simply asked him.

"Would you like to accept Jesus Christ into your life right now?"

He looked a little surprised, and paused for a moment. "You mean," he said, "like, *right here?*"

"Yes," I said. "Right here. Right now. It would be my privilege to lead you in a prayer to ask Christ into your life."

I never push people to do this; I just offer it to them. I will say, "You have a choice. If you don't feel like you want to do this right now, then you don't have to. But if you would like to do this, I would love to lead you in a prayer."

While my young friend was thinking about this, I just stepped back a bit and silently prayed, *Lord, just work in his heart. Right now.* And I waited for him to respond.

Finally, stammering a little, he said, "Well…uh, I…okay."

"Good," I said. "Let's pray right now." And I led him in a prayer and he prayed with me. Sometime later, I checked in with a friend who knows him, and said, "How is he doing?"

"He's doing well," this friend replied. "He's beginning to grow spiritually."

That's not to say I always get a yes, because I don't. But what's the worst-case scenario? Maybe someone will say, "No. I don't want to do that."

"Okay," I'll reply. "I'll be praying for you then, that you see your need for Jesus."

Then I just leave it at that. I leave it in the Lord's hands. But at least I will know that I gave that individual an opportunity to respond, if he or she was ready.

I love the way Philip's story concludes.

> Now as they went down the road, they came to some water. And the eunuch said, "See, here is water. What hinders me from being baptized?"
>
> Then Philip said, "If you believe with all your heart, you may."
>
> And he answered and said, "I believe that Jesus Christ is the Son of God."
>
> So he commanded the chariot to stand still. And both Philip and the eunuch went down into the water, and he baptized him. Now when they came up out of the water, the Spirit of the Lord caught Philip away, so that the eunuch saw him no more; and he went on his way rejoicing. (vv. 36-39)

Saying "he went on his way rejoicing" is a pretty wonderful way to end any story. There is another story of another man in the New Testament that ended with some different words. The Bible says of the man known as the rich young ruler, that "he went away sorrowful."

Why did he do that? Because he was unwilling to do what Jesus asked him to do, and could not bring himself let go of his old life to embrace a new life in Christ.

So one man heard the message and believed, and went on his way, changed, transformed, and full of joy. But another man had the same opportunity, and turned away, going home sad, dejected, and empty.

That's the way it will always be. Some will respond, and some won't. It's not our responsibility to make that eternal decision for them. All we can do is give them the opportunity.

And that's all our Lord asks of us.

NINE
Three Unsung Heroes

In our culture today we have a lot of celebrities but very few heroes.

One person compared the two this way: "The hero is known for achievements. The celebrity is known for being well-known. The hero reveals the possibilities of human nature. The celebrity reveals the possibilities of the press and media. Celebrities are people who make news, but heroes are people who make history. Time makes heroes but dissolves celebrities."[46]

What is a hero? A hero is a person who does something selfless and sacrificial, putting the needs of others above his or her own.

Sometimes heroes are known in their own lifetime for their achievements, but at other times we'll call someone a hero after they're dead and gone. In this case, we might call them an "unsung hero," because we didn't realize how heroic that individual really was until time had passed and given us a different perspective. Perhaps they stood alone, defending a truth or a principle when everyone around them was rushing the opposite direction. Looking back at such a stand with 20/20 hindsight, we say that it was "heroic."

Most families have an unsung hero in their ranks. Maybe it's a wife or a husband or a child with a big heart and a sweet spirit. Sometimes that mantle falls on a godly grandparent, an aunt, or an uncle.

I see an unsung hero as someone who works behind the scenes, and who doesn't really care if another person gets the credit. History, I'm sure, is replete with unsung heroes—men and women who may never be "sung," but who are completely known to God.

In the New Testament, one unsung hero that springs to mind is Andrew. We hear a lot about Peter, James, and John, but we don't know much about Andrew, Peter's brother. But even though he didn't get a lot of "ink" in the New Testament, what we do read about him is significant. Andrew is primarily known as the man who brought others to Jesus.

Thoroughly excited, he brought his brother Peter to the Lord with the words, "We have found the Messiah" (John 1:41).

Later on, he brought a little boy to Jesus, saying, "Here is a boy with five small barley loaves and two small fish…." And in the Lord's hands, that small lunch became a banquet for 5,000.

Just before going to the cross, Andrew—with Philip—brought a delegation of Gentiles to meet the Lord, men who said, "Sir, we wish to see Jesus."

You might say that Andrew is like the patron saint of unsung heroes—the kind of people who habitually fly under the radar, doing what needs to be done, and not worrying about who gets the credit. But here's the thing we need to remember: If we had more Andrews, we would probably have more Simon Peters.

In more recent years, the name Edward Kimble comes to mind.

Kimble was a shoe salesman and a Sunday school teacher, who was concerned about one of his coworkers, Dwight, who didn't know the Lord. Apprehensive at first, he finally mustered the courage, walked up to Dwight and told him about Jesus. As it happened, Dwight was more than ready, and accepted the Lord on the spot.

Oh, and by the way, Dwight later became known as the greatest evangelist of his time. No, we don't know much about Edward Kimble, but we have heard quite a bit about D. L. Moody.

The story, however, doesn't stop there.

Years later when Moody was preaching at a evangelistic rally, a man named Frederick Meyer was deeply stirred, and as a result of hearing Moody preach, decided to become a preacher himself. Subsequently, a college student named Wilbur Chapman accepted Christ while listening to Meyer preach, and later employed a young ball player to help him with his outreaches. The ballplayer's name was Billy Sunday—who also became one of the most renowned evangelists of his day. Billy Sunday went to Charlotte, North Carolina and preached, had a great crusade there. After his success, a group of businessmen came and asked him if he would return the following Sunday. When the evangelist Sunday couldn't do it, they found a lesser-known evangelist named Mordecai Hamm. Hamm came, and put up his big tent in town. And one on one of the last nights of Mordecai Hamm's crusade, a tall lanky dairy farmer came walking up the sawdust aisle to receive Christ. Folks in those parts just knew as Billy Frank. We know him as Billy Graham.

So when you put it all together, Kimble reached Moody…who touched Meyer…who brought Chapman…who helped Sunday…who moved businessmen in Charlotte, causing them to invite Mordecai Hamm…who brought Billy Graham to Christ.

It all started with the simple witness of Edward Kimble. An unsung hero.

The book of Acts has its unsung heroes, too, and in this chapter, I'd like to briefly consider three of them. No, these men weren't household names, but they had one extraordinary thing in common: Each of them touched the life of the man who would become perhaps the mightiest, most celebrated Christian leaders of all time: the apostle Paul.

Unsung Hero #1: Stephen

As we noted earlier in the book, Stephen was a young man brimming with promise. He was chosen to be a deacon in the Church, but was soon boldly preaching the gospel and bringing people to faith in Christ.

It was the boldness that got him into trouble.

When his enemies couldn't refute him or shut him up, they hauled him before the Sanhedrin on false charges, hoping to see him convicted and executed. If Stephen had been a bit more ingratiating, a little more diplomatic, he might have been able to go home for dinner that night. But in that moment before the ruling elite of Israel, he saw an opportunity—an open door to preach the gospel. And it is my belief that he even directed some of his remarks to one of the powerful men in the room that day: Saul of Tarsus.

It seems to me that Stephen may have had a particular burden for Saul. And of course we know the rest of that story, because we looked at it together.

They screamed, stopped up their ears, gnashed their teeth, ran at him like the savage mob they had become, dragged him out of the city, and stoned him to death. Stephen was the first to shed his blood for the testimony of Jesus.

We say, how tragic that his life was cut short. Why do we say that? Because we all assume we're going to live long lives. But who's to say how long we will draw breath on this planet?

While we may tell ourselves that we control our own lives (an illusion right from the beginning) two dates over which we have no control at all are the day of our birth and the day of our death.

Only the Lord knows when we will make our entrance and exit.

I was reminded of this recently when my wife and I were returning from a trip to Florida. Coming home to Los Angeles, we boarded a beautiful, brand new American Airlines jet. We even commented on how nice it was to be in such a clean, fresh plane.

After a perfect takeoff, we'd been in the air for about an hour when the captain's voice came on the intercom. And right away we knew he wasn't kidding around.

"Ladies and gentlemen," he said, "I have an announcement to make."

He went on to tell us that an emergency light on the instrument panel was indicating they did not have control over the plane's flaps. As a result, the flight attendants would now review emergency evacuation directions one more time.

I remember thinking, *I can't believe this. I've used incidents like these in dozens of sermons, and now it's really happening.*

The flight crew told us what we were to do in the event of a crash landing. As it happened, Cathe and I were chosen to go stand by the exit doors. The flight attendant said, "Your job will be to hold the people back, while I get the door open and slide extended." And he went on to show us how he would get the doors open, and what he wanted us to do. Then we went back to our seats.

I turned to Cathe. "Are you scared?"

"No," she said, and I believed her. She looked cool as a cucumber. I wasn't quite so cool as that, and found myself biting my nails just a bit. It wasn't that I was afraid to die, I just didn't want to crash in an airplane, that's all!

As we came in for the landing, we were informed that emergency personnel—including ambulances and fire trucks—were on the scene and standing by.

Thankfully, the flaps ended up working just fine. It was the warning light that was defective! Even so, as we glided to an easy landing on the tarmac, with cheers throughout the cabin, it was a good little wake up call for us. One more reminder that, as James put it, our lives are like a "vapor that appears for a little time and then vanishes away" (James 4:14).

We've all had moments like that in life. Times when you step out onto a crosswalk and a speeding car barely misses you. Or you get that call from your doctor who says, "I have a little concern about this last test we did on you. We want to run it one more time."

In such times, you're reminded of the brevity of life. My counsel is to use such opportunities well, and take the time to re-evaluate where you're headed in life, and whether or not you're living your life well.

No, you don't decide when life begins and you don't decide when life ends, but God does give you the privilege of deciding what you do with that little dash in the middle between those dates.

Stephen's life was short but sweet, but we know that his testimony and martyrdom played a key role in Saul of Tarsus's ultimate conversion.

It's a funny thing about that. We don't read of anybody actually "leading him to Christ." But I think the seed sown in his heart through the faithful preaching of Stephen launched a fierce wrestling match in his heart with the conviction of the Holy Spirit.

In that seminal moment on the road to Damascus, the glorified Jesus Christ said to him, "It is hard for you to kick against the goads."[47] A goad is just a sharpened stick to prod an animal. And Jesus was essentially saying, "Saul, why are you fighting with Me? You're only injuring yourself."

Stephen is an unsung hero who made a huge difference in the conversion of Saul.

Unsung Hero #2: Ananias

Meanwhile, Saul was uttering threats with every breath and was eager to kill the Lord's followers. So he went to the high priest. He requested letters addressed to the synagogues in Damascus, asking for their cooperation in the arrest of any followers of the Way he found there. He wanted to bring them—both men and women—back to Jerusalem in chains.

As he was approaching Damascus on this mission, a light from heaven suddenly shone down around him. He fell to the ground and heard a voice saying to him, "Saul! Saul! Why are you persecuting me?"

"Who are you, lord?" Saul asked.

And the voice replied, "I am Jesus, the one you are persecuting! Now get up and go into the city, and you will be told what you must do."

The men with Saul stood speechless, for they heard the sound of someone's voice but saw no one! Saul picked himself up off the ground, but when he opened his eyes he was blind. So his companions led him by the hand to Damascus. He remained there blind for three days and did not eat or drink. (Acts 9:1-9, NLT)

Talk about having your world rocked! Saul had no idea what to do next. He ended up in Damascus as he had planned, but nothing else in his life was going remotely according to plan. Or…at least, *his* plan.

Saul's entourage had melted away, and his mission was forgotten. Completely blinded by brilliance of his vision, he refused all food and wouldn't take so much as a sip of water. In a hard-charging life that had taken him up the ladder of education, prestige, and influence, he found himself, for the first time, utterly undone.

And that's where Ananias entered the picture.

Now there was a certain disciple at Damascus named Ananias; and to him the Lord said in a vision, "Ananias."

And he said, "Here I am, Lord."

So the Lord said to him, "Arise and go to the street called Straight, and inquire at the house of Judas for one called Saul of Tarsus, for behold, he is praying. And in a vision he has seen a man named Ananias coming in and putting his hand on him, so that he might receive his sight."

Then Ananias answered, "Lord, I have heard from many about this man, how much harm he has done to Your saints in Jerusalem. And here he has authority from the chief priests to bind all who call on Your name."

But the Lord said to him, "Go, for he is a chosen vessel of Mine to bear My name before Gentiles, kings, and the children of Israel. For I will show him how many things he must suffer for My name's sake."

And Ananias went his way and entered the house; and laying his hands on him he said, "Brother Saul, the Lord Jesus, who appeared to you on the road as you came, has sent me that you may receive your sight and be filled with the Holy Spirit." Immediately there fell from his eyes something like scales, and he received his sight at once; and he arose and was baptized.

So when he had received food, he was strengthened. Then Saul spent some days with the disciples at Damascus. (Acts 9:10-19)

You can understand the reticence of Ananias to pay a social call on

Saul of Tarsus—the notorious hunter of believers and killer of Christians. Can you imagine having God send you to find Adolph Hitler's bunker in the latter days of World War II, and giving you a message like this? "Adolf Hitler is now a Christian. He's going to be my chosen vessel and a great soul winner. Go to him now and help him!"

Hitler, converted? Impossible! You would certainly want to make sure that you were hearing the Lord correctly!

That's exactly how Christians in the early Church would have responded to the news that Saul of Tarsus had become a believer. Many would have had friends or relatives Saul had imprisoned or killed. How could such a thing be? It was just too incredible to wrap your mind around.

Even Ananias argued with the Lord a little, saying in effect, "Lord, do You know who this guy is? Do you realize what he's done—and was about to do?"

But Ananias did what God said, and became part of a story that will be told and retold throughout eternity. The fact is, you do have a choice when God gives you a task: you can obey, and reap the wonderful fruits and rewards of that decision, or you can refuse and forfeit the blessing that would have been yours. How big a blessing? That's just it…you'll never know.

We all remember the story of Esther who through God's providence was raised up to be the queen of all the great Persian empire. At one point in the story, her fellow Jews in the empire were being threatened by a wicked man named Haman, and Esther hadn't (yet) made a move in their defense. Her Uncle Mordecai urged her to speak to the king. Yes, he acknowledged, she could choose not to. But there would be consequences.

Mordecai told her: "Don't think that just because you live in the king's house you're the one Jew who will get out of this alive. If you persist in staying silent at a time like this, help and deliverance will arrive for the Jews from someplace else; but you and your family will be wiped out. Who knows? Maybe you were made queen for just such a time as this."[48]

By the way, the same could be said of you.

God has you where you are at this moment for such a time as this. If you refuse to speak to the people God has placed on your heart or do that which God is asking you to do, He will get the job done…with someone else. But you will miss an opportunity that may not come around again.

Back to the book of Acts, I love how Ananias responded to the Lord's command. Verse 17 says, "Ananias went his way and entered the house."

He didn't want to do it. His flesh had rebelled against doing it. He may have been frightened to do it. But he did it.

And what a sight he saw when he walked into the house. There, perhaps on his knees, perhaps lying on the floor, was Saul of Tarsus, the infamous Christian killer. His very name would send chills down the spines of followers of Jesus. And yet there he was, blind, humbled, and broken. Moved with compassion, Ananias went over to Saul and put his hands on his shoulders, saying, "Brother Saul, the Lord Jesus, who appeared to you on the road as you came, has sent me that you may receive your sight and be filled with the Holy Spirit."

It's my guess that in a thousand years Saul would have never imagined hearing a Christian call him "brother." But what a difference a day makes. Or even an hour.

Where were all of Saul's other friends now? His partners in crime? Gone. Scattered. Nowhere to be found. And Saul was about to discover that what he had regarded as his bitterest enemies were in fact his only friends. And all too soon, his so-called friends would be enemies who would try to take his life.

If you want to find out who your true friends and true enemies really are, start telling people about Jesus. When you bring His name up in the workplace or on the campus or in your neighborhood or at that family gathering, wherever you might be, you had better expect opposition. People will become unreasonably angry with you. Sometimes even your fellow Christians will be embarrassed and angry. They may tell you, "Don't be so fanatical. Do you have to talk about Jesus all the time?"

I remember the first time someone called me "brother." I was a brand new Christian, and a guy gave me a Bible and called me "brother Greg." At the time, I didn't like it much. I thought to myself, *I'm not your brother. Who are you?* And I was uncomfortable with the idea.

But in truth, I was his brother. And I had a lot of changing to do.

Ananias is truly an unsung hero of the Christian faith for doing what he did. No, he never preached any sermons that we know of. We don't read of any miracles being performed through his hands. He never wrote an epistle. But he did reach someone who did all of those things, and more.

As I said earlier, if we had more Andrews, we would have more Simon Peters. And if we had more Ananiases, we would have more apostle Pauls.

In his book on the apostle Paul, Charles Swindoll writes these words:

> Ananias has been called one of the forgotten heroes of the faith. Indeed he is. There are countless numbers of them serving Christ behind the scenes the world over. Most we will never meet. We will never know them by name because they are content to remain in the shadows oblivious to the lure of lights and applause. Nevertheless they are heroes. Giants of the faith because of their selfless understated acts of obedience to God.[49]

Later in the book of Acts, Paul himself gave Ananias this tribute: "Then a certain Ananias, a devout man according to the law, having a good testimony with all the Jews who dwelt there, came to me; and he stood and said to me, 'Brother Saul, receive your sight'" (Acts 22:12-13).

And with that, Ananias walks off the stage of Scripture, never to appear again. But Paul, the broken man he met in a darkened room on Straight Street in Damascus, went on to set the world on fire for Jesus. And that's why we call Ananias an unsung hero.

Unsung Hero #3: Barnabas

But there was one more unsung hero who touched Paul's life in an unforgettable way.

> When Saul arrived in Jerusalem, he tried to meet with the believers, but they were all afraid of him. They did not believe he had truly become a believer! Then Barnabas brought him to the apostles and told them how Saul had seen the Lord on the way to Damascus and how the Lord had spoken to Saul. He also told them that Saul had preached boldly in the name of Jesus in Damascus.
>
> So Saul stayed with the apostles and went all around Jerusalem with them, preaching boldly in the name of the Lord. (Acts 11:26-28, NLT)

So often, life is all about timing. And in a critical moment for this new believer, Saul of Tarsus, at a time when the apostles were on the verge of rejecting him and turning him out, a man named Barnabas stepped into Saul's corner.

Effectively, the church leadership was saying to Saul, "You can't worship with us, and we can't give you the authority to teach. Frankly, we just don't trust you."

But when Barnabas heard the story, he said, "You come with me." And they went back to the leadership, this time with a different result. Barnabas laid all of his personal (and substantial) credibility on the line for this untested convert.

That's exactly what every new believer needs. You need to step up, make friends with him, take him to church with you, and introduce him around. Why? Because one of the greatest dangers a new believer faces after making a commitment to Christ is falling through the cracks, and going back to their old friends—and then to their old ways. A new believer needs a brother or sister in the Lord to take them under wing and say, "You're coming to church with me. Let's sit together."

Someone did that for me, not long after I came to the Lord. His name is Mark, and he is one of my personal unsung heroes. After I became a Christian on my high school campus, I really didn't know the believers, and found myself going back to hang out with my old friends again.

Mark walked up to me right out of the blue and said, "Hi. My name is Mark. I saw you go forward at the meeting the other day, and I'm going to take you to church."

At first, I was resistant. "I don't really want to go to church," I said.

But he was persistent. "No, you're coming to church with me. I'm going to pick you up on Sunday. Where do you live?"

He absolutely wouldn't let me off the hook, and we walked together into Calvary Chapel of Costa Mesa, just at the time when the Jesus Movement was at full swing. Bear in mind that I had grown up in a family where no one ever showed me much love or affection. Then I walked into this place, seeing all of those people loving each other and hugging each other and it kind of freaked me out.

I told Mark, "Uh…I really don't want to go in."

Anyway, it was packed out and there didn't seem to be any seats available—which was a relief to me. But wouldn't you know it! Someone in the *front row* recognized me from school, and waved Mark and I down to a couple of seats. I thought to myself, *Oh great. Now I'm in the middle of all this weird love. I don't think I'm gonna like this.*

I made it through that service, however, and, tucked firmly under Mark's wing, he took me to his home. His parents were Christians, and they all spent time with me, encouraging me, reading Bible stories to me, and getting me started.

Mark had stepped into my life when I needed him most.

Aren't you glad God puts people in our lives like that? The name Barnabas means "son of encouragement," and he certainly lived up to his name. And I have been privileged to have a few men like Barnabas—like Mark—in my life through the years as well. When I have a down day and feel like my supply of hope is running on fumes, these are the guys I want to pick up the phone and call.

UPSIDE DOWN LIVING **163**

The apostle Paul had an extraordinary career, but then, he had also been touched by extraordinary men—unsung heroes who met him at critical intersections in his life, and pointed him in the right direction.

Have you had people like that in your life?

More to the point, have you *been* a person like that in the life of someone else?

You may not have received a calling to preach and teach as Paul did. But you can inspire someone like Stephen did. You can pray for someone like Ananias did. Or you can encourage someone like Barnabas did. You can remain available to the Lord and sensitive to His voice, ready to step into the life of someone who might be in great need of a little care, a little wisdom, a little time with someone willing to listen, and not pass judgment.

Someone, somewhere, probably right now, needs you to stand in the gap. Maybe it's a new believer, who's looking around at the brightness and strangeness of this new life and wondering to himself, "What have I done?" You don't have to know every Bible verse, or the answer to all those difficult theological questions. You just need to be a real Christian who can show them what it's like to live in the real world, help them acclimate, and encourage them to become a part of the Church.

I can't emphasize how important this is. Everybody needs help from time to time, because everybody stumbles and falls in some way, shape, or form. Everyone has down days or wakes up on the wrong side of the bed. Even heroes.

James writes: "My dear brothers and sisters, if someone among you wanders away from the truth and is brought back, you can be sure that whoever brings the sinner back will save that person from death and bring about the forgiveness of many sins" (James 5:19-20, NLT).

Be an encourager.

TEN
An Unexpected Conversion

Does it ever seem to you as though God just couldn't (or wouldn't) save certain people?

Most of us, I know, would say, "Obviously, God can do anything." We know (in our head, at least) that He is all-powerful, and that "nothing is too difficult for God."

But having said that, are there people in your life of whom you would say, "There's just no way I can envision that person becoming a follower of Jesus."

This chapter is a reminder to all of us that *no one* is beyond God's reach. In fact, sometimes the very people we imagine to be so far away from the kingdom are closer than we realize.

Perhaps you have an acquaintance that you've spoken to about your faith a couple of times, and his friendly response encourages you. He's nice about it. Pleasant. He gives you eye contact as you speak, and nods his head.

"Well," he will say, "I can see your faith has made you a much happier person. You seem to be fulfilled, and full of joy. I'm glad for *you*."

So you venture to take it a step further, asking, "Would you like to come to church with me this Sunday?"

"No…no I don't think so. But thanks for asking."

"The week after?"

"No…really…."

"Next month?"

"Sorry, I have to run. But it's been really nice talking to you."

Then there's the lady at work, in the workstation right next to yours. Or maybe her office is across the hallway. And she's always hassling you—needling you—about your beliefs. It seems like every Monday at work she has ten new questions to fire at you. At times, she seems downright hostile and angry. She may even make fun of you in front of people because of your faith in Jesus Christ, or try to get you into trouble with management.

Or maybe it's that neighbor of yours…or that unbelieving husband or that wife or son or daughter, and you think to yourself, "She's a million miles from God." Or, "He has no interest at all in the Lord."

I have a little surprise for you. It may be the very opposite. The person who is giving you the hardest time might be very close to coming to the Lord.

There's an old proverb—it's not in the Bible, but it's pretty good—that says, "If you throw a rock into a pack of dogs, the one that barks the loudest is the one that got hit." That's true in life sometimes, too. The ones who protest most loudly about your faith, the ones who argue hardest, the ones who fight most fiercely even taking a baby step toward God may actually be on the very doorstep of the kingdom.

There is no clearer illustration of that principle than in the story before us here in Acts chapter 8.

In the last chapter as we considered three "unsung heroes" who'd had a major impact on the life of Saul (who became Paul), we reviewed some of the details of his dramatic conversion.

In this chapter, I'd like to revisit the mighty transformation that turned a deadly, bitter foe of the Church into its most passionate advocate.

Here was a man who wasn't satisfied with just mocking and criticizing Christians, he wanted to utterly destroy them. He went out of his way to hunt them down—men or women, young or old—and imprison them. He tortured Christians and saw to it that they were executed.

In fact, he presided over the death of Stephen, the first martyr of the Christian church. And when he came to faith, it was like a proverbial lightning bolt out of the clear blue sky. Nobody saw it coming, and most believers greeted the news with skepticism and suspicion—or downright scorn.

Saul's embrace of Jesus Christ, however, wasn't just a flash in the pan like some celebrity conversions we hear about from time to time. He went on to take up a whole new identity as the apostle Paul, a lion for the gospel, and a man who went on to pen two-thirds of the New Testament.

Paul's conversion was such an off-the-charts unlikely event that a British agnostic of the last century thought the whole thing could probably be disproved. And so, in an attempt to undermine the Christian faith, George Lord Lyttelton went to work on his book that he titled, *Observations on the Conversion and Apostleship of Saint Paul.*

After a great deal of careful research, however, Lyttelton (probably to his own consternation) came to the conclusion that the story was true, and became a Christian himself. In the pages of his book, Lyttelton concluded: "Paul's conversion and apostleship alone duly considered are a demonstration sufficient to prove Christianity is a divine revelation."

We will use the expression from time to time, "He was a man who changed the world." But in Paul's case, that was really true; he *did* change the world…and continues to change it to this very day. He blazed a trail, leaving behind many churches and converts. The former enemy of the faith preached to philosophers, Pharisees, rulers, soldiers, sorcerers, sailors, slaves, and most likely to Caesar himself. Called to bring the gospel to his generation, he did so brilliantly. Mighty miracles followed his ministry, and he wrote letters that we regard to day as the very word of God.

But there were some other characteristics of his life I would like to bring to your attention; things we perhaps don't like to talk about.

There's no way around it; before his conversion, Saul of Tarsus was coldhearted, hateful, bigoted murderer. Presiding over the murder by stoning of young Stephen was only a start to the bloodletting. In fact, he was in the very process of hunting out even more believers when the Lord got hold of him.

And when the Lord got hold of Saul, and Saul got hold of the Lord, neither of them let go from that day forward.

Where Did Saul Come From?

Tarsus was a very important city in the Roman world, known for a university that ranked right up there with the universities in Alexandria and Athens—one of the most honored learning centers in the world of that day. As Paul would one day tell a Roman commander, "I am a Jew, from Tarsus in Cilicia, a citizen of no ordinary city."[50]

By education Saul was Greek. By citizenship he was Roman. It was in Tarsus that he studied Greek philosophy and Roman law—knowledge that would come in handy for the ministry that was to unfold so surprisingly before him.

But beneath the layers of Greek and Roman influence, Saul was first a Jew, raised in a very strict religious home. His family tree sprang from Benjamin, the tribe that also gave Israel its first king, also named Saul. As a young man he decided to become a Pharisee, "the strictest sect of our religion" (Acts 26:5). From there, he went on to become part of the Sanhedrin, Israel's legal and religious body, comprised of seventy of the nation's most elite leaders.

To put it on the bottom line, Saul was a rich and powerful man.

He also became an infamous and feared man…for good reason. At some point, he began to feel it was his personal responsibility to eradicate this new sect of fanatics who followed the Man known as Jesus of Nazareth. Not satisfied with simply arresting the Christians who resided in Jerusalem, he went after (and received) extradition orders allowing him to go as far away as Damascus—140 miles to the north of Jerusalem—to find more believers to apprehend and bring back and imprison.

His hatred seems strange to us, because he was such a religious man, who would have claimed a fierce belief in the God of Israel. To this day, I'm always amazed at how people who claim to be believers—sometimes outside the Church, and sometimes inside—can be filled with hate. So critical. So cynical. So small-minded. So mean-spirited.

Vance Havner once said, "If we are too busy using our sickles on one another; we are going to miss the harvest." Even so, we see Christians—or even churches—doing just that: dividing over minor issues and refusing to pull together for the sake of the gospel.

Saul was certainly a religious man, but he was in reality a godless man. He had set a personal goal of wiping the followers of Jesus Christ right off the map. But in the process of carrying out that goal, he had a surprise meeting with the Lord Himself.

A Seed Planted

Somehow, in ways the Bible doesn't really explain, the stoning of Stephen unleashed a tidal wave of persecution against the young church in Jerusalem.

> A great wave of persecution of the believers began that day, sweeping over the Church in Jerusalem, and everyone except the apostles fled into Judea and Samaria. (But some godly Jews came and with great sorrow buried Stephen.) Paul was like a wild man, going everywhere to devastate the believers, even entering private homes and dragging out men and women alike and jailing them. But the believers who had fled Jerusalem went everywhere preaching the Good News about Jesus! (Acts 8:1-4, TLB)

Unwittingly, even before Saul was a part of the kingdom of God, he was working for it. How so? By attacking the Christians, he caused them to spread out. If Saul had not done this, it's entirely possible that the believers in Jerusalem would have become content with a "holy huddle" in Jerusalem, where they had been enjoying success and favor.

And who could have blamed them? It must have been thrilling to be a part of this new church. The teaching was awe-inspiring. The worship was amazing.

This was the Church Jesus Himself started, and it was just blossoming. This thing was first generation, with actual apostles who had walked and talked with Jesus doing the instruction. Why pull the plug on a good thing? Why leave town when all the action was in town?

But that's not what Jesus had instructed them to do, before He ascended into heaven. He had told them to take the message out, out, out, further and further. His exact words had been, "But you will receive power when the Holy Spirit comes on you; and you will be my witnesses in Jerusalem, and in all Judea and Samaria, and to the ends of the earth."[51]

The "Jerusalem" part of that commandment had been working out just fine. But not many seemed inclined to go to out further into Judea or Samaria at that point—let alone "the ends of the earth."

But then Saul came charging in like a bull in a china shop, upsetting everything. As a result, the believers scattered.

It must have made some in the Jerusalem church wonder if Stephen's life and testimony had been wasted, his blood spilled in vain. He had boldly taken his stand before the rulers and elders, and now he was buried in his grave. What had come of it?

In fact, a lot had come of it. More than anyone could have imagined.

Why? Because nobody but the Lord could have seen the tiny seed sown in the heart of Saul of Tarsus.

That ought to be an encouragement to all of us. Maybe you told someone in your high school or college about your faith, and your classmate just blew you off—and insulted you to boot. You walked away, smarting a little, and thinking, "That didn't go well." But as the saying goes, it's not over until it's over. If you have planted a tiny gospel seed, you have no idea when or where it will eventually sprout. Sometimes the message of Jesus Christ is like a little time bomb—that doesn't detonate until later. Perhaps much later.

The individual you've spoken to will say, "I have no interest in what you're saying, and I wish you'd just shut up." But then some crisis hits in this person's life, and that conversation with you comes back to the forefront of his or her mind. Then, what you may have thought was in vain isn't in vain at all.

I think Stephen's words resonated with Saul as he was running from God. As we will discover in a moment, I believe he was fighting with the Lord and resisting the conviction of the Holy Spirit. And he couldn't shake the words of that young man Stephen—the man whose face had shown like an angel.

The Encounter

Then Saul, still breathing threats and murder against the disciples of the Lord, went to the high priest and asked letters from him to the synagogues of Damascus, so that if he found any who were of the Way, whether men or women, he might bring them bound to Jerusalem.

> As he journeyed he came near Damascus, and suddenly a light shone around him from heaven. Then he fell to the ground, and heard a voice saying to him, "Saul, Saul, why are you persecuting Me?"
>
> And he said, "Who are You, Lord?"
>
> Then the Lord said, "I am Jesus, whom you are persecuting. It is hard for you to kick against the goads."
>
> So he, trembling and astonished, said, "Lord, what do You want me to do?"
>
> Then the Lord said to him, "Arise and go into the city, and you will be told what you must do."
>
> And the men who journeyed with him stood speechless, hearing a voice but seeing no one. Then Saul arose from the ground, and when his eyes were opened he saw no one. But they led him by the hand and brought him into Damascus. And he was three days without sight, and neither ate nor drank. (Acts 9:1-9)

The account says Saul was "breathing threats." This could be translated "breathing in and out." In other words, he was living off of hatred and intimidation. The word in the original language gives a picture of a wild beast stalking its prey. Possessed by a raging fury and completely consumed by his vendetta, Paul later confessed that "I stormed through their meeting places, bullying them into cursing Jesus, a one-man terror obsessed with obliterating these people" (Acts 26:11, THE MESSAGE).

Imagine, if you will, someone saying something like this to Saul as he left Jerusalem on his way to Damascus. "Guess what, Saul. Before this day is over, you will personally encounter Jesus Christ. Within three days, you will be His follower." He would have immediately been in that person's face (or found some way of taking him down).

Notice how the Christians are described in Acts 9:2. The text describes Saul getting permission from the high priest to go after "any who were of the Way, whether men or women" that "he might bring them bound to Jerusalem."

I like that phrase "of the Way." That is no doubt based on the statement of our Lord in John 14:6, where He says, "I am the way, the truth, and the life." These early believers were identified as those who believed in THE Way as the ONLY way. And those of us who have put our faith in Jesus are noted for the same thing to this present time.

It's an important distinction in a day when some people are questioning whether or not Jesus Christ is the only way to the Father. Oh sure, they're willing to accept that He is one of many ways. But don't you dare say He is the *only* way. Don't you dare suggest the exclusivity of Christ! And sadly, these are debates you may very well hear *within* churches.

In reality, of course, there can be no debate.

He is the only way, and we who know Him are people of the Way.

Saul was persecuting the people of the Way when he suddenly met the Way Himself. In that instant when he was knocked to the surface of the Damascus highway, he heard the voice of God and saw the face of

God. The others in his party saw the light, but didn't see the Lord. They heard a noise, but they didn't hear the voice.

Here was a man who came into contact with the living, breathing, resurrected Lord Jesus. It's interesting that the others didn't see Him or hear Him, because they weren't His sheep. Jesus said, "My sheep hear My voice."

And that voice said, "Saul, Saul, why are you persecuting Me?"

I wonder if in that moment Saul was afraid to even ask whom the "Me" was. Nevertheless, he did.

"(Gulp). Who are You, Lord?"

And then he heard the answer. "I am Jesus."

Deep down in his heart, Saul must have known right away Who was addressing him as he lay face down in the dirt. And in that moment of ultimate discovery, he also realized he had been fighting tooth and nail against…God Himself.

As we noted in a previous chapter, Jesus said to Saul, "It is hard for you to kick against the goads" (9:5). A goad is simply a sharpened stick, used in those days to prompt an animal to move along a little faster. Instead of stepping on the gas pedal, they poked the animal with a goad. And Jesus was saying to Saul, "That's what you've been doing. You've been kicking against the goads, fighting and resisting the Holy Spirit. Isn't that hard, Saul? Can you see that you're wounding yourself by doing this? And this is why you're behaving in the way that you are. You're trying to fight God."

What had the Lord used as "goads" in Saul's life?

I have no doubt that one of those goads was the Spirit-filled speech of Stephen before the Sanhedrin. Yes, Saul no doubt bared his teeth at that young man's stern word of truth. He probably rushed at Stephen like all the rest of them, and helped drag him to his execution. But even so, something of Stephen's words had penetrated Saul's defenses.

"You stiff-necked and uncircumcised in heart and ears! You always resist the Holy Spirit!"

It was a sharp goad from God Himself, and Saul kicked at it.

Then he saw Stephen die, saw the reflected glory of "the heavens opened," and heard the young martyr call on God to forgive his murderers.

It was another goad, stabbing at Saul, though he couldn't bring himself to admit it.

Then what happened when he laid hands on these believers, men and women who were full of the love of Christ, and loved him and prayed for him even as he sought to destroy them. Was he thinking in the back of his mind, "How could they respond this way? Could this teaching about Jesus possibly be true?"

It was goad after goad, driving Saul into a reckless fury.

After he met the Lord, however, we can immediately take note of three things in the life of the newly converted Saul—aspects that will characterize every follower of Jesus.

He was praying.

Let's look again at the biblical account of Saul's moment of truth with Ananias.

> Now there was a believer in Damascus named Ananias. The Lord spoke to him in a vision, calling, "Ananias!"
>
> "Yes, Lord!" he replied.
>
> The Lord said, "Go over to Straight Street, to the house of Judas. When you get there, ask for a man from Tarsus named Saul. He is praying to me right now. I have shown him a vision of a man named Ananias coming in and laying hands on him so he can see again." (Acts 9:10-11, NLT)

I love that line, "*He is praying to me right now.*" God was listening to the prayers of Saul at the same instant that He was communicating with Ananias…and countless other people besides. The Almighty has no problem giving His undivided attention to everyone who calls on Him—though millions may be accessing His throne at the same moment.

God is really good at "multi-tasking"!

I wonder what Saul was praying about. I have a strong hunch he was asking the Lord for forgiveness. Blind and alone in that room in Damascus, it was dawning at him what he had done…and what he'd been about to do. He had just seen the Lord on the Damascus road, and now he was—possibly for the first time—really seeing himself, and seeing his actions for what they were.

"I have been killing Christians. God, forgive me. Forgive me for the wickedness and blind hatred in my heart and for what I have done."

But I think he probably worshipped as he prayed, as well. "Lord, it's so amazing that I can even talk to You. That You reached out to me. That You care about me." All his life he had tried to be a good religious boy, careful and devout. He had kept the law to the best of his ability, but knew in his heart that he had fallen short. But now, he had entered into a relationship with God—something beyond what he had ever experienced before. He was praying, and maybe for the first time in his life, knew those prayers were getting through.

Every Christian should be praying.

He was preaching.

Verse 20 tells us that "Immediately he preached Christ in the synagogues, that He is the Son of God."

He couldn't restrain himself! He was so full of awe and wonder and joy over what the Lord had done in his life that he couldn't keep still about it.

He was suffering.

Notice verse 23: "Now after many days were past, the Jews plotted to kill him."

Regarding the future apostle Paul, God had said to Ananias, "He is a chosen vessel of Mine…. For I will show him how many things he *must suffer* for My name's sake" (vv. 15, 16). Saul knew from Day One that he was going to suffer as a representative of Jesus Christ.

Through the years of Paul's ministry, God used him in mighty ways:

traveling across the known world, opening new frontiers to the gospel, performing miracles, discipling earnest young believers, writing letters that would become part of the Word of God forever.

But he also suffered. Listen to this litany of trials that the apostle sent to the Church in Corinth:

> I have worked harder than any of them. I have served more prison sentences! I have been beaten times without number. I have faced death again and again.
>
> I have been beaten the regulation thirty-nine stripes by the Jews five times.
>
> I have been beaten with rods three times. I have been stoned once. I have been shipwrecked three times. I have been twenty-four hours in the open sea.
>
> In my travels I have been in constant danger from rivers and floods, from bandits, from my own countrymen, and from pagans. I have faced danger in city streets, danger in the desert, danger on the high seas, danger among false Christians. I have known exhaustion, pain, long vigils, hunger and thirst, going without meals, cold and lack of clothing.
>
> Apart from all external trials I have the daily burden of responsibility for all the Churches. Do you think anyone is weak without my feeling his weakness? Does anyone have his faith upset without my longing to restore him?
>
> Oh, if I am going to boast, let me boast of the things which have shown up my weakness! (2 Corinthians 11:23-30, PHILLIPS)

You and I love all the exciting parts of the Christian life—the adventure and the joy and the fellowship and the great teaching. But we don't like that part about suffering. Yet Paul himself wrote, "All who desire to live godly in Christ Jesus will suffer persecution."[52]

If you want to be used by God to make a difference in this world, you will be attacked. If you want to just be a little wallflower and sort of mix in with the crowd and never stand up for your faith in Christ, I don't know that you will have that much opposition. But if you say, "I want my life to count for eternity. I want to stand up for Jesus Christ wherever I am," you will certainly face opposition—in a thousand different forms and probably from unexpected sources. Sometimes it will come at you from the outside, from nonbelievers. But there will be times when it will also come from directions that you won't expect—from the inside, and from so-called believers.

To the Philippians, Paul wrote: "I want to know Christ and the power of his resurrection and the fellowship of sharing in his sufferings, becoming like him in his death."[53] Out there in that blinding heavenly light on the Damascus road, he had asked the Lord two questions. First, he had said, "Who are You, Lord?" And upon receiving that answer, he replied with, "Lord, what do You want me to do?" In effect, he spent the rest of his life discovering the answer to that.

There was nothing commonplace about Paul's life as a follower of Jesus. He accomplished incredible things for his Lord, but he also suffered greatly.

One time, after he was stoned by a mob in Lystra, Scripture seems to indicate that he briefly died and entered heaven.[54] In his second letter to the Corinthians, he described being "caught up to the third heaven… caught up into Paradise and heard inexpressible words, which is not lawful for a man to utter."[55]

Now if you had gone to heaven and were allowed to come back and tell the story, you might find yourself becoming just a little arrogant. So Paul went on to say, "And lest I should be exalted above measure by the abundance of the revelations, a thorn in the flesh was given to me, a messenger of Satan to buffet me, lest I be exalted above measure" (2 Corinthians 12:7).

Preachers and commentators through the years have tried to guess what that "thorn" might have been in the apostle's life, but no one really knows. Most believe it was some kind of physical disability—perhaps an eye condition that hindered his sight. (At least one verse in Scripture—Galatians 4:15—seems to imply that.) But whatever it was, he went to Jesus on three separate occasions and begged Him to take it away.

But the Lord said no.

He said to His servant, "My grace is all you need. My power works best in weakness" (2 Corinthians 12:9, NLT).

So Paul wrote, "So now I am glad to boast about my weaknesses, so that the power of Christ can work through me. That's why I take pleasure in my weaknesses, and in the insults, hardships, persecutions, and troubles that I suffer for Christ. For when I am weak, then I am strong" (vv. 9-10, NLT).

God can work mightily through human weakness, suffering, and disability—sometimes even more effectively than through a person who is "whole" in our culture's eyes, and has never experienced much hardship in life.

Your life might be going reasonably well, and you tell someone about Jesus and they say, "Well look at you. Your life is great. Everything turns out right for you. Why wouldn't you be happy?" But then if you face calamity, if you have a loved one die unexpectedly, if you have a physical infirmity you are struggling with, and you can still rejoice, praise God, and maintain a peaceful spirit, now that, my friend, is a powerful witness.

After all, how will they find out that God's grace is sufficient for their needs, unless they first see how His grace has been sufficient for *your* needs?

ELEVEN
Reaching Beyond Our Own Circle

Cornelius was a centurion living in Roman-ruled Palestine.

The fact that he was a Gentile, not a Jew, doesn't mean that much to us today, living as we do in the great melting pot called the United States of America. But in the culture of the first century, if you were a Jew, you did your best to avoid all contact with non-Jews.

Why would you behave that way? Because as a believer in the true God of Israel, you would have been brought up to believe that contact with people outside of your faith would contaminate you. The non-Jews, or Gentiles, didn't believe in the Lord or acknowledge His laws and commandments. The rest of the world worshiped other gods. In the Roman culture, they might even worship Caesar himself—a terrible and blasphemous thought for anyone who served Jehovah, the true God. So, as much as possible, the Jews would keep themselves separate from the people of other nations.

Simon Peter was a loyal Jew, who still followed Jewish ways and traditions, as he had from childhood. But since the death, resurrection, and ascension of the Lord Jesus, he had a bit of a problem. Just before the Lord departed from the disciples and was taken into heaven, He gave His inner circle some rather specific instructions.

> "But you shall receive power when the Holy Spirit has come upon you; and you shall be witnesses to Me in Jerusalem, and in all Judea and Samaria, and to the end of the earth." (Acts 1:8)

The disciples had received that power, and they had certainly become His bold witnesses in Jerusalem, unashamedly declaring the name of Jesus. When the great wave of persecution broke over the Church following the death of Stephen, the Church was scattered throughout Judea and Samaria[56]…so the gospel spread even further. In fact, Philip had great success in Samaria, leading many to Jesus.

But what about that last, troubling phrase in the Lord's final instructions—the part about being His witnesses "to the ends of the earth"? Wouldn't that involve preaching to Gentiles, people of other nations?

Of course that is exactly what the Lord meant. But as we reach the tenth chapter of Acts, that hadn't happened—yet. And if that situation had been allowed to continue, Christianity might well have been swallowed back into Judaism. People who wanted to follow Christ would have first had to become Jews, following all the old ways and adhering strictly to the Law.

That's not what God had in mind.

And that's not why Jesus had died on the cross.

Jesus Himself had said, "For God so loved the *world* that He gave His only begotten Son, that *whoever* believes in Him should not perish but have everlasting life."[57]

Six years had passed, however, and (as far as we know) Peter and the other apostles had not yet ventured to take the gospel beyond their fellow Jews.

Even so, the Holy Spirit was working, and God's power had been flowing through the apostle Peter in some dramatic ways. In Acts chapter 9, we read that he was traveling about the country, visiting fellow believers. In Lydda, he healed a paralytic man named Aeneas, creating a wave of excitement that had many people in that town turning to the Lord.

In the nearby town of Joppa, the Lord used him to minister to a disciple named Tabitha, actually raising her from the dead.

Peter asked them all to leave the room; then he knelt and prayed. Turning to the body he said, "Get up, Tabitha." And she opened her eyes! When she saw Peter, she sat up! He gave her his hand and helped her up. Then he called in the widows and all the believers, and he presented her to them alive. (Acts 9:40-41, NLT).

Now being used by the Lord in such a dramatic way as that is bound to make an impression on your heart! Peter had become a channel of the Lord's mighty, resurrection power, and through his ministry, a dead woman had been raised to life. The life of Christ flowing through his ministry…bringing life out of death! That had to be an eye-opener for Peter. God was up to something amazing.

But at that point, he didn't realize *how* amazing.

In his encounter with Cornelius in Acts 10, the outreach of the Church of Jesus Christ was about to break wide open…forever.

A Hungry Heart

In Caesarea there lived a Roman army officer named Cornelius, who was a captain of the Italian Regiment. He was a devout, God-fearing man, as was everyone in his household. He gave generously to the poor and prayed regularly to God. One afternoon about three o'clock, he had a vision in which he saw an angel of God coming toward him. "Cornelius!" the angel said.

Cornelius stared at him in terror. "What is it, sir?" he asked the angel.

And the angel replied, "Your prayers and gifts to the poor have been received by God as an offering! Now send some men to Joppa, and summon a man named Simon Peter. He is staying with Simon, a tanner who lives near the seashore."

As soon as the angel was gone, Cornelius called two of his household servants and a devout soldier, one of his personal attendants. He told them what had happened and sent them off to Joppa. (Acts 10:1-8, NLT)

Cornelius was a Roman officer stationed in Caesarea, a Roman outpost on the Mediterranean coast of Palestine, some thirty miles north of where Peter was staying in Joppa. As a centurion he was a man of authority, commanding a group of one hundred soldiers. We learn from history that only a select number of outstanding men were even qualified to be considered as centurions. Roman historian Polybius described centurions as men who were not so much adventurous and daredevils, as much as natural leaders known for their steadiness and dependability in the field of battle.

Cornelius was such a man, disciplined, responsible, and courageous. As a Roman, he would have been taught to follow the Roman pantheon of gods—basically adapted from the conquered Greeks. He had even been taught to worship Caesar as a god. As a Roman officer he would have known all of those beliefs and practices—and been expected to follow them.

But it is evident from this story that the religion of his people had left him with an empty, unsatisfied heart. Through the years of his duty in Palestine, watching the conquered Jewish people around him and their devotion to the God of Israel, Cornelius had evidently come to a radical conclusion: "I believe these people are worshiping the true and living God."

So even though he wasn't a Jew himself, he began praying to the God of Israel, and giving money to the poor in God's name.

In the book of Jeremiah, the Lord said, "You will seek Me and find Me, when you search for Me with all your heart. I will be found by you, says the LORD." And Jesus Himself declared, "Ask, and you will be given what you ask for. Seek, and you will find. Knock, and the door will be opened. For everyone who asks, receives. Anyone who seeks, finds. If only you will knock, the door will open."[58]

God will reveal Himself to the true seeker, wherever he or she may be in all the world. And because Cornelius sought God with all his heart, the Lord dispatched an angel with instructions on how the centurion was to meet up with Simon Peter, to get the answers to his questions.

Why didn't the angel just cut to the chase and directly give him the gospel? "Hey Cornelius, you need to believe in Jesus, who died for your sins on a cross, and rose again on the third day." Why give him all of those MapQuest directions to Joppa, and instructions on how to find Peter?

Because preaching the gospel isn't primarily the job of the angels.

It's our job.

Angels do their work behind the scenes at the bidding of the Lord—protecting us, guiding us, sometimes even speaking to us. But the primary way that God reaches people is through people. We are told in Romans 10, "How, then, can they call on the one they have not believed in? And how can they believe in the one of whom they have not heard? And how can they hear without someone preaching to them?" (vv. 14-15, NIV).

God wanted Peter to reach Cornelius—for Cornelius's sake and for Peter's! The Lord wanted to use the conversion of Cornelius, a Gentile, to open Peter's eyes to the fact that there was a big wide world out there that needed to hear the gospel.

In fact, there still is.

A Surprise Summons

Meanwhile….

Don't you love how our sovereign God works? At any given moment, God is always working in billions of lives on trillions of levels to accomplish His purposes. As Cornelius's men were nearing Joppa with a surprise invitation for Peter, Peter was about to receive a distinct "heads up" from the Holy Spirit.

> The next day as they were nearing the city, Peter went up on the flat roof of his house to pray. It was noon and he was hungry, but while lunch was being prepared, he fell into a trance. He saw the sky open and a great canvas sheet, suspended by its four corners, settle to the ground. In the sheet were all sorts of animals, snakes, and birds [forbidden to the Jews for food].

Then a voice said to him, "Go kill and eat any of them you wish."

"Never, Lord," Peter declared, "I have never in all my life eaten such creatures, for they are forbidden by our Jewish laws."

The voice spoke again, "Don't contradict God! If he says something is kosher, then it is."

The same vision was repeated three times. Then the sheet was pulled up again to heaven.

Peter was very perplexed. What could the vision mean? What was he supposed to do?

Just then the men sent by Cornelius had found the house and were standing outside at the gate, inquiring whether this was the place where Simon Peter lived!

Meanwhile, as Peter was puzzling over the vision, the Holy Spirit said to him, "Three men have come to see you. Go down and meet them and go with them. All is well, I have sent them."
(Acts 10:9-20, TLB)

God was using this startling vision of a sheet full of creepy, crawly creatures as a means of awakening His servant to a neglected responsibility: It was time for Peter to overcome his personal prejudice, and bring the gospel of Christ to the Gentiles.

His response?

"*Never, Lord.*"

Now isn't that interesting? As I think about Peter's answer, it strikes me that there are certain word combinations that work nicely, and other combinations that don't work at all. "Yes, Lord" would have been just fine. "How, Lord?" would have also been acceptable. "Where, Lord?" would have been appropriate. Even "Why, Lord?" would have been understandable. But one response a believer should never utter, is "Never, Lord" or "No, Lord."

Memories of the Valley

I was working on this chapter, considering this very point, on the day my thirty-three year old son Christopher died in an automobile accident. (I have the date—and even the time—recorded on my computer document.) I remember that I had completed most of it earlier that day.

In that day, in that moment, we received the worst news a parent could ever receive: that our son had been killed in an accident on the freeway.

I wasn't able to preach for weeks, and I asked a number of my pastor friends to step up to the pulpit for me. I eased back in with a series of messages that I have put in a book, *Hope for Hurting Hearts*. It was written in "real time" as we walked and are still walking through the hardest time of our lives.

David spoke of walking through "the valley of the shadow of death," and knowing that the Lord was with him (Psalm 23). We have found the Lord with us as well. So, what I put in *Hope for Hurting Hearts* could be described as a "dispatch from the valley."

Our hearts are still broken, we still grieve, and from what I have learned from others who have walked this road before me, there is a lot of sadness, pain, and grieving to come. We have had our faith tested like never before, but I must tell you that God has been faithful, giving us the "grace to help in time of need."

Sometimes it's a day-by-day process, but more often, hour-by-hour. As the old hymn says: "I need Thee every hour," and my family and I do.

After a couple of months passed following Christopher's unexpected departure to heaven, I felt it was time to resume the series I had been teaching in the book of Acts. Christopher himself had been listening to the series, and had designed the art for the CD package.

So I went back to the computer file, back to the very place I had been when I received the news.

And I had just typed, "Never, Lord."

That is how I felt when I heard the news. "No! Not this, Lord! I don't want this. I don't accept this. *No.*"

There are times when we will feel that way about the will of God. Even Jesus, when He was in the Garden of Gethsemane, recoiled from what was ahead. He said, "If it is possible, let this cup pass from Me." Why did He say that? Because Jesus, who was sinless and perfect and holy, was looking into the abyss of all the wicked things that have or will transpire on this world—past, present, and future. He was seeing everything that is sinful, vile, hellish, cruel, wicked, and unholy, and knew He would have to bear all of that sin upon Himself during those six hours of hanging on a Roman cross.

Dr. Luke tells us that while He agonized in the Garden that night, "His sweat became like great drops of blood falling down to the ground."[59] Medical experts think that Jesus might have been experiencing something that today we call *hematidrosis.* This is an unusual condition when a person is under such severe stress that they actually sweat blood and perspiration. And that may have been what was happening to Jesus as He staggered under the terrible grief, pressure, and revulsion of what was about to take place to Him in a matter of mere hours.

The gospel of Mark, however, tells us that He said something else, prior to "If it is possible, let this cup pass from Me."

He said, "Abba Father."

This is the affectionate cry of a child. It is a term of trust and childlike faith, like saying, "Daddy" or "Papa." If there was any other way, if there could have been any other plan…everything within Him longed for that.

Sometimes in our lives, it *is* possible for the cup to pass. And by that I mean that sometimes God plucks us out of difficult situations in which we find ourselves. We read of the disciples on the storm-tossed Sea of Galilee, how they cried out for help, and how Jesus stood up in the boat and calmed the storm. Or we read of blind Bartimaeus, sitting along the Jericho Road, and crying out at the top of his lungs for Jesus to have mercy on him and heal him. And that is just what happened.

Sometimes when a crisis overwhelms us and we call out to God, He will step in and change our circumstances. We've all seen it happen. I know people in our church family who have been told by doctors that they have incurable cancer, that there is no hope at all, and to get their affairs in order. We have prayed for these people, and we have seen God heal. We know God can do this. I have seen people in the direst circumstances have their situations dramatically reversed by the power of God. And I think we always should pray for these things, pray that the Lord will remove the cup from us.

Often He will.

But there are other times when He will say, "No, My child, you must drink it. You have to go through it. The cancer will run its course. Your loved one will pass away. But it's not the end, it's just a transition. Your loved one will be with Me on the Other Side, and you will be with them again."

Do we want that to happen? Of course we don't! We want the people we love to be with us always. We might find ourselves saying, "Never, Lord." But ultimately, we have to say, "Yes, Lord. Your will be done."

If I could somehow change the circumstances and get Christopher back, would I do that if I could? In a heartbeat! But I don't have that option. And if we believe in the providence of God, we know that the Lord is in control of all things, even those events that hurt and grieve us. Either He directly causes those circumstances, or allows them to happen for purposes that we may never grasp or understand this side of eternity.

So what do we say? "Lord, I don't like this. I don't understand this. I don't want this." But in the end we also say, "Yes, Lord. I will trust You—even in this."

In response to the vision of eating unclean foods, Peter had said, "Never, Lord!" Being a good Jew, he didn't want to eat food that wasn't kosher—and he didn't want to leave his comfort zone and go to non-Jews with the message of the gospel.

It might be the same with us. We might find ourselves writing off whole groups of people that we don't like, don't agree with, or don't want to be around. If God asked us to reach out to these people or be kind to these people or minister to these people, our instinctive response might be, "Never, Lord! Not them. Not there. Not now. Not me. Not that!"

But we really don't have that option, do we? If we call Him "Lord," then we really can't say "never" to Him. Either He's Lord, or He's not.

Profiles in Prejudice?

It's interesting that all of this took place in Joppa. That name might ring a bell for people who know their Bible.

In the book of Jonah, we read about a prophet named Jonah who received a clear and specific assignment from the Lord to go the great city of Nineveh and warn the residents about the judgment of God. Jonah, however, replied (in effect) with "Never, Lord," and got into a ship to flee the country and run from the presence of the Lord.

The first place he headed to was Joppa.

Jonah, like Peter, was a good Jew who didn't want to preach to the Ninevites because they were a cruel and evil people, and bitter enemies of Israel. And his secret fear was that if he warned them, God might spare them from the judgment He had planned and let them live. And he didn't want that! In fact, he would have preferred the whole nation to go down in judgment.

So when God told him to go to Nineveh, he went the other direction… to the seaport of Joppa. He found a ship going to far-away Tarshish, paid the fare, and tried to get as far away from God as he could.

If you don't know "the rest of the story," I suggest you read the little Old Testament book of Jonah. After three days of serious meditation in the gullet of a great fish, the reluctant prophet changed his "Never, Lord," to "Yes, Lord."

Now here is Peter, centuries later, in the town of Joppa, hearing the Lord say, "Go reach out to these people." And he was resistant…at first.

Could it be that we might have a little of that prejudice, too? Sometimes we might say, "I don't want to reach out to my enemy. What if she becomes a Christian? Then I'd have to see her at church and be friendly to her!" We might not say that out loud, but we might think it! Or maybe we would say, "I don't want to reach out to that family member. He hurt me so deeply! In fact, I'd be kind of glad if he went to hell. He deserves it! But if I tell him about Jesus, and he repents, then he'll be my brother, and join me in heaven."

But the fact is, God might be calling us to go to our very enemies with the Good News. And though everything in our flesh might resist that idea, there will be blessings beyond what we can imagine for our obedience.

Jonah finally (and reluctantly) obeyed. And what was the result of that obedience? It may have been the greatest revival in human history. The entire mega-city of Nineveh, the capital of a great empire, repented and turned to the God of Israel. Then, just as Jonah had feared, the city was spared from the judgment of God.

Peter had a choice, too. He didn't think much of the idea of meeting and greeting Gentiles—especially representatives of a Roman army officer.

He could have run from God like Jonah. But he didn't. He obeyed the vision of God, and went with the men back to Caesarea to see Cornelius.

In the Home of a Gentile

They arrived in Caesarea the following day. Cornelius was waiting for them and had called together his relatives and close friends. As Peter entered his home, Cornelius fell at his feet and worshiped him. But Peter pulled him up and said, "Stand up! I'm a human being just like you!" So they talked together and went inside, where many others were assembled.

Peter told them, "You know it is against our laws for a Jewish man to enter a Gentile home like this or to associate with you. But God has shown me that I should no longer think of anyone as impure or unclean. So I came without objection as soon as I was sent for. Now tell me why you sent for me." (Acts 10:24-29, NLT)

As the story continues, Peter goes on to share the gospel with this Roman soldier, his household, and friends. Cornelius comes to faith in Jesus Christ, and the Holy spirit is poured out upon this home. In this way, the book of Acts shows us how the gospel finally came to the Gentile world. And the rest, as they say, is history.

It reminds me of another breakthrough that I was a part of, about forty years ago. The man at the center of this story was named Charles—known to his friends as Chuck. Chuck, with his wife Kay, had pastored a number of small churches, and felt called to teach God's Word in an understandable way. Finally, he ended up at a little church in Orange County known as Calvary Chapel.

In those days, the counterculture revolution was in full swing. Babyboomer kids were collectively losing their minds, there were protests in the streets, "sex, drugs, and rock and roll" was the mantra of the day…and parents thought America had lost an entire generation.

Pastor Chuck looked at these crazy hippies and for the most part really didn't want much to do with them. But his wife Kay, one of the unsung heroes of the Jesus Movement, had a real heart for the hippie kids and she prayed for them. I found out later that my friends and I used to hang around by Chuck and Kay's house and, unbeknownst to me, they would pray for us when we walked by their home. Of course, I was still a nonbeliever at that point, and had no idea I was being prayed for.

Kay had it in her heart to reach this youth culture. Influenced by his wife's interest and compassion, Chuck too became intrigued. One day their daughter Jan brought home a living, breathing hippie, and he stood there in their front room in all of his hippie-ness. You know: beads, long hair, beard, and the whole getup.

Chuck and Kay sat in the living room with him, and began asking him questions. As it turns out, this hippie was a Christian, and he talked about how God was reaching out to his friends and they were coming to faith. Out of that conversation, Chuck and Kay wanted to open up their church to the hippies, and find a way to reach that whole emerging subculture.

So Chuck went and told his board of elders, "We're going to open the Church up and invite the hippie kids to come." The elders said, "No way. These kids don't even take baths. They'll soil the new carpet with their bare feet!"

So the next Sunday morning Chuck was at the front door of the Church with a basin of water and a towel, ready to wash all the kids' feet so they could come to church.

He won that battle, and the kids started coming in. And what resulted from that deliberate outreach? Calvary Chapel Costa Mesa became one of the churches impacted by what we would later call "the Jesus Movement"—a genuine spiritual revival. Young men who came to faith during this time started countless churches—and I'm one of those guys. What we know today as contemporary Christian worship and music were also born in this time. It was a sea-change in America's spiritual history, and began when one man was willing to overcome his personal prejudice, and say, "Yes, Lord."

I'm not saying that Chuck Smith started the Jesus Movement. As a matter of fact, it was Jesus that started it—and it happened in other parts of the country and world as well. But Chuck was certainly a key individual in this great revival that began in Orange County, California, and spread to other parts of the nation and the world.

Going back to Acts 10, is there a "Cornelius" in your life? Is there someone rubbing up against your world who makes you feel uncomfortable because he or she is so "different," or holds values that are so opposite from your own? Does the thought of reaching out to that person with the Good News about Jesus make you want to run in the opposite direction? Maybe this is an individual you would regard as an enemy, and deep down you're not even sure if you *want* them to find forgiveness in Christ and go to heaven.

My mom was married and divorced seven times. I felt like I had a full-time ministry just sharing the gospel with my mother's old husbands! I tracked down Oscar Laurie, the man who had adopted me, and had the privilege of leading him to faith in Christ. (To hear that whole story you will need to read my autobiography, *Lost Boy*.)

I was very thankful for the opportunity to share Christ with Oscar, but as time went on, there was another man who kept coming to my heart.

And I had a much harder time thinking about reaching out to Eddie.

This is the man my mom left Oscar for when I was in high school in New Jersey. I came home from school, and the car was filled with all our luggage.

Mom said, "We're moving to Hawaii."

"Where's Dad?" I asked.

"Dad's not coming."

We arrived in Hawaii, she divorced Oscar, and suddenly I had to get used to another man in the house, a man I had never met before.

Eddie.

He was a big guy, over six feet tall. He owned a bar, and he was a raging alcoholic. This is the man who almost killed my mother. When they were both drunk one night, he took a wooden statue and clouted her on the head with it, knocking her unconscious to the floor.

With my mother lying on the floor, bleeding and near death, Eddie told me to go to my room. If I hadn't, he probably would have killed me. Slipping out of the house, I ran to a neighbor's place and called an ambulance. My mother survived.

After I became a Christian, however, I shared my faith with Oscar, and sensed the Lord leading me to go share with Eddie.

I didn't want to do that.

I had a big "No!" right in the middle of my heart. I thought to myself, *He's a bad man. I never want to talk to him again. I never want to see him again.*

Nevertheless, I went—only because the Lord had asked me to do it. I would like to say that it was glorious encounter, and that afterwards he got down on his knees and accepted Christ. But I can't say that.

He listened to me, and was pleasant about it. "Well, Greg," he said, "I'm glad to know this has happened for you."

I happened to be preaching that night, just a short distance away at the Waikiki Shell, a venue for outdoor concerts near Diamond Head.

Telling Eddie about it, I said, "Why don't you come?"

"Well, I can't come."

"Why not? I'll come pick you up and take you."

"Greg…I don't want to come."

"It's just *right there*," I said, pointing. "It's almost a stone's throw."

"I don't want to come."

So he said no, and that was that. There was nothing else to do. I had shared the gospel with him, and I had to leave the results in the hands of God. The point is, I went to him. I went to him because I felt that is what the Lord wanted me to do. And if I had said "No, Lord," I would have regretted that choice for the rest of my life.

There are probably people like that in your life—people who have hurt you, mistreated you, disappointed you, or treated you unjustly. And because of past events, you find yourself thinking, *I don't even want to talk to that person again, let alone share the gospel with them*.

One thing I believe we can learn from Peter in Acts chapter 10 is that there are blessings beyond what we can even conceive for simply obeying the prompting of the Lord. Share the Good News with that "Cornelius" in your life, and see what the Lord will do. They may react like Eddie, turning you away, or they may respond like Oscar, and find eternal salvation. The results are in the hands of God.

Our job is to overcome our reluctance and personal prejudice and say two of the most powerful words we could ever utter.

"Yes, Lord."

TWELVE
The Power of Prayer

As you read these words, you may find yourself facing a personal crisis.

It might be a lack of employment, a foreclosure on your home, or a deep loss in your investments. Maybe you have a marriage that is falling apart or a prodigal son or daughter who is away from the Lord right now. You could even be facing a life-threatening illness, and find yourself paralyzed by fear as you ponder an uncertain future.

So what are you to do?

The Bible says you are to pray.

The apostle Paul gave the Church in Philippi these life-transforming words:

> Don't worry about anything; instead, pray about everything. Tell God what you need, and thank him for all he has done. Then you will experience God's peace, which exceeds anything we can understand. His peace will guard your hearts and minds as you live in Christ Jesus. (Philippians 4:6-7, NLT)

In the backwash of emotions and mental turmoil following the death of my thirty-three year-old son, Christopher, I have lived by these words.

In times of deep sadness, when those waves of grief roll over me, I pray. Sometimes my prayers aren't very long—little more than quick cries to God. *God, help me. Lord, give me strength.*

And He does. He gives me the strength that I need for the moment.

God promises that He will give you a peace that *passes* understanding—not necessarily a peace that will always give understanding.

Even so, when you're overwhelmed, that's the time to pray. I don't even want to contemplate what life would be like if I didn't have the privilege of taking my sorrows and cares and worries to the Lord.

In Psalm 61, David wrote:

> Hear my cry, O God;
> Attend to my prayer.
> From the end of the earth I will cry to You,
> When my heart is overwhelmed;
> Lead me to the rock that is higher than I.
> (vv. 1-2)

In other words, when your heart is overwhelmed, start looking for higher ground. In times of prayer, God lifts us and gives us His strength.

That is what we see the Church doing in Acts chapter 12. As the chapter opens, the believers in Jerusalem faced a pretty bleak scenario. They were in one of those situations where if God didn't come through for them, it was going to be a complete disaster.

We don't like situations like that. We like to have a backup plan in case things go south. In fact, we'd like to have a backup plan for our backup plan. But sometimes the Lord allows us to be caught up in a set of circumstances with no backup plan, no back door, no emergency exit, and no way out but through Him.

In times like that, as David said, our hearts are overwhelmed. And we cry out to God in our distress.

Acts 12 gives an exciting account of the power of prayer, and in this chapter, we'll consider four principles about praying in a way that brings results.

Prayer that prevails.

Herod's Vendetta

Now about that time Herod the king stretched out his hand to harass some from the Church. Then he killed James the brother of John with the sword. And because he saw that it pleased the Jews, he proceeded further to seize Peter also. Now it was during the Days of Unleavened Bread. So when he had arrested him, he put him in prison, and delivered him to four squads of soldiers to keep him, intending to bring him before the people after Passover.

Peter was therefore kept in prison, but constant prayer was offered to God for him by the Church. (Acts 12:1-5)

As the story begins, a shocking wave of persecution has shaken the young church to its core. Back in Acts 7, young Stephen had been martyred, and in the attacks that followed many of the believers had been scattered through Judea and Samaria. But God continued to work in spite of—and even through—that tragedy.

As we have noted, the comfortable "holy huddle" the believers had enjoyed in Jerusalem was shattered by that campaign of violence and intimidation, and the believers spread out across the land with the Good News about Jesus (which they were supposed to be doing in the first place).

Then things seemed to settle down for a while—until the evil King Herod decided he wanted to boost his poll numbers with certain elements of Jewish population. The interlude of peace was shattered as "the king stretched out his hand to harass some from the Church" (Acts 12:1).

He laid hands on James, the brother of John, and one of the men who had been closest to Jesus during his three-year ministry, and had him summarily executed.

Apparently, the king's strategy worked. The enemies of the Church were very happy about that move, and Herod's approval numbers soared. In fact, the strategy worked so well he looked for a way to push his numbers even higher. So he arrested Peter, one of the principle leaders of the Church, intending to execute him as well—after a bit of political grandstanding at a show trial.

With Peter behind bars, Herod wanted to make very sure that Peter didn't get out of prison. Something very strange had happened when the high priest had thrown Peter and the apostles into the public jail, as recounted in Acts 5:

"During the night an angel of the Lord opened the doors of the jail and brought them out. 'Go, stand in the temple courts,' he said, 'and tell the people the full message of this new life'" (vv. 19-20, NIV).

Herod undoubtedly had his own prison, and his own security apparatus. But just to be on the safe side, he detailed an extra-armed guard to keep Peter under lock and key—until he could publicly put him to death.

Act 12:4 tells us that Herod delivered Peter to "four squads of soldiers to keep him, intending to bring him before the people after Passover."

So Peter was behind two gates, chained to two guards, and guarded by fourteen more. So what did the Jerusalem church do? Flood Herod's switchboard? Call their member of congress? Organize a protest and picket the palace? No, we have no record of such a thing. There were no petition drives, product boycotts, street demonstrations, bumper stickers, or tearful appeals to the media. (By the way, I am not necessarily critical of any of those expressions in their proper place.)

Verse 5 gives us their entire strategy: "Peter was therefore kept in prison, but constant prayer was offered to God for him by the church."

We have a secret weapon in the Church. And it is called prayer. Though all other doors may remain closed, one door is always open: the door into the presence of God through prayer.

So often, however, we save this as our last resort—what we do when "all else fails." But this church prayed as a *first* resort, and it was by far the most powerful and effective thing they could have done.

Now let's see if we can identify some principles about the prayer they offered on Peter's behalf.

Four Principles of Effective Prayer

#1: They offered their prayer to God.

"Constant prayer was offered to God." (v. 5)

Does that seem just a little too obvious? Isn't all prayer offered to God? Not necessarily. Often in prayer there is little thought of God. Our mind can be so taken up with what we need that we never actually think of the Lord Himself. Sometimes in our prayer we pray to impress others. Jesus warned us to not be like the Pharisees, who would stand on the street corner and put on a show when they prayed.

Maybe you're in a prayer meeting and you're praying out loud. Somehow, the words just come flowing out, and some part of your mind is thinking just how profound you sound. You think to yourself, *Man, this is a great prayer. This is better than anybody else's prayer.* As if it was some kind of contest!

Jesus told a story about a Pharisee who got caught up in his own self-congratulating verbiage as he prayed. And the Lord said of him, "The Pharisee stood and prayed thus with himself" (Luke 18:11). In other words, this man's prayers never went any higher than the ceiling; he was praying with himself, and God wasn't even part of the equation. That's possible for you and me, also. We can rattle off or recite some "prayer" but never really have an encounter with the living God.

We want to truly offer our prayers to Him.

My granddaughter Stella is just learning to pray. So before a meal we will say, "Okay. Let's pray. Let's fold our hands and close our eyes." So she does that. And sometimes I will look while we're praying and she'll have her eyes open or be eating something! We are teaching her to close her eyes, so that she will learn to think about God for a few seconds before she starts poking at the food.

But obviously, you don't have to close your eyes when you pray… or fold your hands…or kneel. Scripture speaks of many postures in prayer, but what really counts isn't posture at all, it is the attitude of the heart. You can be praying when you're walking down the sidewalk, driving on a highway (eyes open, please), or taking a shower.

What God looks for is the movement of your heart toward Him.

Yes, the Church's prayer in Acts 12 was offered up to God. But here is a corollary to that point. As we present our prayers before God, we must align our will with His. In other words, if you want to see your prayers answered in the affirmative, your goal should be to pray according to God's will, as you best understand it.

Easier said than done, by the way.

How do we discover God's will? One of the best ways I can think of to do is to be in the Scriptures every day, seeking His face as you read His Word. That's what the prophet Daniel did in Babylon, as he prayed for the return of his captive nation to Israel. He had read in the book of Jeremiah that the captivity was to last seventy years, and as that time reached its conclusion, he "turned to the Lord God and pleaded with him in prayer and fasting" (Daniel 9:3, NLT). He prayed for God's forgiveness and mercy on the nation, knowing he was on firm ground for doing so.

The best way you and I are going to discover the heart and mind of God is through a consistent, diligent study of the Bible. And as you know more and more about God's desires, your prayers will more and more reflect those desires.

Jesus made this amazing promise: "If you abide in Me, and My words abide in you, you will ask what you desire, and it shall be done for you" (John 15:7). Another translation says, "But if you make yourselves at home with me and my words are at home in you, you can be sure that whatever you ask will be listened to and acted upon."[60]

We like the sound of that, don't we? Especially the latter part—"whatever your heart desires." But don't miss the big "IF" at the beginning of that sentence. "IF you maintain a living communion with Me, and My words are at home in you…." In other words, if you are investing daily time studying His Word and growing in your understanding of the nature and character of God, you will begin praying for what He wants. True prayer is not bending God my way. It is bending myself His way.

#2: They prayed with passion and persistence.

Look at verse 5 again. "Constant prayer was offered to God for him by the church." What kind of prayer? *Constant* prayer. Another way to translate it would be "earnest prayer." In fact, the word used here to describe their prayer is the same word used to describe the prayer of Jesus in the Garden of Gethsemane. That was a prayer of passion. It was an agonizing prayer. And that's the way this church prayed for their leader, Peter.

Many times our prayers have no power because they have no heart. If we put so little passion in our prayers, we can't expect God to put much passion into answering them.

They didn't pray, "Lord, save Peter…or whatever."

Sometimes we can be so wrapped up in our own thoughts and concerns that we really don't give our full attention to prayer. Someone will tell us of a crisis they're facing, and we may send up a quick, "Lord help them," but if the truth were known, we don't really care that much. We don't pray with passion, and we don't pray continuously.

Jesus taught, "Ask, and it will be given to you; seek, and you will find; knock, and it will be opened to you."[61] A better translation of the original language, however, would read: "Keep on asking. Keep on seeking. Keep on knocking."

If someone keeps on knocking at your door, you might say, "Okay, okay, hold on! I'm coming." And you open the door just to shut them up. But God isn't irritated at all when you keep knocking, knocking, and knocking at His door. He likes it. He likes opening the door to you, His much-loved child. In fact, He tells you to be persistent and to keep at it.

You and I tend to pray for something once or twice, and then say, "Well, I guess God isn't going to answer this prayer." No! Keep praying about that matter on your heart. In Luke 18:1, Jesus taught His disciples that "men always ought to pray and not lose heart."

So the church in Jerusalem kept praying with great passion and persistence for Peter, knowing he was in peril for his very life.

Sometimes we will say, "My prayer wasn't answered." But in reality, we just didn't *like* the answer. "No" is as much an answer to prayer as "yes" is. God answers prayer in one of three ways: yes, no, and wait.

But we don't like to wait. In a society of instant gratification where we get everything on demand, we don't have a lot of patience to spare. Nevertheless, the Lord's timing is perfect, and we have to accommodate ourselves to His schedule, His priorities, His reading of the seasons of our lives.

You see, sometimes God says "go," sometimes God says "slow," and sometimes God says "grow."

When Paul, for instance, prayed for release from his "thorn in the flesh," God answered that prayer. But it wasn't with a yes. God's answer was, "My grace is sufficient for you." So effectively God was saying to Paul, "I will use this set of circumstances in your life to cause you to grow."

Moses wanted to deliver the Israelites out of the bondage of Egypt, and it was a great idea—even a God idea. The problem was, his timing was off by about forty years. So through a set of circumstances that came into Moses' life, God was effectively telling him, "Slow."

But sometimes God says go.

As in, "Go *now*."

For all the times when God asks us to wait for the answers to our prayers, there are other times when they're answered so fast it shocks us. The petition is barely out of our mouths when we see the answer walk in through the front door.

#3: They prayed together.

The Church met together at the home of Mary, mother of John Mark, to plead with God for Peter's release.

There is power in united prayer. Jesus said, "If two of you agree on earth concerning anything that they ask, it will be done for them by My Father in heaven. For where two or three are gathered together in My name, I am there in the midst of them" (Matthew 18:19-20). The term translated "agree" here doesn't just mean agreement in general. It's not as though three Christians could get together and pray for something stupid and expect to receive it. As I mentioned earlier, your will needs to be in lined up with God's will, and your prayers in accordance with what He teaches in His Word. So this verse assumes that those who pray together are all in alignment with the will of God and praying with a God-given burden.

So if you have a crisis or a need in your life, you go to your Christian friends and say, "Here's what's going on in my life. Will you pray about this with me? Can we agree together on this?" That is what the Church did at John Mark's house. They prayed together.

#4: They prayed with doubt...and God heard them anyway.

Yes, these believers prayed to God, prayed with passion, prayed constantly, and prayed together. But Scripture always paints a true picture, and it's obvious that these good, sincere men and women harbored doubts in their hearts about God's answer.

That's the only thing we can conclude when we see them so blown away by the literal answer to their prayers.

You have to love the way Dr. Luke tells the story:

All the time that Peter was under heavy guard in the jailhouse, the Church prayed for him most strenuously.

Then the time came for Herod to bring him out for the kill. That night, even though shackled to two soldiers, one on either side, Peter slept like a baby. And there were guards at the door keeping their eyes on the place. Herod was taking no chances!

Suddenly there was an angel at his side and light flooding the room. The angel shook Peter and got him up: "Hurry!" The handcuffs fell off his wrists. The angel said, "Get dressed. Put on your shoes." Peter did it. Then, "Grab your coat and let's get out of here." Peter followed him, but didn't believe it was really an angel—he thought he was dreaming.

Past the first guard and then the second, they came to the iron gate that led into the city. It swung open before them on its own, and they were out on the street, free as the breeze. At the first intersection the angel left him, going his own way. That's when Peter realized it was no dream. "I can't believe it—this really happened! The Master sent his angel and rescued me from Herod's vicious little production and the spectacle the Jewish mob was looking forward to."

Still shaking his head, amazed, he went to Mary's house, the Mary who was John Mark's mother. The house was packed with praying friends. When he knocked on the door to the courtyard, a young woman named Rhoda came to see who it was. But when she recognized his voice—Peter's voice!—she was so excited and eager to tell everyone Peter was there that she forgot to open the door and left him standing in the street.

But they wouldn't believe her, dismissing her, dismissing her report. "You're crazy," they said. She stuck by her story, insisting. They still wouldn't believe her and said, "It must be his angel." All this time poor Peter was standing out in the street, knocking away.

Finally they opened up and saw him — and went wild! (Acts 12:5-16, THE MESSAGE)

That story gives me hope, because I'm not always a man of great faith. There are many times when I will pray for something—even something I truly believe to be in God's will—and yet wonder in my heart (and sometimes worry) if it will really happen. It's encouraging to know that even when we are weak, God can still intervene and answer our prayers. Even though the prayer of the Church for Peter that night was weak, it was mightier than Herod. And it was mightier than hell.

Despite their lack of faith, God came through.

In some branches of the contemporary church, we're told that we must have complete faith when we pray, and even if we have a single doubt it won't happen.

Oh, please. Just stop.

I don't care who you are, we're all going to have times when our faith isn't as strong as it ought to be. But God is faithful, and will answer our prayers even when our faith is shaky and our hearts are gripped with doubt.

I love the story in the book of Mark about the dad with a demon-possessed son who came to Jesus for help. Broken-hearted, knowing his faith wasn't what it ought to be—and yet desperate for help—"the father of the child cried out and said with tears, 'Lord, I believe; help my unbelief!'"[62]

And Jesus immediately healed the boy.

How much faith did Lazarus have when God raised him from the dead? Not much! The weeping people around the tomb weren't exactly overflowing with faith, either. The point is that God can—and will—work even when we don't have as much faith as we ought to have. That's not to excuse us from having faith. In fact, "without faith it is impossible to please God."[63] We should pray with faith and we should pray with persistence. But obviously these believers were shocked when God actually answered their prayer, and saw the answer standing right before them.

Speaking of faith, you really have to admire the way Peter weathered this storm. There he was, chained up in Herod's maximum-security cell, surrounded by guards, knowing that his fate hung in the balance…and he slept like a baby. He was sleeping so deeply that the angel "struck Peter on the side and raised him up" (Acts 12:7). In other words, the angel had to give a little punch and then haul him to his feet.

But even on his feet, Peter still wasn't with it. The angel had to hurry him like a mom hurrying a sleepy child with a school bus to catch. "Get your shoes on, Peter. Grab your coat, Peter. Come on, Peter, let's get going."

Peter had been able to sleep in a crisis, knowing that whatever the outcome, the Lord would be with him. Either he would be rejoining His Church family, or he would be joining James, Stephen, and the Lord Jesus on the other side. Psalm 4:8 says, "I will both lie down in peace and sleep; for You alone, O LORD, make me dwell in safety."

Psalm 127:2 says, "He gives His beloved sleep." And that's what He gave to Peter in the middle of a frightening situation.

Once Peter was finally delivered from prison and found himself out on the street, the angel left him. I find that interesting. He needed a miracle to escape the prison, the shackles, and the guards. But he didn't need a miracle to reach Mary's house. He didn't need an angel guide through the streets of Jerusalem, he could get there on his own.

Sometimes we get confused and try to do God's part—or expect God to do ours. There is a place for the miraculous, and a place for our response to that work of God. For instance, Jesus raised Lazarus up from the dead. Only God could do that. But someone else loosed the man from his grave clothes and let him go. Jesus took the five loaves and two fish and fed 5,000 men with it, but others distributed the food and picked up the pieces afterwards.

Often in our own strength we try to do what only God can do. Only God can convert a soul. I can't, and neither can you. None of us can. But sometimes we imagine we'll "help the Lord out a little" with gimmicks or pressure tactics, trying to do what only the Holy Spirit can do.

But on the other hand, there are certain things that God will not do. Only we can do it. Only I can obey God. Only I can choose to apply discipline in my life and do the right thing. Only I can repent of my sin. The Lord will not do those things for me. He wants me to take those steps—for Him.

God will not force me to do His will, He will give me the choice. And then I must decide.

So Peter finds himself delivered and free, and makes his way over to Mary's house and knocks on the gate. Back at Herod's prison, the iron gate had opened for him automatically—just like the supermarket! But now, at Mary's house, he can't seem to get in the front door. It's kind of funny—all the doors open for him to get out of prison but he can't get into a prayer meeting!

The New King James Version says that "when they opened the door and saw him they were astonished." *They*. In other words, when they finally decided to check out what Rhoda had told them, the whole group went together to open the door.

And there stands Peter. And they went wild. They were so excited to see the living, breathing, big-as-life answer to their prayers.

Note the way Acts chapter 12 begins and ends. The chapter opens with a seemingly all-powerful, unstoppable King Herod who stretches out his hand "to harass some from the church." He seizes James, and kills him. He arrests Peter, planning to put him on trial and kill him, too.

Seen from the perspective of those verses, life looks pretty grim. A good man murdered. A beloved leader imprisoned, on death row. Herod has on his side the power of the government, the sword, and the threat of prison. The bad guys win.

Or do they?

The Church has on their side the Creator of the universe and the secret weapon He has given to them—and to us—the mighty power of prayer. Acts 12 ends with Herod giving a speech to the citizens of Tyre and Sidon. And after his speech was done the people were so taken with it they began to chant in unison, "It is the voice of a god and not of a man! The voice of a god and not of a man!"

Herod is standing there saying, "Thank you, thank you, very much." He's soaking it up, taking it all in, reveling in his own self-importance. The Jewish historian Josephus points out that at this particular event, Herod was dressed head to toe in silver, so the sun flashed and sparkled from his garments. It was apparently a very impressive sight; the king looked like a god to the people, and he freely accepted their adulation.

But listen how the story ends.

Then immediately an angel of the Lord struck him, because he did not give glory to God. And he was eaten by worms and died.

But the word of God grew and multiplied.
(Acts 12:23-24)

What a difference. The chapter opens with James dead, Peter in prison, and Herod triumphing. It closes with Herod dead, Peter free, and the Word of God triumphing.

You see, it isn't over until it's over.

So keep praying.

Never give up.

THIRTEEN
The Problem of Pain

Without question, the Christian life is the greatest life you could ever live.

And why is that?

I can't even count all the ways! God takes a life that was empty, aimless, and headed toward certain judgment, and turns it around and transforms it. He forgives us of all of our sin, and if that wasn't enough, credits the very righteousness of Jesus Christ into our spiritual bank account. He removes all of our guilt, and fills the void in our lives with Himself, as He literally takes up residence in the very center of who we are. Most importantly, He changes our eternal address from a place called hell to a place called heaven.

This all comes as a result of the power of the gospel proclaimed and believed. And when we do believe, we are gifted with a new desire to glorify God with our lives.

It's absolutely true that when you trust Christ as Savior, God removes a whole lot set of problems you used to have—including the nagging guilt and that empty sense of aimlessness in life that used to haunt you.

But we need to understand something else: There will be a whole new set of problems that will take the place of your old problems. Because the day that you put your trust in Jesus Christ, you enter into a battle—warfare that will last for the rest of your life. Why? Because not only is there a God who loves you and has a plan for your life, there is also a devil who hates you, and fiercely opposes God's plan. Some are surprised to find that the Christian life is not a playground, but a battleground. And that is why the apostle Paul said, "Endure hardship as a good soldier of Jesus Christ."[64]

I bring this up because some have believed in what we might describe as a watered-down gospel. This diluted version of the true gospel promises forgiveness, but rarely tells you of the need to repent of your sin. It's a gospel that promises peace and plenty, but never warns of persecution. It's a gospel that says God wants you to be healthy and wealthy, and never have any problems to speak of. It's a gospel that says you can so wrap yourself in God's favor that there will always be a parking space available for you at the mall.

My friend, that is *not* the gospel of the New Testament. I can assure you, the last thing on Paul's mind was "How can I find a great parking space?" He had other objectives that gripped his heart and soul.

What am I saying here? That God wants you to be sick, poor, and miserable? That He doesn't want you to be happy? No, that's not my point. I believe that happiness will come as you really follow the Lord. But it is a by-product—a fringe benefit—of belonging to God in Christ.

The essence of the Christian life is knowing God and walking with Him. It's about sticking with Him when the sky is blue and also when it's filled with clouds or choked with smoke. It's about walking with the Lord through thick and thin, and pressing on through every heartache and trial that happens to come our way.

Storm Warnings

Jesus made it clear that storms will enter every life. But it is through these storms and hardships and tribulations that we will enter God's kingdom.

As Dr. Luke phrased it Acts 14:21-22: "And when they had preached the gospel to that city and made many disciples, they returned to Lystra, Iconium, and Antioch, strengthening the souls of the disciples, exhorting them to continue in the faith, and saying, 'We must through many tribulations enter the kingdom of God.'"

We don't always like to read a verse like that. It's probably not a passage we want to put in calligraphy on a plaque and hang by our front door. We would *rather* the passage read, "Through many days of perpetual happiness, we enter the kingdom of God." But that isn't Scripture, and that isn't life. Trials and tribulations will come.

Job said it well: "Man who is born of woman is of few days and full of trouble." Another version translates it like this: "How frail is man, how few his days, how full of trouble!"[65]

In the wrap-up to His Sermon on the Mount, Jesus told a story about two men who built two homes. They may have been at the same time and close together. They might have even had the same floor plan. One of the builders however, erected his home on shifting sand, while the other built his home on a stable rock foundation.

Then the storms came, with wind and driving rain hitting both of those houses—hard! The house that had been built on sand collapsed and fell in upon itself, while the one built on the rock stood firm. The obvious moral of the story is to build your life on a foundation that will last, like the one we find in the pages of God's Word.

But here's an application we sometimes miss.

The storm came to *both* lives. The wind beat on *both* houses. The rain poured on *both* building sites. The man who was wise and carefully chose a stable foundation got hit with the same hurricane-force winds as the man who foolishly took shortcuts and didn't bother to plan ahead.

We will all experience storms in life. Good things will happen to us, as well as tragic and inexplicable things. Every life will have its share of pain.

As much as we would like to believe otherwise, none of us can take an extended vacation beyond the reach of human suffering and tragedy. Former British Prime Minister Benjamin Disraeli summed up life in this pessimistic way: "Youth is a mistake. Manhood is a struggle. And old age a regret."

The Russian novelist and philosopher Tolstoy condensed four attitudes people have towards life's problems and human suffering.

#1: There are those who view life as all bad, and get drunk to forget it.

#2: There are those who view life as all bad, and struggle against it.

#3: There are those who view life as all bad, and by suicide remove themselves from it.

#4: (And Tolstoy included himself in this one.) there those who view life as all bad, but live on, irrationally accepting it as it comes.

I would like to suggest a fifth category that both Disraeli and Tolstoy missed in their negative evaluations:

There is a God who, despite the worst tragedy, can bring good out of bad!

That is what the Bible teaches, and that is what I believe. That's not to say that God will make bad good, because bad is bad. But it is to say that good can *come out* of bad. As Romans 8:28 affirms: "And we know that in all things God works for the good of those who love him, who have been called according to his purpose."[66]

A better translation would be, "He is causing all things to work and to continue working together for good." Life is a process, and we are finite beings who live moment to moment. We can't see around the bend, we can't discern God's ultimate purposes.

Good Out of Bad

Right now, as you look at some recent hardship or tragedy that has befallen you, you might well say, "I don't see *any* good in this." But then maybe a month from now, you will see a little good. And then a little bit later, you will see a little more. Most likely, it won't be until you have departed this life and entered eternity that you will finally see the big picture and the complete good. But until that day, God promises that He can bring good out of bad.

Some people actually imagine that as believers in Christ, we are somehow exempt from human suffering. I hate to break it to you, but inexplicable and heartbreaking things happen to good and godly people. Christians get cancer, die in auto accidents, lose their jobs, and experience practically all of the problems that people outside of Christ experience.

Scripture acknowledges that you and I may be surprised by the trials we encounter. The apostle Peter wrote: "Dear friends, do not be surprised at the painful trial you are suffering, as though something strange were happening to you" (1 Peter 4:12, NIV). Even so, we frequently are surprised when we encounter problems and difficulties—problems in our career, with our family, with our kids, or in our marriage.

After my son Christopher's death, I even had people coming up to me and saying, "I can't believe that this happened to you, *of all people*." The idea being, I suppose, that because I'm a pastor and preach the gospel, that I should somehow get a free pass on the suffering of the rest of the human race.

But the Bible makes no such promise. Not to anyone.

In Romans 5, Paul says, "Because of our faith, Christ has brought us into this place of undeserved privilege where we now stand, and we confidently and joyfully look forward to sharing God's glory.

"We can rejoice, too, when we run into problems and trials, for we know that they help us develop endurance. And endurance develops strength of character, and character strengthens our confident hope of salvation. And this hope will not lead to disappointment. For we know how dearly God loves us, because he has given us the Holy Spirit to fill our hearts with his love."[67]

It's just a little bit hard to fit some of those words together, isn't it? How can the words "problems and trials" fit into the same passage with the assurance of how dearly God loves us? If God loves me, why doesn't He remove my trials and problems?

Answer: Because God loves you.

We mentioned the death of Lazarus in the previous chapter. You may remember that when Mary and Martha found out about how ill their brother was, they sent word to Jesus, simply saying, "The one that You love He is sick" (John 11:3).

That may have been the eight-word message that they sent to Jesus, but there was much between the lines! "*Lord, remember us? Mary, Martha and Lazarus. Here in Bethany. We're Your friends. You come and hang out at our home whenever You're in town. Remember Martha? She's the one who makes the killer meals. Mary is the one who sits at Your feet. And Lazarus is Your friend! It's Your own dear friend, Lord, who is sick.*"

They probably thought that Jesus would just speak the word and Lazarus would be healed instantaneously. Or that the Lord might rush back from wherever He was staying, and lay His hand on Lazarus' fevered brow.

But instead, we read that Jesus delayed His arrival. In fact, when Jesus received the message, He replied, "Lazarus's sickness will not end in death. No, it happened for the glory of God so that the Son of God will receive glory from this" (John 11:4, NLT).

So even though Jesus loved Mary, Martha, and Lazarus, He stayed where He was for the next two days. You know the rest of the story, and how it ended. Jesus allowed Lazarus to die, but raised him from the dead. The most important issue in the story, however, was that God wanted to use that difficult life circumstance to bring greater glory to His name.

It's true that God loves us and works all things together for good. The problem arises with our definition of "good," and how we feel He should demonstrate His love in our lives. We think that good means no pain, no suffering, and no hardship. We imagine the best good to a problem-free life, with the sun always shining and the birds always singing.

Now don't get me wrong: that sounds pretty appealing to me, too. And truthfully, we will have many beautiful days of joy, peace, happiness, and good times. But there will also be many trials. As Jesus said in John 16:33 (NLT), "Here on earth you will have many trials and sorrows. But take heart, because I have overcome the world."

Why Does God Allow Suffering?

Here's the problem in a nutshell: Our definition of good is what benefits us in the here-and-now, not in the bye-and-bye. In other words, we are interested in what will benefit us temporarily, but God is interested in what will benefit us eternally. We are interested in what will make us happy for a while, but God is far more interested in what will make us holy.

So here is the key. Jesus loves us, and He wants to be glorified through our lives. In view of that reality, He will not always remove suffering, because it can make us stronger and bring us closer to Him. Even though we would never choose it, suffering can give us a greater platform for glorifying God and pointing others toward Him.

Why does God allow suffering? Let's consider just a few reasons.

Adversity levels us, and keeps us humble.

Success or prosperity has a tendency to make people proud and self-sufficient. We may not feel an overwhelming need for God when we have our salary, our investments, our career, our 401k, our homes, our health, and our family. But when the economy goes south or the stock market crashes or our home burns, we have the opportunity to turn back to God with all our hearts, being reminded of what really matters in life.

The truth is, you and I shouldn't always be so afraid of pain. There is something worse than pain: it is a prosperity that leads us to forget about God.

As they were (at long last) poised to enter the Promised Land, God warned the Israelites that the real danger to their lives had just begun.

> "Be careful that you do not forget the Lord your God…. Otherwise, when you eat and are satisfied, when you build fine houses and settle down, and when your herds and flocks grow large and your silver and gold increase and all you have is multiplied, then your heart will become proud and you will forget the Lord your God, who brought you out of Egypt, out of the land of slavery." (Deuteronomy 8:11-14, NIV)

Prior to this point, Israel had wandered in a desolate wilderness for forty years, completely dependent upon God for *everything*. Every day they would step outside of their little tent, and there would be manna waiting for them, just like the morning paper. Room service direct from heaven! And God gave them fresh water to drink, a cloud to guide and shade them by day, and a pillar of fire to light their camp by night.

Yes, wilderness living came with plenty of hardships. But those very difficulties compelled them to look to the Lord every day, depending on Him for everything.

But then He brought them to the brink of the Promised Land, and they could look across the Jordan and see lush green hills, rippling fields of wheat, flowing rivers, and trees loaded with fruit. They could hardly wait to get in! But God said, "Be careful! Watch out, or you'll get fat and sassy and forget all about Me. Then your troubles will *really* begin."

We've all experienced it; when our lives are hit with uncertainty, danger, or pain, we fall to our knees and cry out to God. In the last chapter we read about the church in Jerusalem after James had been killed and Peter had been arrested. They prayed with great passion! And so it is with you and me. God can use adversity to bring us closer to Him.

C. S. Lewis writes: "God whispers to us in our pleasures, He speaks in our conscience, but He shouts in our pains: It is His megaphone to rouse a deaf world."

Sometimes, we're just not ready to listen to God. He whispers to us in our pleasures, but we don't pay attention. He speaks to us our conscience, but we tune Him out. So He has to use a megaphone, and in our pain, we finally begin to listen. As the psalmist said, "Before I was afflicted I went astray, but now I keep Your word…. It is good for me that I have been afflicted, that I may learn Your statutes."[68]

Adversity teaches us eternal truths we might not otherwise learn.

For most of us, our basic objective in life is to avoid pain at all costs. We want to be comfortable. Even dentists know this! Have you seen the ads for "pain free dentistry"? Isn't that an oxymoron? Every time I have been to a dentist, I have felt a certain degree of pain. Don't get me wrong, I have a great dentist, and I'm not blaming him. It's just the nature of what they do.

Bottom line, we just want to dodge pain whenever we can. We want to get in better shape and look cool in our new gym outfit, but we don't want to sweat and strain.

"No pain, no gain"? Alas, it's true. And what is true of the gym or health club is also true of life. Our pain reminds us of a deeper need: the need for God in our lives. And God will teach us lessons in those valleys that we would never have learned on mountaintops—things we need to know, and to share with others.

To quote C. S. Lewis again, "Pain removes the veil; it plants the flag of truth within the fortress of a rebel soul." God wants to plant His flag in your rebel soul. He wants to get control of your life. And with that control comes the deep inner peace and sense of purpose and meaning our heart craves.

Adversity gives us new compassion for others who are in pain.

In case you hadn't noticed, pain, disappointment, and heartache are all around us, as common to the atmosphere of our planet as nitrogen and oxygen. If you preach to people who are hurting, you will never lack for an audience.

It has been said, "Success builds walls, but failure builds bridges." If you have experienced pain, grief, failure, or depression, and by God's grace and help you've come through that valley, your companionship and counsel are like gold for someone who might still be groping their way through that valley. If I was going to take a hiking trip on a certain trail in the Sierras, I'd want to talk to someone who has actually taken that particular hike, not someone who has only thought about it or read about it in a book.

Paul, who certainly experienced his share of valleys in his earthly journey (and high mountaintops, too!), shared this perspective with the Corinthians:

> All praise to the God and Father of our Master, Jesus the Messiah! Father of all mercy! God of all healing counsel! He comes alongside us when we go through hard times, and before you know it, he brings us alongside someone else who is going through hard times so that we can be there for that person just as God was there for us. We have plenty of hard times that come from following the Messiah, but no more so than the good times of his healing comfort—we get a full measure of that, too. (2 Corinthians 1:3-5, THE MESSAGE)

When we go through adversity, we can help others who are going through it as well.

So coming back to the question I raised earlier. *Why me? Why should I go through a time of suffering or loss?*

Maybe the question should be, Why NOT me? As I have continued to grieve over my son's abrupt departure for heaven, God has given me a very unique platform to bring the comfort to others that He has brought to me. Never in all the years of my ministry have I had so many hurting people write to me and talk to me. There are some who are listening to me now who would have never listened to me before.

So I thank God for that.

Am I glad that all of this has happened so I can have this new ministry? No. But am I glad God can bring some good out of the pain and comfort that I am experiencing? The answer is yes.

Would I trade it all to have my son back? In all honesty, the answer is yes. But I have not been given that option. So I press on, and preach in my pain, looking forward to that day when I will see my son again.

A Day in the Life....

With Paul and Barnabas' missionary journey in Acts 13 to 14, Paul takes center stage in the book of Acts, as Peter begins to fade from view. Paul's travels always make for interesting reading, because he basically stirred up a hornet's nest wherever he went! It didn't matter where he was or with whom he was traveling, the pattern went something like this: He would enter a city and preach the gospel. Some people would be touched by the message and either believe, or want to know more. But others would become jealous, angry, or hostile, and oppose Paul's gospel—often with violence.

There was never a dull moment with Paul.

I wish we could say the same for many churches in our country. Sadly, there are plenty of dull moments, because these churches aren't really making much of an impact on anyone.

How different it was with Paul. Wherever he went, something happened, be it a conversion, a miracle, or a riot. It was said of Paul and Silas in Acts 17:6, "They turned the rest of the world upside down and now they are here disturbing our city."

God, give us more disturbances like this! It was G. Campbell Morgan who said, "Organized Christianity which fails to make a disturbance is dead." So is the Church shaking the world today? I fear that far too often the world is shaking the Church.

Let's take a moment to consider one day in the life of Paul.

While they were at Lystra, Paul and Barnabas came upon a man with crippled feet. He had been that way from birth, so he had never walked. He was sitting and listening as Paul preached. Looking straight at him, Paul realized he had faith to be healed. So Paul called to him in a loud voice, "Stand up!" And the man jumped to his feet and started walking.

When the crowd saw what Paul had done, they shouted in their local dialect, "These men are gods in human form!" They decided that Barnabas was the Greek god Zeus and that Paul was Hermes, since he was the chief speaker. Now the temple of Zeus was located just outside the town. So the priest of the temple and the crowd brought bulls and wreaths of flowers to the town gates, and they prepared to offer sacrifices to the apostles.

But when Barnabas and Paul heard what was happening, they tore their clothing in dismay and ran out among the people, shouting, "Friends, why

are you doing this? We are merely human beings—just like you! We have
come to bring you the Good News that you should turn from these worthless things and turn to the living God....

Then some Jews arrived from Antioch and Iconium and won the crowds to their
side. They stoned Paul and dragged him out of town, thinking he was dead. But
as the believers gathered around him, he got up and went back into the town.
The next day he left with Barnabas for Derbe. (Acts 14:8-15, 19-20, NLT)

There's nothing like a miracle to get a day rolling. Paul spotted a man
who had never taken a single step in his whole life and called out, "Stand
up!" As it turned out, the formerly crippled man didn't slowly and pain-
fully pull himself to a standing position, he *leapt* immediately to his feet,
and immediately started walking. It was a miracle of seismic propor-
tions, and shook the little town of Lystra like an earthquake.

The city's pagan residents immediately concluded that they had a
couple of visiting Greek gods on their hands, and tried to sacrifice to
them.

What amazes me is how quickly they turned from worship to war.
One moment they wanted to honor and adore Paul, and in the next
moment they were trying to stone him to death. Talk about being
fickle. It reminds you of the crowds who cried out, "Hosanna to the
Son of David" on Sunday, and "Crucify Him" on Friday. How quickly
people can turn.

The fact is, Satan is going to hit us in two primary ways as we seek to
serve the Lord. One of those ways will be an overt outward attack.

They stoned Paul and dragged him out of town, thinking he was dead.
(14:19, NLT)

Why are we insulted? Why are we persecuted? Why do people oppose us for what we say and what we believe? Here's the simple answer:
Because we live godly lives. The Bible says, "All who desire to live godly
in Christ Jesus will suffer persecution."[69]

Your very presence and belief in God and what His Word teaches bothers people today. They don't like it, and when they have opportunity, they will oppose you. You are a bright light in a dark den. You are salt in an open wound. Jesus said in John 15:18-19, 20, "If the world hates you, you know that it hated Me before it hated you. If you were of the world, the world would love its own. Yet because you are not of the world, but I chose you out of the world, therefore the world hates you.…If they persecuted Me, they will also persecute you."

A story is told of British preacher John Wesley, who was riding along a road one day when it dawned on him that three whole days had passed in which he had suffered no persecution. Not a brick, not so much as an egg had been thrown at him for three days as he traveled from place to place and preached the gospel.

The thought started to worry him. Finally he got off his horse, got down on his knees, and cried out, "O God, could it be that I have sinned and I am backslidden?" And he began to pray aloud, asking God to show him if he had somehow, somewhere gone astray.

As the story goes, some man out of Wesley's view had watched all this, thinking, "That preacher is crazy. I'll show him!" Picking up a brick, he hurled it at Wesley while he was praying, just missing the evangelist's head.

When Wesley saw that brick he jumped up, and said joyfully, "Thank God, all is well! I still have His presence."

That's one method of Satanic attack: a direct, verbal or even physical assault. But there's another, subtler way the enemy will try to stop us. In Acts 14, we have an example of the more indirect approach, when the people proclaimed Paul and Barnabas gods, bringing them garlands and seeking to sacrifice to them.

In our lives, we may hear words like these in our ears: "Wow, you're really making big strides for Christ. You are a man of God or a woman of God. Your words really resonate. You've grown so much. You're doing so well."

Why would the devil butter you up like this? Because He knows all too well that "Pride goes before destruction, and a haughty spirit be-fore a fall."[70] More men and women have been brought down by pride than probably any other sin. Lucifer knows a little bit about that, since that is the very thing that brought him down as well.

What happened to Paul after this vicious attack?

The answer is: Perhaps more than we would think at first glance!

A Preview of Heaven

They stoned Paul and dragged him out of town, thinking he was dead. But as the believers gathered around him, he got up and went back into the town. The next day he left with Barnabas for Derbe. (vv. 19–20, NLT)

Many commentators believe that Paul may have actually died there in Lystra, and was raised from the dead.

In 2 Corinthians 12, Paul writes about an experience of being caught up into the third heaven. So apparently, at some point in the apostle's life, he died, went to heaven, and came back again. And some surmise it may have been at this very time, lying in the dirt outside of Lystra.

Here is how the apostle described this incredible experience to the believers in Corinth:

I know a man in Christ who fourteen years ago—whether in the body I do not know, or whether out of the body I do not know, God knows—such a one was caught up to the third heaven. And I know such a man—whether in the body or out of the body I do not know, God knows—how he was caught up into Paradise and heard inexpressible words, which it is not lawful for a man to utter. (2 Corinthians 12:2-5)

Paul experienced a preview of heaven.

When you go to a movie, you have to sit through some trailers—some sneak previews—before the main feature comes on. And maybe you'll watch one of those carefully packaged excerpts and say to your spouse, "That looks good, let's go see that." Or then again, you might say, "They couldn't pay me to see that movie." Sometimes the trailers are better than the movies themselves!

Paul was allowed a little preview of things to come. A glimpse of heaven. But what did he mean by "the third heaven"? Where's that? Here is what Paul most likely meant: the first heaven is the sky above us, the clouds, and our atmosphere. The second heaven would be the solar system, the galaxies, and the host of stars in the night sky. The third heaven, then, is the dwelling place of God.

In our imaginations, of course, most of us think about that "third heaven" being somewhere way out there beyond the furthest galaxy. It may be. Then again, it may be much closer than we could possibly realize. The Bible doesn't say where it is. It just tells us it exists. And it may be that this future dwelling place of all believers is not as far as we think.

But whether it be near or far, we know one thing. It is Paradise.

The word "paradise" is used only three times in all the New Testament. One time here, another time by the apostle John, describing his vision of heaven, and the third time by the Lord Jesus, speaking to the thief who was crucified beside Him. He promised the dying man, "Today you will be with Me in Paradise."

Heaven is a real place, a place that will fully engage all of the senses of our resurrected bodies. D. L. Moody said, "Heaven is as much a place as Chicago. It is a destination. It is a locality." It isn't just a state of mind or state of consciousness. It's a *place*. Jesus said, "I go to prepare a *place* for you." Heaven is a place of feasting and fellowship, activities and worship, adventure and overflowing joy.

But even though Paul was granted a little foretaste of what was to come, he had to return to earth and to the pain of a body battered and bloodied by stones hurled in hate. He opened his eyes to see the concerned faces of fellow believers all around him.

Then he simply got up, and went back into town. And the next day he and Barnabas continued their missionary journey. In other words, he dusted himself off and went back to work. No wonder these guys turned the world upside down! What a commitment to the gospel of Jesus Christ!

After preaching at Derbe, we're told that Paul returned to Lystra—the very town where he had been stoned and left for dead—as well as Iconium and Antioch. What was he doing? The Bible says he was "strengthening the souls of the disciples, exhorting them to continue in the faith, and saying, 'We must through many tribulations enter the kingdom of God.'"

Continue in the faith.

He didn't say, "Continue in the feeling." No, he said, "Continue in the faith…even when it doesn't make sense. Continue in the faith… knowing that God is with you, walking you through all of it, and one day He will take you by His hand and draw you into His very presence. Continue in the faith…when the skies are blue and also when they are filled are with clouds. *Press on.* Even if your health isn't what it once was. Even if your loved ones have gone before you. Press on because you will see them again.

And in that final day that some would call "the end," we will see that it's only just the beginning, and we will realize that it was worth it all.

A million times over.

FOURTEEN
Songs in the Night

At some points in our lives, praise comes easily. At other times, quite honestly, it will be a sacrifice, and not easy at all.

Job offered a sacrifice of praise on the darkest afternoon he could have imagined in his worst nightmare: all of his possessions and all of his children ripped away from him in rapid, successive blows. His soul must have felt like it had been jammed through a shredder.

Yet here is how the Bible records his response:

> Then Job stood up and tore his robe in grief and fell down upon the ground before God. "I came naked from my mother's womb," he said, "and I shall have nothing when I die. The Lord gave me everything I had, and they were his to take away. Blessed be the name of the Lord." (Job 1:20-21, TLB)

That is about the clearest example in all of Scripture of what the New Testament calls a *sacrifice of praise*: "Through Jesus, therefore, let us continually offer to God a sacrifice of praise—the fruit of lips that confess his name" (Hebrews 13:15, NIV).

That means that you should offer it if you feel it, or if you don't feel it at all. And notice that it not only says offer a sacrifice of praise, it says "the fruit of your lips." That means you don't just *think* thoughts of praise, you *verbalize* them.

As in, out loud.

I remember the first time I said, "Praise the Lord." It seemed like a very awkward phrase to utter, even though all of my Christian friends would say it. One day I thought, *Well, here goes. I'm going to say that, too*. I actually consciously thought about it, and had a difficult time getting it out.

"Uh…. P—P…Prai...Praise the Lord."

Actually, after I'd said, it felt kind of good. So I said it again. "Praise the Lord!"

It's a wonderful thing when it just flows from your heart through your lips. Say it where you are, right now. *Praise the Lord*. See, it's nice isn't it? That is what you were created to do. You were created to give glory to God. That is the highest use of your lips, mouth, and vocal chords, to give honor and glory to God.

God wants to hear our praise. As an illustration, let's consider a husband who really loves his wife. Does he tell her?

"Well, no. But she *knows*."

"Does she? How does she know that.

"Because I think about it all the time."

That's good…but you might consider verbalizing it. Letting your mouth form the words and saying them right out loud. You don't have to be poetic. You don't have to write a sonnet. Saying "I love you" works just fine.

Now God, in contrast to a wife or husband, *is* a mind reader, and knows very well (and in great detail) what you're thinking. Even so, He wants you to give a sacrifice of praise that is the fruit of your lips. We need to give God what He deserves, and that is glory. Psalm 29 says, "Give unto the LORD the glory due His name; worship the LORD in the beauty of holiness."

Far too often, however, we're like those ten lepers in Luke 17:11-19, who called out loudly to Jesus for intervention. He graciously heard their prayer and healed all of them of the dreaded disease of leprosy. But as may remember, all ten went on their way…and only one returned to give thanks. And Jesus said in response, "Didn't I heal ten of you? Where are the other nine?"[71]

We're often quick to ask God for help during times of crisis, but very slow to offer thanks after He intervenes in answer to our cry. Our attitude is, "Thanks, God. See You next crisis."

After Jesus healed the ten lepers, we read this of the one who returned to offer a sacrifice of praise: "With a loud voice he returned and glorified God falling at His feet and giving Him thanks" (v. 17). That phrase translated "loud voice" in our English Bible is from two words from which we get our English words *megaphone*. He was loud with His praise to God.

So Why Do I Praise God?

#1: Because He controls all the circumstances that surround my life.

Sometimes we understand those circumstances, and at other times they utterly baffle us. Yes, we live our lives and make our plans, but God will always have His way. There's nothing wrong with making plans for tomorrow or next month or next year. But just remember the Lord may change your plan. He, not you, is in control of your life.

We are told in Psalm 16:9: "A man's heart plans his way, but the LORD directs his steps." Jeremiah tells us: "I know, O LORD, that a man's way is not in himself, nor is it in a man who walks to direct his steps."[72]

We call this the providence of God, and while doesn't mean bad things won't happen to good and even godly people, it does mean that even when bad things happen, God can bring good out of bad. Romans 8:28 reminds us that "all things work together for good to those who love God, to those who are called according to His purpose." The good that God promises, however, will not be fully realized until we get to heaven.

There some things we can look at in life and say, "That was bad, but now as I look back in retrospect, I can see the good that has come from it." But then there are other times in life when we will never see or understand the good. And it won't be until we get to the other side and see the Lord face to face that we will understand these things.

#2: God loves me and always looks out for my eternal benefit

Let me emphasize the word "eternal."

What I'm enduring at this moment may be terribly difficult—more difficult than I think I can bear. Yet Paul tells us in 2 Corinthians 4:17–18, "For our present troubles are small and won't last very long. Yet they produce for us a glory that vastly outweighs them and will last forever! So we don't look at the troubles we can see now; rather, we fix our gaze on things that cannot be seen. For the things we see now will soon be gone, but the things we cannot see will last forever" (NLT).

What you and I sometimes perceive as "good" could potentially be bad…and what we sometimes perceive as "bad" could potentially be good.

We think, for instance, that having perfect health and lots of money and influence is good. I'm not suggesting there's anything wrong with any of those good blessings from the hand of our Father. But what's good for one person is not always good for another. If you don't believe that, just consider the lives of many of the people after they win the lottery. Coming up with the winning numbers may be something they have hoped for or dreamed about for years. Yet I have read so many stories of lives—and even whole families—that have literally been destroyed through the immediate accumulation of vast amounts of wealth. It has devastated them, blasting what little happiness in life they might have had before their "lucky day."

What would be perceived as the greatest thing that could happen was actually a curse for some of these people. But then on the other hand, we know people who are blessed with affluence and influence and material things and seem to handle it very well, blessing others and being blessed themselves. God is the one who determines these things.

By the same token, sometimes what we think of as bad or disastrous today may ultimately be good because it changes who we are, ultimately making us more like Jesus. Sometimes what we think of as good can be very bad for us, if it causes us to forget God and instead trust in ourselves instead.

Which brings me to point number three.

#3: I must realize that God is wiser than I am.

God always deals with me for my eternal good. What are those circumstances in my life that will result in my becoming more like Jesus? Frankly, I don't know. But the Lord (who does know) will sort all these things out. So it's not for me to fret over. What I am to do is to glorify Him.

Here before us in Acts 16 is a beautiful story of two men who did just that.

When the Spirit Says "No"

In our last chapter, we considered aspects of Paul's first missionary journey. In Acts 16, we encounter Paul—with Silas, his new traveling partner—on his second such journey.

Deeply concerned for the new churches he had left behind in Asia Minor, Paul proposed a trip where they would revisit those new fellowships, offering encouragement and checking on their progress.

But there was one small problem: God had a different game plan than Paul had. And to Paul's surprise, the Lord stopped them from going where they had wanted and intended to go.

> Paul and Silas traveled through the area of Phrygia and Galatia, because the Holy Spirit had prevented them from preaching the word in the province of Asia at that time. Then coming to the borders of Mysia, they headed north for the province of Bithynia, but again the Spirit of Jesus did not allow them to go there. (Acts 16:6-8, NLT)

I find that fascinating. How did the Holy Spirit stop them? Scripture doesn't tell us. But suffice it to say, God said no…and He made His point clearly.

Sometimes the Lord will do that with us. We make our plans as best we can, and we'll say, "Lord, I think I should do this."

And sometimes He will say no.

How will He communicate that?

There are many, many ways God can stop us, slow us, or turn us. Sometimes it might be through the warning of a friend whom we respect. He or she will say, "I've thought about this and prayed about it but—I have a little check in my spirit. I don't think you should do this right now." At other times it might be through a simple lack of peace in our lives. It may be a vague sense of uneasiness, a feeling that "something isn't right." On the surface, all of the circumstances might line up and all the conditions might check out just fine…but we just can't get peace in our heart.

Be careful about violating that sense of unease! The book of Colossians tells us that we should let the peace of God arbitrate, or settle with finality, all matters that arise in our mind.[73] And if you are starting to do something or go somewhere and you don't sense God's peace or God's blessing, you should learn to tune in and listen to that.

Sometimes we'll be blocked from pursuing a particular course simply because of circumstances. It might be as simple as a cancelled flight, a car that won't start, a sudden case of the flu, or an expected financial provision suddenly drying up. Whatever it might be, something happens circumstantially that stops you or turns you.

And you realize that God has said, "No. Don't go that way."

Perhaps you had some long-held plans or dreams, but the Lord finally made clear to you, "No, that's not what I had in mind for you. That's not My plan for you."

You wanted to go into ministry, but God instead called you into business. Or you wanted to go into business, but God intervened and called you into ministry.

You wanted to be married, and instead God called you to be single. Or you'd always seen yourself pursuing a single life, when God suddenly brings someone into your life, and your plans change.

You hoped to have a large family, but you only had a small one. Or you always intended to have a small family, but God saw fit to bring you a large one.

Your life has developed differently than you ever expected, wanted, or intended, but you need to understand that God has His purposes in these things.

In such a way, Paul and Silas were directed from their intended course into another path.

"Come Over and Help Us"

...Then coming to the borders of Mysia, they headed north for the province of Bithynia, but again the Spirit of Jesus did not allow them to go there. So instead, they went on through Mysia to the seaport of Troas.

That night Paul had a vision: A man from Macedonia in northern Greece was standing there, pleading with him, "Come over to Macedonia and help us!" So we decided to leave for Macedonia at once, having concluded that God was calling us to preach the Good News there. (Acts 16:7-10, NLT)

So Paul and Silas made the trip to Philippi—a city that wasn't on their original itinerary, but was on God's itinerary all along. Later, of course, Paul wrote an epistle to the believers called "Philippians," which has brought immeasurable comfort and encouragement to the Church of Jesus Christ through the centuries.

Philippi, a city in eastern Macedonia (modern Greece), was a colony of Rome with a very small Jewish population. You needed ten Jewish men to start a synagogue, but apparently there weren't that many in the city. I conclude that because when Paul and Barnabas or Silas would blow into town, the first thing they would usually look for was the local synagogue. And that's the place where they would begin preaching and launch their ministry in any given town.

With no synagogue to attend on the Sabbath, however… "We went outside the city gate to the river, where we expected to find a place of

232 UPSIDE DOWN LIVING

prayer. We sat down and began to speak to the women who had gathered there."[74]

So they preached the gospel there, and a lady named Lydia came to faith. The Bible says Lydia was "a seller of purple," which doesn't mean much to us today. What it actually meant was that she traded in purple garments and linens—purple being the material of status and wealth at that time. It's obvious that Lydia was a well-known and influential woman in Philippi, and in God's providence, she became the very first convert in the city. When she heard the gospel, she accepted Christ right on the spot, and others believed with her.

What a glorious start to this outreach in a new city!

But the devil never yields territory without a fight, and it wasn't long before opposition began to rise up. And what began as a mere annoyance ended up with shocking brutality.

It should never surprise us. Whenever and wherever the gospel is proclaimed, Satan and his demons will oppose it in some way, shape, or form. In Philippi, it began with something weird…that became intolerable!

> One day as we were going down to the place of prayer, we met a demon-possessed slave girl. She was a fortune-teller who earned a lot of money for her masters. She followed Paul and the rest of us, shouting, "These men are servants of the Most High God, and they have come to tell you how to be saved."
>
> This went on day after day until Paul got so exasperated that he turned and said to the demon within her, "I command you in the name of Jesus Christ to come out of her." And instantly it left her. (Acts 16:16-18, NLT)

Now what she was saying was true enough, but you really don't want the devil to do your PR work. And as this woman's antics went on day after day, it began to irritate Paul. Finally he couldn't take it anymore. He turned to her, cast the demon out of her, and that was that. The distraction stopped immediately, and the slave woman was delivered from an evil spirit.

You'd think everyone might have been happy with that result.

But not so.

The masters who had been exploiting the girl for her fortune-telling abilities saw that their source of income was immediately gone. Furious with Paul and Silas, they grabbed them and dragged them down to the town square.

> "The whole city is in an uproar because of these Jews!" they shouted to the city officials. "They are teaching customs that are illegal for us Romans to practice."
>
> A mob quickly formed against Paul and Silas, and the city officials ordered them stripped and beaten with wooden rods. They were severely beaten, and then they were thrown into prison. (vv. 20-23, NLT)

Obviously there was some serious anti-Semitism in this city. What did Paul and Silas do? What was their offense? They preached the gospel and healed a woman with an evil spirit. And their reward? They were publicly stripped, and severely beaten with rods.

Have you ever seen anyone beaten with a baton or a club? It isn't a pretty sight. Paul and Silas had to be bruised and bloodied by this point.

And then their already bad day got even worse.

They were thrown into prison.

> The jailer was ordered to make sure they didn't escape. So the jailer put them into the inner dungeon and clamped their feet in the stocks.
>
> Around midnight Paul and Silas were praying and singing hymns to God, and the other prisoners were listening. Suddenly, there was a massive earthquake, and the prison was shaken to its foundations. All the doors immediately flew open, and the chains of every prisoner fell off! The jailer woke up to see the prison doors wide open. He assumed the prisoners had escaped, so he drew his sword to kill himself. But Paul shouted to him, "Stop! Don't kill yourself! We are all here!" (vv. 23-28, NLT)

So after being beaten with wooden rods, they were thrown into a filthy, dark, underground hole, with their legs clamped in stocks. That means that their naked backs were in the dirt, and their legs were put in stocks, pulled as far apart as possible, causing excruciating pain. Archeologists believe they have discovered this dungeon that Paul and Silas were in—a small, windowless room in the inner part of the dungeon—from which there could be no escape. Needless to say, there were no sanitation facilities in such a place.

It was a hellhole.

What would you do if you ended up in a place like that? What did Paul and Silas do? We read, "At midnight they offered praises to God."

Now *this* was a sacrifice of praise. Circumstantially, there was nothing to rejoice about. They had been unjustly arrested, stripped and humiliated in the public square, savagely beaten, and thrown into the darkest, dirtiest hole in the city of Philippi.

How easily we could have read that they groaned at midnight, and we would have understood it. And really, who could have blamed them if they had cursed the men who beat them or the jailer who had imprisoned them?

But they didn't.

No, they sang hymns and praises to God.

In agony at midnight is not my idea of an ideal time for a worship service. And yet the Bible promises that God can give songs in the night. We are told in Psalm 42:8, "But each day the Lord pours his unfailing love upon me, and through each night I sing his songs, praying to God who gives me life" (NLT).

There is something about nighttime that can amplify our problems. Have you noticed that? When you're getting ready to go to sleep, your problems can suddenly crowd in on you and seem larger, more pressing, and more frightening than they really are.

We need to let those weights and worries push us into the presence of our Father, who loves us. Just before we fall asleep, we come to Him in prayer and say, "Lord, I have all of these problems, and You know about each and every one of them. Tell You what…I'm going to go to sleep now, and I'm just going to let You worry about them through the night, because You're awake all night anyway."

Now of course God doesn't worry about my problems at all. But He is deeply concerned about *me*. The Bible speaks about "casting all your care upon Him, for He cares for you." And again, counsels us to "Cast your burden on the LORD, and He shall sustain you."[75]

In the darkness, in their dungeon, in their stocks, in their bruises and great pain, in their misery, Paul and Silas did what nobody would have expected them to do.

They praised God. They sang hymns of thanksgiving.

And the Bible says they had an audience!

> Around midnight Paul and Silas were praying and singing hymns to God, and the other prisoners were listening. (Acts 16:25, NLT)

The word that is used here for listening could be translated *listening very, very carefully*—or even listening for pleasure. The prisoners that night were straining their ears, because they couldn't believe what they were hearing coming up from the maximum-security cell.

I was watching a commercial on television the other day for a hearing device. (I don't need one myself…yet.) It's designed to look like one of those hands-free Blue Tooth devices people use to talk on their cell phones. But this isn't a phone; instead, it amplifies sound around you, so you can hear the TV, etc., etc. But the *real* reason you want to wear something like that is so that you can eavesdrop on other people's conversation! The commercial shows a lady getting her mail at the mailbox, and covertly listening to two of her neighbors across the street.

But I don't think those other prisoners needed listening devices or hearing aids to hear Paul and Silas in the inner dungeon. My hunch is that these men were going for broke, singing aloud with all their hearts.

Everyone was listening in, because they'd never heard anything like this before. Maybe Paul and Silas were even doing a cool little harmony deal, like Simon and Garfunkel. Probably not. I think the big attraction was they would even be singing the praises of God in such a dark, oppressive, horrible place.

It's the same with us. There is a lost world all around us, and they are both watching us and listening to us. They're watching and listening when things go well for us, and when they don't go well. And sometimes they say things like this: "Well, you Christians are so thankful to God when everything is going your way. What about when crisis hits you? What about when tragedy befalls you? How are you going to deal with it?"

When they see you and I giving praise to God even in difficult circumstances, even when our hearts are breaking, it opens up a door for a ministry opportunity. And suddenly certain people will listen to what we have to say who would not have listened to us otherwise. This is one of the good works God can accomplish through our pain and our suffering.

It's also a reason why I believe corporate worship to be so important. It's a powerful witness when a nonbeliever comes into a church auditorium and sees people singing praise to God with full hearts and voices. Do you know why? In today's culture, people don't sing together very much anymore. Have you noticed that? We don't sing the Star Spangled Banner at basketball games. Nobody even does the Pledge of Allegiance anymore. Somehow, it's become unusual for people to lift their voices together and really sing a melody. We've come to avoid that as a culture—at least, here in America.

But then we come to church, and we get caught up—together—in the worship of our great God. And we sing out loud, sometimes with our hands lifted high, glorifying the Lord together. That's a compelling testimony to a nonbeliever, and the Lord blesses it in a special way.

The Bible tells us that in some mysterious way, the Lord actually inhabits the praises of His people.[76] Jesus said, "For where two or three are gathered together in My name, I am there in the midst of them."[77]

That doesn't mean that God isn't with us wherever we go, for indeed He is. Nevertheless, the Bible tells us that God manifests His presence in a unique way when we gather together for corporate worship.

The fact is, when we worship God on earth, we are in tune with what is happening in heaven—where joyful praise rises continually before God's throne.

Another thing that happens when we gather for worship is that we gain a fresh perspective on our lives. When we walk into a worship service, our problems and worries may seem huge to us—even overwhelming. But when we begin to praise our great God, when we lose ourselves in the wonder of His might and majesty and faithfulness and love, we regain an accurate perspective. God seems greater in our eyes, and our problems smaller.

David said, "Oh, magnify the LORD with me, and let us exalt His name together" (Psalm 34:3). When I magnify something, I see it up close. It fills all my vision. And in times of corporate worship, I see God for who He is, and my problems for what they are. I remember that the all-powerful, all-knowing God of the universe loves me and holds me in the palm of His hand. I recall that He leans down to listen to my prayer, and willingly receives the sacrifice of praise that I offer to Him.

And so that is what Paul and Silas did. They began to praise God.

Actually, the apostle Paul would have the opportunity to perfect his prison musical ministry, because he emerged from that Philippi dungeon only to be arrested and imprisoned again and again. He wrote the book of Philippians from a prison cell—a book that resonates with joy, praise, and thanksgiving to God.

If Paul had written Philippians from a beautiful beach in the Caribbean, it would have been one thing. But the fact that he wrote it from prison, with no assurance of when or if he would be released, makes his arguments even more powerful. In the last pages of that book, the apostle writes:

> Always be full of joy in the Lord; I say it again, rejoice! Let everyone see that you are unselfish and considerate in all you do. Remember that the Lord is coming soon. Don't worry about anything; instead, pray about everything; tell God your needs, and don't forget to thank him for his answers. If you do this, you will experience God's peace, which is far more wonderful than the human mind can understand. His peace will keep your thoughts and your hearts quiet and at rest as you trust in Christ Jesus. (Philippians 4:4-7, TLB)

These aren't just some pleasant thoughts or sweet sentiments Paul is passing along here; it comes with the force of a command from God Himself. We are to rejoice and give thanks to God, no matter what our circumstances. Romans 8:37-39 gives us the assurance that "in all these things we are more than conquerors through Him who loved us. For I am persuaded that neither death nor life, nor angels nor principalities nor powers, nor things present nor things to come, nor height nor depth, nor any other created thing, shall be able to separate us from the love of God which is in Christ Jesus our Lord."

On this occasion, Paul and Silas weren't praying for deliverance or even asking for anything from the Lord. They just glorified God and left the results in His hand. How were they able to do that? When you think about it, Paul may have had a little bit of a home court advantage here. As we have seen, he had already had the experience of dying, going to heaven, and coming back again. So the thought of being killed there in that prison really didn't bother him much.

He was basically saying, "I'm just going to praise the Lord. If they kill me, I get to go back to heaven—this time for keeps! If they let me go, and I get out of here, I'll preach the gospel everywhere I go. Whatever happens, this is a win-win scenario."

On this particular night, however, God chose to deliver Paul and Silas from the dungeon.

> Suddenly there was such a violent earthquake that the foundations of the prison were shaken. At once all the prison doors flew open, and everybody's chains came loose.[78]

When the prison guard saw this, he knew it was curtains; losing your prisoners meant you would be executed yourself. So he already had his sword out of the sheath, getting ready to plunge it into his own chest. Suddenly he heard a voice from the inner dungeon. Paul, the prisoner, was shouting: "Don't hurt yourself! We're still here."

When given the opportunity to flee, they stayed.

Had the jailer been tuned into Paul and Silas's midnight praise meeting along with the other prisoners? Had he been listening to the songs of praise rising up from the bowels of his stinking prison? I wonder if he thought to himself, "If only God could save someone like me. But I'm too hard. I'm too jaded." He had probably heard about that servant girl who had been following Paul and Silas around, shouting, "These men are the servants of the Most High God. They will show you the way of salvation."

Could it be true? Could even he, a hardened Roman official find the way of salvation? Listen how he responded to the news that Paul and Silas hadn't escaped.

> Then he called for a light, ran in, and fell down trembling before Paul and Silas. And he brought them out and said, "Sirs, what must I do to be saved?" (vv. 29–30)

I love the change in tone! When he had these men beaten and placed into stocks in his dungeon, there had been no respect, no consideration, and no mercy.

Now it is, "Sirs…." (A little more respect there!)

"Sirs…what must I do to be saved?" It's a direct question, and Paul gives an answer just as direct: "*Believe on the Lord Jesus Christ and you will be saved*." The man believed right there on the spot. And we see immediate evidence of his changed and transformed heart:

> Even at that hour of the night, the jailer cared for them and washed their wounds. Then he and everyone in his household were immediately baptized. He brought them into his house and set a meal before them, and he and his entire household rejoiced because they all believed in God. (vv. 33–34, NLT)

So after hearing the gospel, the man's whole family believed and was baptized. The jailer brought his prisoners into the light, washed their wounds, and set a meal before them.

Just that quickly, Paul and Silas's circumstances changed—wounds tended, shackles broken, and chains discarded. They sat down to a late night supper in warm candlelight, with a joyous family.

Most of us would have started singing our praises to God right then, and it would have been right for us to do so. But would we have been singing just an hour previous to that scene, in a world of pain, darkness, stench, misery, and uncertainty? Would we have praised God then?

The sweetest—and ultimately, the most powerful—songs of praise to God are those sung in the dark.

FIFTEEN
Reaching the iGeneration

Since its introduction a couple of years ago, Apple has sold multiple millions of its iPhones. What Steve Jobs and Apple did was to essentially reinvent the phone, pulling together media, messaging, music, and an endless supply of applications in a fun and user-friendly package.

There was so much hype about this product before it was released that some dubbed it the "Jesus-phone", which shows how technology truly has become a god to some people. It should surprise no one that the inevitable competitors have stormed the marketplace with their own "me too" versions of the iPhone.

The iPhone phenomenon is based on the runaway success of the iPod, which revolutionized the personal digital music market. Prior to its debut, there were a number of other MP3 type devices available, but none had the ease of use and coolness factor of the iPod.

The whole idea is that with this device, you can control your own little universe. You can have your photos, music, and contacts all in one place. We don't have to wait to hear our favorite song on the local radio station anymore, we can just plug in our iPods and have our music when we want it.

This device has become so much a part of our culture that even the president was asked, "Mr. President, what's on your iPod?" The questioner just assumed the president had one (doesn't everybody?), and that by revealing what he listens to, we might gain a better insight into who he is.

We truly have become the iGeneration. We order our private universe and expect that the world will somehow revolve around us. The iGeneration even has its own morals, which we seem to make up as we go.

iGeneration Morality

A Los Angeles-based research organization recently released a study dubbed, "A Report Card on the Ethics of American Youth." The researchers said that the teenagers' responses to questions about lying, stealing, and cheating "reveal entrenched habits of dishonesty for the workforce of the future." Boys were found to lie and steal more than girls. (No surprise there!) Overall, 30 percent of the students admitted to stealing from a store within the past year, a 2 percent rise from 2006. More than one third of boys (35 percent) said they had stolen goods, compared to 26 percent of girls.

An overwhelming majority—83 percent of public school and private religious school students— admitted to *lying* to their parents about something significant. The study found that "cheating in school continues to be rampant and it's getting worse." Amongst those surveyed, 64 percent said they had cheated on a test, compared to 60 percent in 2006. And 38 percent said they had done so two or more times.

The iGeneration feels this is acceptable behavior—and even ethical.

This study pointed out that despite these high levels of dishonesty, these same kids have a high self-image when it comes to ethics. Some 93 percent of students indicated satisfaction with their own character and ethics, with 77 percent saying that "when it comes to doing what is right, I am better than most people I know."

The people who did the survey did point out, however, that many of the participants may have been lying(!).

You might think this is all new, but it isn't at all. We are not the first "iGeneration." The Bible tells us that "nothing is new under the sun." Malcolm Muggeridge said, "All new news is old news happening to new people."

Scripture describes a time in history when "Everyone did what was right in their own eyes." That would be a pretty accurate description of American culture right now. We all have our own rules and ideas that flex and change with how we feel in a given moment. And you don't have to be a genius to see the problems that result from such a national mindset, as crimes, drug and alcohol use, and divorce rates climb higher and higher by the day. You can even find the roots of the current economic meltdown in the self-centered, me-first attitudes of iGeneration.

So, how do we fix it?

The prophet Isaiah might well have been speaking of these very times when he wrote: "Destruction is certain for those who say that evil is good and good is evil; that dark is light and light is dark; that bitter is sweet and sweet is bitter" (Isaiah 5:20).

That's exactly where our culture is today. We mock what is good and pure and celebrate what is wicked and sinful. You can even hear it in the language, can't you? "Bad" is good. "*That car is soo…bad!*" (Which is meant as a compliment.) The kids have a phrase now for something that is *really* good.

It's sick! As in, "*That movie was sooo…sick!*" (In other words, it was really good.) And you advertise a high-calorie dessert by describing it as "decadent, sinful, or wicked." (Read: "It's really tasty!")

Our world is truly "upside down." How do you reach such a world for Jesus Christ? How do you present the saving truths of the gospel to a generation such as this?

Athenian Idol

Acts 17 tells the story of the apostle Paul presenting the gospel to the first century. But it might as well have been the *twenty-first century*, for despite the rapid advances in technology, the essential heart of man remains the same.

Without question, Paul was one of the greatest communicators of all time. And Acts 17 is a page right out of his playbook. In this passage, we see how Paul adapted his message to the intellectuals of Athens, Greece, at a place known as Mars Hill.

Mars Hill was where the elite would gather—the intellectuals, the philosophers, the affluent, the politicians, and the powerful. They all gathered on Mars Hill to talk about the latest news, fads, ideas, and trends. In fact, we read in Acts 17:21, "The Athenians and the foreigners who were there spent their time in nothing else but either to tell or to hear some new thing."

Another translation of that same verse says, "Downtown Athens was a great place for gossip. There were always people hanging around, natives and tourists alike, waiting for the latest tidbit on just about anything."[79]

So the hip people in ancient Athens weren't all that different from today's generation—everyone wanted to access the very latest, newest information on trends and hot topics. No, the Athenians didn't have iPhones or Twitter, or but they knew how and where to tune in on the latest gossip and fads—and it was all in the heart of the city at a place called Mars Hill.

Evidently waiting for his traveling companions to catch up with him, Paul took himself on a little walking tour of the city. And seemingly everywhere he looked, he saw images erected to a huge array of gods and goddesses. You might say Paul was taking the spiritual measure of Athens as he walked those streets. It becomes apparent a little later that he even took time to dip into some of their philosophers. Processing this information, he began to formulate a plan to bring the light of Jesus Christ to the heart of that cosmopolitan cultural center.

> Now while Paul waited for them at Athens, his spirit was provoked within him when he saw that the city was given over to idols. Therefore he reasoned in the synagogue with the Jews and with the Gentile worshipers, and in the marketplace daily with those who happened to be there. Then certain Epicurean and Stoic philosophers encountered him. And some said, "What does this babbler want to say?"

Others said, "He seems to be a proclaimer of foreign gods," because he preached to them Jesus and the resurrection.

And they took him and brought him to the Areopagus, saying, "May we know what this new doctrine is of which you speak? For you are bringing some strange things to our ears. Therefore we want to know what these things mean." For all the Athenians and the foreigners who were there spent their time in nothing else but either to tell or to hear some new thing.

Then Paul stood in the midst of the Areopagus and said, "Men of Athens, I perceive that in all things you are very religious; for as I was passing through and considering the objects of your worship, I even found an altar with this inscription: TO THE UNKNOWN GOD. Therefore, the One whom you worship without knowing, Him I proclaim to you." (Acts 17:16-23)

Let's focus in on several precepts Paul employed for reaching that generation—principles we can use effectively to this very day.

Principles for Reaching the iGeneration

#1: We must have a burden for the people we're speaking to.

Verse 16 tells us that Paul's "spirit was provoked within him when he saw that the city was given over to idols." That phrase *spirit* was provoked could also be translated "his soul was exasperated, irritated, or even roused to anger" by what he saw. You could put it like this: "He was hot and mad."

It grieved Paul to see the absolute absence of the living God in this celebrated city—and all of the false and demonic substitutes in the place of worship that rightfully belonged to Him alone.

Have you ever found yourself becoming angry over the godless direction of our contemporary culture, and as you see young people buying into all of the God-substitutes offered at every turn?

There is a place for righteous anger.

Even Jesus, who was God among us, became angry at times. We know, for instance, that He displayed anger when He made a whip of cords and drove the moneychangers out of the temple. It incensed Him to see religious charlatans ripping off God's people—preying on them instead of praying for them.

Yes God has anger, and there is a place for righteous indignation among His people. And as Paul walked the streets of Athens and felt the indignation rising within him, he made up his mind to do something about it.

Here's the problem in our day: Far too often people outside of the Church, outside of the faith, only know believers for what we are *against*, rather than what we are *for*. They know us for what we oppose. And while there is certainly a place for that as we seek to be salt and light in our culture, people also need to know what we believe with all our hearts. What we're truly excited about.

The world needs to hear about Jesus, God's love and forgiveness, and the hope of heaven. People may disagree with me, but it's my contention that most people in our culture today haven't heard the gospel. Some would say to me, "Greg, how can you say that? I think Americans have heard the gospel over and over and over."

I beg to differ. I believe that many of the so-called presentations of the gospel coming from pulpits and over the airwaves in our country are missing some essential ingredients. I suggest to you that most people have never heard the *real* gospel.

You and I have to do something about that. We need to bring them the authentic biblical message, as Paul did.

Even so, we could talk all day long about various techniques we could employ in telling others about Christ. I could address difficult questions unbelievers raise and how to best answer them. But none of that is going to really matter if you don't care about lost people.

Do you have a burden for those that don't yet know the Lord? Sometimes it seems as though we regard non-believers as the enemy, rather than people who simply need to hear the truth.

Let me be a little blunt about it: One of the reasons we don't share the gospel more often is because we really don't care. So I think we need to start by saying, "Lord, You know my heart. Give me a heart for people who don't know You."

In verse 16 we read that Paul's spirit was provoked. Stirred. Moved. Agitated. And in the very next verse, the text says: "Therefore he reasoned in the synagogue with the Jews and with the Gentile worshipers, and in the marketplace daily with those who happened to be there."

In other words, he cared. And then he acted.

It was Alexander Mclaren who said, "You tell me the depth of a Christian's compassion and I will tell you the measure of his usefulness."

Do you have compassion?

#2: To reach our culture, we must go to where people are.

Paul went right to where these people were and brought the gospel to them. He went to the synagogue. He went to the marketplace. Later, he went right to the beating heart of the culture when he addressed an audience at Mars Hill. He adapted to the situation in which he found himself, and this is something we should all do.

I'm not much of a fisherman, but I know this much: You use different kinds of bait to catch different kinds of fish. It's the same when you go fishing for the souls of men and women. You offer something that people understand, something that they can relate to—and that is exactly what Paul did.

Jesus gives us the classic example of this strategy as He presents the gospel—Himself—to two very different people in John 3 and in John 4. In the first instance, we have the record of Jesus speaking to the heart of an elderly religious leader named Nicodemus. In the following chapter, Jesus offers words of life to an unnamed immoral woman of Samaria.

In the first encounter with the well-known Jewish leader, the Lord essentially "cuts to the chase" and says to him, "You need to be born from above. Your religious views and beliefs are not enough. You need a spiritual rebirth, Nicodemus, and you need it now." To the immoral, burned-out woman of Samaria, who had tried to find fulfillment in relationships with a succession of men, He appeals to her inner thirst, speaking of a water that is alive and will satisfy her deepest longings.

He adapted His message to each situation, each individual, and so it is throughout the gospels with everyone He encounters.

Over in Mark chapter two, we have two accounts that present an interesting contrast. In the first we have the story of men who brought their friend to Jesus, and in the second, we have the story of a man who brought Jesus to his friends.

In Mark 2:1-12, four friends had a companion who was a paralytic, confined to a cot. They wanted Jesus to heal him, but Jesus was teaching in a home that was packed to the rafters and they couldn't get in. Undeterred, these men climbed up on the top of the roof, opened up a hole, and lowered their friend down on a cot so he was right in front of Christ. Seeing their persistence, Jesus rewarded it by touching the man and raising him up so he could walk again—and forgiving his sins in the bargain! So the men brought their friend to Jesus, and that friend found healing and salvation. This suggests that sometimes we need to invite our friends to church or to a crusade or special evangelistic event, where they will have an opportunity to meet the Lord.

The very next story in Mark 2 provides a contrast to the story of the paralytic. In verses 13-17, Mark tells us about the tax collector Matthew who responded to the call of Jesus. As a result of meeting the Lord, Matthew threw a party, inviting Jesus and all his old buddies.

It must have been a rowdy crowd. Just imagine the street out in front of Matthew's house, with all kinds of interesting vehicles parked there—skateboards and cool choppers and lowered cars and Rolls Royces and everything in between. And right in the middle of the party, Matthew says, "Okay guys, listen up! I want to introduce you to my new Friend, Jesus Christ." He brought Jesus to his friends.

We need to infiltrate our culture in similar ways. Far too often, however, we isolate from our world instead of infiltrating it. Living in a comfortable Christian subculture as we do, we regard it as a good day when we have little to no contact with one of those dreaded nonbelievers! But that's not the heart of our Lord, is it? He wants us to invade the world of non-believers with the message of Jesus Christ.

We need to bring our friends to Jesus, and Jesus to our friends. The Lord never said that the whole world should go to church; He did say that the Church should go to the whole world!

Paul had a burden to reach a group of people he had apparently never encountered before. Verse 18 says: "A group of Epicurean and Stoic philosophers began to dispute with him. Some of them asked, 'What is this babbler trying to say?'"

As it happened, those were the two dominant philosophies in Athens at that time. The Epicureans derived their world view from their founder Epicurus, and believe the world came about by chance—a life with no afterlife or future judgment. Epicurus taught that the chief goal of man was to obtain the maximum amount of pleasure and the minimum amount of pain. It's a philosophy that's still very big in today's world—the basic belief that you only go around once in life, and you've got to grab for the gusto. If it feels good, do it. If it doesn't feel good, don't do it, and be sure to avoid anything that would hurt you or cause you pain. You might say that the Epicureans were the "party animals" of the first century.

Many people today subscribe to that point of view. They live for pleasure…for the party…for the experience…for the rush…for the buzz…for whatever they think will bring them pleasure, avoiding anything that would bring discomfort. We don't call these people Epicureans today, but the philosophy is very much with us.

Then there were the Stoics. Their founder was known as Zeno, and in contrast to the Epicureans, they shunned the mere pursuit of pleasure. Stoic philosophy taught self-mastery—that the goal of life was to reach a place of indifference to pleasure or pain. Zeno taught that life is filled with both good and bad, and since you can't avoid the bad, you just grin and bear it. Stoics believed god was in everyone and everything—people, trees, plants, rocks, you name it. So your goal in life was to just get through your allotted years to the best of your ability. Today, you can see elements of the Stoics in both Zen and New Age adherents.

Both of these philosophies were wrong in that they rejected God. Not only were these people ignorant of truth, but they were also elitist and smug about it. Listen to what they said in verse 18, talking about Paul. "*What does this babbler want to say?*" I like the British spin that J. B. Phillips put on this verse in his paraphrase:

"*What is this cock sparrow trying to say? …He seems to be trying to proclaim some more gods to us, and outlandish ones at that!*"

They called Paul a babbler, a charlatan. They said he was like a parrot, just repeating bits and pieces of what others say.

In Athens at that time, if anything was "new" it at least merited a hearing; so they invited Paul to come speak to them. Little did they realize, of course, that they were inviting one of the greatest communicators in church history to come give a little inspirational talk.

I'm sure Paul must have smiled and said the Greek equivalent of "You bet!" He gladly seized the moment, walking through that open door.

#3: We must first arouse the interest of our listeners.

Let me say it another way: To reach the iGeneration, you must build a bridge not burn one! Sometimes the game is over before it even starts because of the verbiage we use. We'll say something that makes no sense to the interested person at all, or we'll make some comment that is unnecessarily offensive to them before the conversation has even begun.

"*Hey, you, sinner. Come over here. Yeah, you. Philistine! I want to talk to you. You are idolaters and worship false gods and you're going to burn and go to hell, so you'd better repent.*"

The person turns around and walks away in huff, and we say, "Oh man, no one ever wants to hear the gospel anymore!"

No, they just don't want to hear *you* anymore. Because you haven't learned how to have your speech seasoned with grace, as the Bible says.[80] You haven't learned the truth of the passage that says, "The goodness of God leads a person to repentance."[81]

Yes, you need to deliver the goods, and communicate the vital information of the gospel. But at the same time, can you at least try and be nice about it? Can your words be loving? Can you build a bridge and actually arouse the interest of your listener?

That's what Paul did—in a masterful way.

> Then Paul stood in the midst of the Areopagus and said, "Men of Athens, I perceive that in all things you are very religious; for as I was passing through and considering the objects of your worship, I even found an altar with this inscription: TO THE UNKNOWN GOD. Therefore, the One whom you worship without knowing, Him I proclaim to you...." (Acts 17:22-23)

What a diplomatic way to hook their attention…and draw them into his message.

He could have just as easily said, "Men of Athens, this is a dark city, you're a bunch of sorry pagans, and you're all going to burn." But instead, he essentially said, "Hey, I've been around town and couldn't help noticing that you have a lot of gods here. Man, you guys are really religious." One historian estimated that there were as many as 30,000 images erected to deities throughout Athens. Can you imagine? These gods needed their own phonebook. So Paul used that fact, and led into his message by admitting that the Athenians were certainly "religious."

We don't use the word "religious" much anymore.

We'll ask someone, "Do you believe in God?" And they may answer, "Well, I'm not religious. I'm not a part of an organized religion. But I am a very spiritual person. I'm into spirituality." Now you might be thinking, "*What is that supposed to mean?*" But instead of critiquing their comment, you could begin a conversation something like this:

"You're a spiritual person? That's great, because I am, too. Since you care about spirituality, I'd really like to hear your view on the meaning of life. Would you share that with me?" Then *listen* to what they have to say.

After you've heard them out, you might go on and say, "Tell me, according to your beliefs as a spiritual person, what do you think will happen to you after you die?" Again, listen carefully. And then say, "I'd like to give you my view"—and then share the gospel with them. Instead of burning that bridge—"Oh, you're a spiritual person"—you actually use it as a bridge, and transition into giving your testimony of coming to Christ, and how He has changed your life.

Paul said…"I perceive you are a religious people." In reality, they were a pagan people. But Paul wanted the opportunity to speak to them about the Lord Jesus, so he led his talk with words that would open doors to them, rather than slamming a door in their faces.

That phrase, "you are religious" could be translated "you are fearers of God." But the word he chose for "God" was unusual. Instead of the common word *theos*, which means God in His greatness, he chose the word *damon*—or even demon. By doing so, he implied that the gods they worshipped were lesser concepts than the great idea of God. And he indicated that by employing a different term. In other words, he said, "You worship different kinds of gods." He did not equate the God he worshipped with the gods they worshipped.

Why do I bring this up? Because sometimes in our attempts to relate to someone outside the faith, we compromise the truth. I have even heard some well meaning but misguided Christians say, "Well, we all worship the same God, but we call Him by different names."

No! We do *not* all worship the same God. You cannot interchange, for instance, the name Allah for Yahweh, the God of the Bible. My God is the God of Abraham, Isaac, and Jacob; He is the God who loved the world and sent Jesus Christ, His only begotten Son. Be careful to never use another word for God, and say that "it's all the same."

We're talking about a delicate balance here. You want to keep every bridge of communication open that you can, but in that attempt you don't want to cross over the line and actually compromise the truth. Here's the way Paul put it to the Corinthians:

> I have become a servant of everyone so that I can bring them to Christ. When I am with the Jews, I become one of them so that I can bring them to Christ. When I am with those who follow the Jewish laws, I do the same, even though I am not subject to the law, so that I can bring them to Christ. When I am with the Gentiles who do not have the Jewish law, I fit in with them as much as I can. In this way, I gain their confidence and bring them to Christ. But I do not discard the law of God; I obey the law of Christ. (1 Corinthians 9:19-21, NLT)

There is only so far that I will go in seeking to reach a person for Christ. I will not lower my standard in order to extend my reach. I won't compromise my core values in order to appear cool. Even though I want very much to communicate, *I want to be biblical even more than I want to relate.*

#4: We need to be culturally relevant.

In the middle of his brief presentation on Mars Hill, Paul quoted a secular philosopher in order to build a bridge to his audience.

> ..."In Him we live and move and have our being, as also some of your own poets have said, 'For we are also His offspring.'" (v. 28)

When it comes to being culturally relevant, preachers are often the worst offenders—sometimes speaking with verbiage no one understands. Just imagine how words like these sound to someone who has no background in the Bible or "insider" Christian lingo: "Did you know that you are lost? You are reprobate. You need to be saved. You need to be redeemed. You need to be justified. You need to be washed in the blood and become a part of the body of Christ."

All of that may be true…but as far as some people are concerned, you might as well be speaking Swahili. Am I suggesting we not use biblical terminology? No. Am I suggesting we define it? Yes! We can't assume our listener has any idea what we are saying. In our biblically illiterate culture of today we need to break down what we're saying in a way that is understandable to the person we're speaking to.

Paul was clearly doing that. And then he transitioned into the actual message of the gospel.

#5: We must preach Jesus Christ, crucified and risen from the dead.

Speaking of God, Paul declared to the Athenians: "'He has appointed a day on which He will judge the world in righteousness by the Man whom He has ordained. He has given assurance of this to all by raising Him from the dead'" (v. 31).

This brings me back to a point I raised earlier. I have heard so-called presentations of the gospel that make no mention of the cross. It's my opinion that if your message—be it to one person or a hundred—doesn't contain the message of the life, death, and resurrection of Jesus, then you have not authentically preached the gospel. Sometimes in our attempts to "cross over" we don't bring the cross over!

There is power in the message of the cross. Paul said to the believers at Corinth: "For I determined to know nothing among you except Jesus Christ, and Him crucified."[82] He even added that we can deprive the message of the gospel of its power by adding things to it that don't belong.

After I have preached in a crusade I have had people say to me, "I can't believe all those people responded. Your message was so *simple*."

Would you believe that I actually work at keeping it simple? Because I understand that the less I tamper with the pure gospel of Jesus Christ, the more effective it will be. There is great power in the simple message!

#6: We need to preach the whole gospel.

In his presentation of the gospel, Paul used a word we rarely hear these days.

Repent.

Look again at verses 30 and 31:

"Truly, these times of ignorance God overlooked, but now commands all men everywhere to repent, because He has appointed a day on which He will judge the world in righteousness by the Man whom He has ordained. He has given assurance of this to all by raising Him from the dead."

God *commands* people to repent. He doesn't suggest it, advise it, or even hope it. He commands it. Why? Because a judgment is coming, and we must repent, changing our minds and changing our direction—if we want to escape that judgment.

There was a time—a generation back—when you would hear criticisms like this: "You preachers always preach hellfire and brimstone." That actually may have been a problem once. But now? I don't think so! When is the last time you heard a hellfire and brimstone message? For that matter, when is the last time you heard a preacher use the word "hell"?

We've become afraid of that word. We think to ourselves, "If I say 'hell' I might offend someone." That could very well be true. But if you don't say it, you will offend God. The fact is, I'm not going to fully appreciate the full measure of the good news if I don't first know the bad news. And the bad news is I am irreparably separated from a holy God whom I can never reach or please apart from Christ. And if I don't repent of my sin I will face a certain judgment. But Jesus took that judgment upon Himself when He went to the cross.

That is the message people need to hear. You need to repent.

There are people today who have responded to a heavily diluted, gospel-lite message, who say they believe in Jesus but really have no idea what that means!

That is why we need to break the terms down. What does it mean to believe? When I say "believe in Jesus," some people would say, "Sure, I believe in Jesus. Jesus is great. I believe He lived, He died, even that He rose again. So therefore, I'm a Christian. Right?"

Not necessarily.

If we were to interview Satan (which I would never want to do), and we were to ask him, "Now Lucifer, let me ask you a question. Do you believe that Jesus Christ is the Son of God?"

He would say, "Yes."

"Do you believe He died on a cross?"

"Yes."

"Do you believe He rose from the dead?"

"Yes."

"Do you believe He is coming back again?"

"Yes."

Satan certainly believes in God. But also hates Him and stands to oppose Him at every opportunity. James 2:19 says, "Even the demons believe—and tremble!"

So we're not talking about mere intellectual assent here. To believe means to put your complete faith and trust in Christ and Christ alone. And "Whoever believes in Him should not perish but have everlasting life."[83]

Believe means "to take hold of something."

But it also means to let go of something.

To believe is to hold on to Christ for salvation, and it is to let go of your sin…to repent. However, because this is seldom emphasized, there are people today who say they believe in Jesus but go on living in open sin. I believe that these people have a false assurance of their salvation—a very, very dangerous place to be in.

People need the whole gospel, as Paul delivered it to the intellectuals on Mars Hill.

#7: We need to trust God for the results.

Paul delivered a gospel witness, wedged in a culturally relevant message that was engaging and acceptable to the ears of Greek philosophers. And the results on that day? Did 3,000 believe like we read about in Acts 2 after Peter preached on the day of Pentecost?

Well…no. Here is what the Scripture says:

"And when they heard of the resurrection of the dead, some mocked, while others said, 'We will hear you again on this matter.' So Paul departed from among them. However, some men joined him and believed, among them Dionysius the Areopagite, a woman named Damaris, and others with them" (Acts 17:32-34)

I am so glad those verses are in the Bible. The fact is, even the apostle

Paul didn't hit it out of the park every time. Nevertheless, he was faithful to God, and he held high the lamp of the gospel of Jesus Christ in a dark, Christless city.

You don't always define effective communication by results. You set out to communicate in an honest, gracious way, depending on the power of the Holy Spirit, and leaving the results to God. Faithfulness is the key. Paul spoke well and wisely that day in the Areopagus. But not everyone believed.

We see three reactions of the people at Mars Hill—and they are common reactions to the gospel to this very day.

First, we read that *some mocked.*

They snickered. In fact, that word "mocked" could be translated "they sneered and burst out laughing." Can you imagine doing this to Paul? The great apostle preaches and you laugh out loud like it's a joke?

There should be no surprise in that.

The Bible tells us that "the message of the cross is foolishness to those who are perishing, but to us who are being saved it is the power of God" (Romans 1:18). To these educated fools the message of Jesus seemed so silly and unbelievable. They laughed it off. Some will do that even to this day. They will laugh in your face when you tell them about Christ. It may be offensive and it may hurt your feelings, but it will happen, and we shouldn't be surprised.

Second, *some delayed.*

That's the more common reaction you will encounter if you are faithfully sharing the gospel. Some of those philosophers said, "We will hear you again on this matter." These are the people who say, "Let's talk about it later. Let's not deal with it now. I like what you're saying, and I want to know more about it. But…not now."

This is pretty typical. People will delay and procrastinate, trying to put off any decision for another time. And then, sadly, "later" becomes forever.

Third, *some believed.*

Some repented and changed their minds. Dionysius gave his heart to Christ. He was actually one of the judges of the Areopagus—an intellectual and a ruler in the city. Damaris came to the Lord as well, a woman who had become disillusioned with the empty gods of Greece. The Bible says that a few others also believed. So God did the work that He wanted to do, accomplishing it through the faithfulness of His servant Paul to proclaim the Good News.

Let me use a simple acronym to describe what Paul did on Mars Hill—one little word that may help us remember some of the principles we have identified in this chapter.

The acronym is the word SHARE.

"**S**" reminds us to be *sensitive* to the leading of the Holy Spirit. Paul was burdened for these people of Athens, lost as they were in a maze of false gods and deceptive philosophies. He truly cared about them, and did something about it. It's a reminder to all of us to be open to the leading of God's Spirit, and to watch for the opportunities that He will open up for us.

"**H**" stands for *honor* and respect others. Don't unnecessarily offend the men and women God leads you to speak to. Don't come off as holier than thou, as though you were somehow better than them. The truth is, I am not "better" than anyone. But I'm certainly better off to have Christ in my life! So when you speak to someone, do so with humility, gentleness, and kindness. You're representing Jesus Himself.

"**A**" stands for *arouse* the interest of your listener. Try to get their attention.

"**R**" stands for *reveal* sin. Having established a dialogue, don't compromise what you believe. When Jesus was speaking with the Samaritan woman at the well, He gently nudged her toward admitting her emptiness and need, and spoke of what He had to offer. But then at one point He confronted her with her life of sin. He told her plainly that she'd had five husbands, and that she was currently living with a man who wasn't her husband. That took her aback; it apparently wasn't common knowledge, and she thought she had covered it up pretty well.

Yes, He was gentle, considerate, and respectful. But He also put His finger squarely on that black spot in her life. We too, need to share the gospel with love and compassion. But sooner or later we need to say, "Friend, I've got to tell you this. You are a sinner. You have broken God's commandments, and there is nothing you can do to fix that." That is an essential part of our presentation.

"**E**" stands for *explain* the way of salvation. Having done these other things, now take time to patiently break it down, telling the person how to believe in Jesus Christ. People need that explanation, because often they really don't get it. And even if they don't accept it right then, they might come around later.

There is life and power in the gospel message. The Bible describes it like a seed that's dropped into the soil. It might not germinate right away…but it may a few hours or days or even weeks later. Just drop it in there, and let the Holy Spirit do the work of cultivation.

The individual might initially respond to you and say, "I don't agree with you."

That's fine. Just plant the seed and pray, waiting on the Lord. Sometimes that conversation may come back to them at some odd time—while they're driving or they're in the shower or crawling under the covers at night. They come under the conviction of the Holy Spirit, and realize they need God—and need Him desperately.

I have heard so many stories of people who have come to the Lord *after* we have had a crusade in a city. They don't come forward at the crusade, but maybe a week later they pray the prayer in their room alone.

We have the assurance that God's Word will not return void. We can sow seeds with confidence, water them in prayer, and let the Master Gardener do what He does best.

Bring forth life out of death.

SIXTEEN
Gun Lap

Okay, it's the twenty-first century, and I have one question that's been burning in my heart.

Where is my spaceship?

Wasn't I promised a spaceship in my youth by the time we reached the twenty-first century? I have to explain. I was raised on all those crazy cartoons like *The Jetsons*; the futuristic family with spaceships, robotic maids, and things like that.

So…where is my personal hovercraft and my robot butler? Here we are, in the twenty-first century, and we're still lumbering about in four wheeled automobiles that run on gas. We haven't even perfected an electric car yet, much less one that actually flies. So I'm a little disappointed, to say the least.

Back in the 1950s and 60s, there was lots of talk about The Future. Disneyland (home of "Tomorrow Land") had an exhibit called "the house of the future." You would sit in this chair and the house would move around you, morphing from the house of yesteryear, to the house of today, to the house of The Future. It all looked so cool. I can even remember them talking about a new technology coming, an oven that would heat your meal in just minutes!

A microwave oven? Big deal. That seems low tech to me now. My reaction today is more like, "Are you kidding me? I have to wait two minutes to get this thing hot? I don't have two minutes to spare!" But back in the 50s and 60s, there was a utopian dream in America where we thought the future would be wonderful and idyllic. Education, technology, and science would usher in the solutions to all of our problems.

You don't hear people talk that way much anymore. We've come to the collective realization that the utopia we imagined when we were kids will never come to be. Right now, we're just concerned about preserving what prosperity and freedom we have left in our nation.

What we as believers look forward to is infinitely better than any plastic manmade technological utopia. We look forward to the day when Jesus Christ will rule this world in righteousness, and we will rule and reign with Him, living forever in new resurrected bodies that will never age, and never die.

Who needs the Jetsons?

Regarding that future day, Jesus taught us to pray "Your kingdom come, Your will be done, on earth as it is in heaven." Technology will not deliver us from evil. Political systems will not redeem us. The environmental movement will not save the planet. No man-made solutions will bring us the answers for which we long.

Only Christ will do those things, when He comes back and establishes His kingdom on earth. He was and is—and always will be—the only answer.

Until then, however, we're alive on earth at this particular time in history because God in His wisdom and love *placed* us here.

We're alive…so we might as well live our lives to the full.

So let's take stock for a minute or two. What if this year was to be your last year on earth? If you had only one year left to you, how would you live your life? Would you live it any differently than you lived the previous year? This is something we need to come to grips with, because we as believers want to deal with reality. We want to face the facts of the brevity of life on earth and the reality of life in the future. We want to consider these things, and order our lives accordingly.

It was Moses who wrote: "Teach us to number our days aright, that we may gain a heart of wisdom."[84]

None of us knows the allotment of our days. You may have many, many years left in the hourglass of your life, one year left, or maybe even only a part of a year.

One person wrote this about the passing of time: "Ready or not, your life will all come to an end. There will be no more sunrises. No minutes, hours, or days. All the things you collected, whether treasured or forgotten, will be passed to someone else. Your wealth, your fame, your temporal power, will shrivel to irrelevance. It will not matter what you owned or what you were owed. Your grudges, resentments, frustrations, and jealousies will finally disappear. So too your hopes, ambitions, plans, and to do lists will expire. The wins and losses that once seemed so important to you will fade away. It won't matter where you came from or what side of the tracks you lived on. It won't matter whether you were beautiful or brilliant. Even your gender and skin color will be irrelevant.

"So what will matter? How will the value of your days be measured? What will matter is not what you bought but what you built. Not what you got but what you gave. What will matter is not your success but your significance. What will matter is not what you learned but what you taught. What will matter is every act of integrity, compassion, courage, or sacrifice that enriched, empowered, or encouraged others to emulate your example. What will matter is not your competence but your character. What will matter is not how many people you knew but how many will feel a lasting loss when you are gone. What will matter are not your memories but the memories that live in those that loved you. What will matter is how long you will be remembered, by whom, and for what. Living a life that matters doesn't happen by accident. It is not a matter of circumstance but of choice. Choose to live a life that matters."[85]

I don't know if the person who wrote those words was a Christian, but there are certainly elements of biblical truth in those words. Tragically, there are many today who live silly, shallow, wasted lives.

As heartbreaking as it might be, a good life cut short is not the greatest tragedy of all. The greatest tragedy is a God-given life that is largely squandered and wasted.

Don't waste your life. Don't waste your year. *Don't waste today*. Make every day count.

In a brief, heartfelt farewell message to the elders of the Ephesian church, the apostle Paul presented a perspective on life that's just as valid today as it was when he spoke it to that little band of men…two thousand years ago.

"You Know How I've Lived…"

From Miletus he sent to Ephesus and called for the elders of the Church. And when they had come to him, he said to them: "You know, from the first day that I came to Asia, in what manner I always lived among you, serving the Lord with all humility, with many tears and trials which happened to me by the plotting of the Jews; how I kept back nothing that was helpful, but proclaimed it to you, and taught you publicly and from house to house, testifying to Jews, and also to Greeks, repentance toward God and faith toward our Lord Jesus Christ. And see, now I go bound in the spirit to Jerusalem, not knowing the things that will happen to me there, except that the Holy Spirit testifies in every city, saying that chains and tribulations await me. But none of these things move me; nor do I count my life dear to myself, so that I may finish my race with joy, and the ministry which I received from the Lord Jesus, to testify to the gospel of the grace of God." (Acts 20:17-24)

In transit to Jerusalem and what would be a major crossroads in his life, Paul called for the elders of the Church of Ephesus to meet him in Miletus, a point some fifty miles south of their city. Paul knew in his heart that it would be his last meeting with these leaders, and he wanted to it to be in person, face-to-face.

In his words to these elders, Paul summed up some of the priorities that laid so heavily on his heart. He was passing on a legacy that day, and I can't imagine that anyone's attention wandered in the course of that final meeting. And though these truths were initially addressed to leaders of a particular church, they have immediate relevance for every Christian.

In a broad sense, every one of us is called to lead in some way, shape, or form, whether in our church, at home, on our job, or among our friends. Each one of us has been given a certain sphere of influence, and people who look up to us. So these words of Paul resonate with all of us.

In giving this farewell message to the Ephesians, Paul sums up the life of a Christian in five different categories or pursuits. He compares the Christian who serves the Lord to a runner in a race, a steward, a witness, a herald, and a watchman.

Five Portraits of a Believer

A Runner in a Race

"...I want to finish my race with joy." (v. 24)

The analogy of running was one that Paul favored, and he used it several times in his writings. He told us, for instance, that we need to run to win in the race of life. In 1 Corinthians 9:24 he said, "Remember that in a race everyone runs, but only one person gets the prize. You also must run in such a way that you will win" (NLT).

When I'm in some competitive sport, I always try to win—though it hardly ever means I actually do! But at least I try, and I enjoy the competition.

In the race of life, we need to run it to win. When we watch people in the Olympics, we primarily celebrate the ones who win the gold, don't we? We don't want to run this race of life—the one and only life we've been given to live—to receive fourth place or honorable mention.

Whom are we competing against in this race? It's not each other!

Our true opponents in this life are the world, the flesh, and the devil. We fight against them, ever seeking to overcome and defeat them. And we run to win.

Paul also told us that we can all too easily get off track in this race of life—or have someone cut in on us and throw us off our stride. In Galatians 5:7 (NIV) he writes, "You were running a good race. Who cut in on you and kept you from obeying the truth?"

Sometimes poor choices in friends and companions may nudge us off course, off track. They tend to drag us away or sidetrack us from our commitment, rather than encouraging us to pursue it with all our hearts. You know how it is: There are certain people in your circle of acquaintances or friends who always inspire you and encourage you to be more like Jesus. Then there are others who somehow seem to distract you from thinking about spiritual things when you're around them; they slow you down in your race, bump you out of your lane, or cause you to veer in the wrong direction.

Paul also cautions runners in the race of life to keep facing forward, and avoid looking back. In Philippians 3:14–16 he tells us, "Friends, don't get me wrong: By no means do I count myself an expert in all of this, but I've got my eye on the goal, where God is beckoning us onward—to Jesus. I'm off and running, and I'm not turning back. So let's keep focused on that goal, those of us who want everything God has for us. If any of you have something else in mind, something less than total commitment, God will clear your blurred vision—you'll see it yet! Now that we're on the right track, let's stay on it."[86]

How have you run this past year? Have you made progress, or did you go backwards? Did anyone cut in on you? Did you lose your focus or lose sight of your priorities? Did you get off track?

In his message to the Ephesian elders, Paul poured out his heart and said, "I want to finish my race with joy."

The older I get, the more I think about finishing my race. It's great to jump off the starting line with a burst of energy. But what good will it be if I falter or turn aside before I get to the finish line? I can look back to the time when I came to Christ, and think of others who became believers at the same time I did. And now…many of these men and women have become sidetracked—or they're out of the race altogether. Some have made a mess out of their lives through a series of foolish and sinful choices. They had a great start, and some fast early laps, but something happened, and they're no longer in the race.

Think about it: If you're in a race that has ten laps, and you're in the lead for nine of them, what would happen if you just walked off the track in the middle of the tenth lap? You'd be disqualified! And all of that running through all of those years would come to nothing. It's is not enough to start well; we need to finish well. But Paul's not only talking about crossing the finish line, he says he wants to finish the race with joy!

I can also think of a number of people I know who have run the race of life very well, and have actually picked up their stride. They are a tremendous example to me.

Paul knew that he was in the final lap of his race—sometimes called the gun lap, because the starter's pistol sounds once again as the first runner begins the final turn.

I know there are people who say they enjoy running, and that makes no sense to me at all. I'll be honest with you; I don't *enjoy* any kind of exercise. I *do* it, but it's always reluctantly and under protest. My favorite part of a workout is when it's done!

Looking back, I've come to realize that I always seemed to do better in athletic events when I had an audience. I'd run better in a track meet if I someone in the stands cheering me on (particularly a pretty girl). Now I'm married and have my wife to cheer me on! It's a fact that most of us run a better race if we know someone's watching us.

Guess what? You truly *are* being watched in this race of life. Those who have gone before you and have already finished their races are watching you. In Hebrews 11 we read about those great men and women of God who served Him faithfully down through the millennia. Transitioning to chapter 12, the writer begins: "Therefore we also, since we are surrounded by so great a cloud of witnesses, let us lay aside every weight, and the sin which so easily ensnares us, and let us run with endurance the race that is set before us, looking unto Jesus, the author and finisher of our faith, who for the joy that was set before Him endured the cross, despising the shame, and has sat down at the right hand of the throne of God."

Another translation renders Hebrews 12:1-2 like this:

> Do you see what this means — all these pioneers who blazed the way, all these veterans cheering us on? It means we'd better get on with it. Strip down, start running—and never quit! No extra spiritual fat, no parasitic sins. Keep your eyes on Jesus, who both began and finished this race we're in. Study how he did it. Because he never lost sight of where he was headed—that exhilarating finish in and with God—he could put up with anything along the way: cross, shame, whatever. And now he's there, in the place of honor, right alongside God. When you find yourselves flagging in your faith, go over that story again, item by item, that long litany of hostility he plowed through. That will shoot adrenaline into your souls![87]

Keep running, and look to Jesus as the One you're running toward. He is watching you, and He is urging you on. And it may be that our loved ones who have gone before us are watching as well.

A steward

Back in Acts 20:24, Paul speaks of "The ministry that I received from the Lord."

A servant or slave owns very few possessions. And in the same way, I need to realize as God's servant that everything I have is on loan from Him. My life. My health. My career. My ministry. My possessions. My children. My future. It all belongs to God.

So what's my objective as a steward of His possessions? To find out how God can bless *my* dreams and ambitions and goals? No, my objective is to discover His goals, His purposes, and align myself with these. It only makes sense; I'm His servant!

Some people think of the Christian life as "bringing Jesus along for the ride." They see Him as a celestial big buddy. These are the folks that put that bumper sticker on their car: "God is my co-pilot."

I have only one response to that assertion: *No, He's not*. My friend, God has no desire to be your co-pilot. He doesn't even want you in the cockpit!

God wants to be in sole control of your life. He's the Master, I'm the servant. He's the Shepherd, I'm the sheep. He's the Potter, I'm the clay. I am the property of Jesus Christ, and I became that when I put my faith in Him. As Paul tells us in 1 Corinthians 6:20. "For you were bought at a price; therefore glorify God in your body and in your spirit, which are God's."

Most of us can get pretty excited about all the "fringe benefits" of being a follower of Jesus. I know I'm going to heaven, I have an inner peace that passes all human understanding, I know God has a plan for my life and promises to protect me and provide for me.

All of that is very, very good.

But what about the part that says I'm a servant, and I'm to do His will no matter what? I don't always like *that* part. If you happen to feel that way, maybe you as a servant need to know a little bit more about your Master.

The Master you follow is also a Friend who loves you.

The Potter who molds you is also a Father who adores you.

And the more you know of the Lord and His plan and purpose, the more willing you will be to do what He wants you to do.

In Luke 17, Jesus told about a parable about servants who were given a task to fulfill. And at the end of the story in Luke 17:10 Jesus said, "Likewise when you have done these things which you are com-manded to do, say, 'We are unworthy servants. We have only done what our duty was.'"

True servants of Jesus want more than anything else to please and obey their Lord. We want to be faithful servants of the Lord who loves us.

A witness

In Acts 20:24, Paul speaks about testifying "to the gospel of the grace of God."

A witness describes what he or she has seen. If there's an accident, witnesses are sought out to give an account of what they've witnessed or observed. They're not called to make up a story, elaborate the facts, or make it exciting, dramatic, or entertaining. They're expected to simply state what they observed. That is what believers are to do as well: To testify of what God has done for us. As John wrote, "We proclaim to you what we have seen and heard, so that you also may have fellowship with us. And our fellowship is with the Father and with his Son, Jesus Christ."[88]

This is where your personal testimony comes in—where you simply tell people about what Jesus has done for you. My wife and I were out with some friends the other night, and after dinner we were sitting at our table, talking. Suddenly a man walked up to me and said, "Hey dude, can I bum a cigarette off of you?"

I said, "Sorry. I don't smoke."

Then he turned to my friends, "Can I bum a cigarette off of you?"

They said, "No, we don't smoke either."

"Okay. Wow. Cool, man." And he just stood there. He didn't leave. I was thinking to myself, *You need to leave now.* And then I thought, *Maybe he's here for a reason. Maybe the Lord wants me to share the gospel with him.* And so I said, "You know, I used to smoke a lot."

"Oh really?" he said.

"Oh yeah. I smoked. And I actually partied and used drugs. All kinds of stuff like that. But I stopped doing it because I found something better."

"Oh, you found religion."

"No. I didn't find religion."

"No? What did you find?"

"It's a personal relationship with Jesus Christ." So I engaged the guy, and used my own personal story to tell him of what God had done for me. We talked for a while, and then he left.

Here's the thing about testifying. You don't have to necessarily work yourself up to do it. If you are walking with God, it just overflows. It's sort of like a sponge that's so full of water that if you twist it or even just poke it water comes out. You're just full of the Lord, because He's working in your life, you're studying His Word, and you're growing in your faith. It's a natural and easy thing for you to testify of the grace of God in your life.

A herald

In verse 25 Paul says: "And indeed, now I know that you all, among whom I have gone preaching the kingdom of God, will see my face no more."

The term "gone preaching" means to declare a message as the herald of a king. A witness, as we have seen, tells what he has observed, and what has happened to him. By contrast, a herald speaks whatever the king tells him to declare. In other words, a herald is a messenger of the king sent to deliver a specific message. It's not up to them to edit that message—either adding to it or taking away from it. They are simply to deliver it.

In the same way we are all called to deliver the message of the gospel of Jesus Christ. It's not our place to edit out certain parts of the message that we feel might offend someone, like mention the mention of hell or the coming judgment—or, for that matter, leaving out the part about God's love and grace. As a herald of the King, it's our job to deliver God's gospel just as He gives it to us in Scripture.

Paul follows this with a warning:

> For I know this, that after my departure savage wolves will come in among you, not sparing the flock. Also from among yourselves men will rise up, speaking perverse things, to draw away the disciples after themselves. (vv. 29-30)

I have found that people who are into false teaching don't go out into the culture and try to win people to faith. In fact, they don't seem to have the ability to do it, because their teaching is so weird or convoluted. Instead, what they do is to infiltrate the ranks of strong, growing churches, and attempt to draw believers away into their strange doctrines. They will say, "Do you want to get into the deep things of God? Into some really heavy-duty truth? Come over to this little meeting we're having at our house." And they lure people away in a clandestine, secretive way.

That is what Paul was talking about. "They will come in among you…to draw away the disciples after themselves." It's a warning for all of us, and we need to be prepared and equipped to deal with these false teachers. Most of all, we just need to know the truth!

I believe that if you have a good working knowledge of the Bible, you will be able to detect the false rather quickly because you are so familiar with the genuine article.

So it is with us. When you are conversant with the Word of God and something weird comes along, you'll say, "There's something strange or off-base about that…something that's not quite right. As a student of God's Word, you'll realize that what you're hearing doesn't line up with the clear teaching of the Bible, and a little warning bell will go off in your spirit.

Our objective as a herald of the King is to simply deliver the gospel as it is presented in God's Word. We don't need gimmicks or deceptive methodology, nor do we need to make any apologies. We can be completely upfront about it, and tell anyone who will listen, "Here it is," as we deliver it lovingly, clearly, compassionately, and most importantly, *biblically*.

A watchman

Finally, Paul compares himself to a watchman. In verse 26 he says, "Therefore I testify to you this day I am innocent of the blood of all men."

What is he saying here? In making this statement, Paul alludes to passages in Scripture about the role of watchman who would patrol the city walls, keeping his eyes open for possible enemies. If he saw danger approaching, perhaps the approach of an enemy army, he would immediately cry out a warning.

A contemporary equivalent might be a lifeguard at the beach. He or she scans the horizon to make sure everyone in the water is safe. These people need to be always on the alert and perform their jobs with diligence, because lives are at stake.

Paul draws on a reference in Ezekiel chapter 3, where God says, "Son of man, I have made you a watchman for the house of Israel; so hear the word I speak and give them warning from me. When I say to a wicked man, 'You will surely die,' and you do not warn him or speak out to dissuade him from his evil ways in order to save his life, that wicked man will die for his sin, and I will hold you accountable for his blood" (vv. 17-18, NIV).

This is serious stuff. This is life and death. So if I know the truth of the gospel and meet somebody who doesn't know it, I have a responsibility as a witness, as a herald, and as a watchman to proclaim it. If know a believer is going astray or doing things contrary to what the Bible teaches, I have a responsibility to warn that individual of what could potentially happen. I don't do this because I hate them. I do it because I love them, and want to help and protect them.

The Motive

Paul closes this challenging and insightful message to the elders of Ephesus with the motive of why we should do all of this.

Here's why. In verse 35 he says,

> "I have shown you in every way, by laboring like this, that you must support the weak. And remember the words of the Lord Jesus, that He said, 'It is more blessed to give than to receive.'"

I love that statement. Have you discovered its truth yet?

I think about Christmas time, and our tradition of giving presents, in honor of the One who gave the greatest Gift of all. When you're very young, you concern yourself with "What I'm going to get." But as you get older, your focus shifts more and more to the joy of giving, and you find that it truly is more blessed or more happy to give than it is to receive.

We need to learn to be generous with everything that God has given to us—our resources, our energy, our time, and our talents and gifts. Why? Because you can't out-give God. Listen to what Jesus said in Luke 6:38. "If you give, you will receive. Your gift will return to you in full measure, pressed down, shaken together to make room for more, and running over. Whatever measure you use in giving—large or small—it will be used to measure what is given back to you."

Some who have never learned the joy of giving want to hoard what God has given them, thinking they'll "make it last longer" and that it will give them security. They couldn't be more mistaken. Our security comes from God Himself, not from the gifts He gives us. If we have Him, we have everything.

Proverbs 11:25 says, "The one who blesses others is abundantly blessed; those who help others are helped."[89]

It helps me when I can help you. It blesses me when I can bless you. Sometimes people come up to me as their pastor and say, "Oh, Greg thank you for your sacrificial service. Thank you for all that you do." And of course I appreciate someone being so thoughtful to say that. But the truth is, I receive so much more than I ever give. And the more I attempt to give, the more the blessing comes back to me in ten thousand ways.

Before we wrap up this chapter, let's do a quick fly-over of the points we've covered. Paul met with the elders of Ephesus, and told them solemnly that this was the last time he would ever see their faces—until they were all together again in heaven. His words, then, were weighty words, and he wanted them to understand those priorities that were closest to his heart.

Number one, he said, we're all runners in the race of life, and our objective is to finish our race with joy. With that in mind, let's run to win and not let anyone or anything cut in on us or somehow steal our prize.

Number two, we are stewards or servants. Our sole responsibility here on earth is to please and serve our Master, not ourselves.

Number three, we are witnesses. We're here to testify of what God has done in our life.

Number four, we are heralds, commissioned to deliver a specific message from the King Himself.

Lastly. We are watchmen. We have a responsibility to warn those who live their lives apart from God that there will be consequences for that. But watchman can also see good things on the horizon as well as enemies, and we can freely declare the hope, help, and blessings available when men and women turn to God and place their lives in his hands.

The Holy Spirit had evidently revealed to Paul the knowledge that he wouldn't be back to Ephesus again. As a result, he was very purposeful in his meeting with the elders. He wanted to make sure that they truly understood his encouragements and his warning, because he wouldn't have a second chance to tell them again.

That's the truth for all of us every day. We don't know the length of our days here on earth. And if we speak to someone this afternoon, who knows if we will ever see that person again? That's why it's so important to walk in the power and the leading of the Holy Spirit, always being ready to speak the words He gives us to say.

Make every day count, and at the end, yours will be life well lived.

SEVENTEEN
Christ's Call to Courage

Paul was in prison.

Again.

But it's not as though he hadn't been warned!

Though he had been cautioned again and again not to go back to Jerusalem, Paul felt that Jerusalem was the very place where God wanted him. He would do his best not to make a scene or cause a riot, but he simply believed that was the next step on the journey the Lord Jesus had given him to travel.

But of course, he found trouble anyway.

Just as the prophet Agabus had predicted in Acts 21:10-11, Paul made his journey to Jerusalem and—for all his precautions—was apprehended and incarcerated.

In a trial before the Sanhedrin, Paul had managed to set Jerusalem's two main religious parties—the Pharisees and the Sadducees—at odds with one another, starting what boiled over into a minor riot.

We pick up the story in Acts 23.

> Then there arose a loud outcry. And the scribes of the Pharisees' party arose and protested, saying, "We find no evil in this man; but if a spirit or an angel has spoken to him, let us not fight against God."
>
> Now when there arose a great dissension, the commander, fearing lest Paul might be pulled to pieces by them, commanded the soldiers to go

> down and take him by force from among them, and bring him into the barracks.
>
> But the following night the Lord stood by him and said, "Be of good cheer, Paul; for as you have testified for Me in Jerusalem, so you must also bear witness at Rome."
>
> And when it was day, some of the Jews banded together and bound themselves under an oath, saying that they would neither eat nor drink till they had killed Paul. Now there were more than forty who had formed this conspiracy. (vv. 9-13)

When the meeting of the Sanhedrin degenerated into a violent chaos, the Romans had to rush onto the scene and rescue him. The upshot of it all was that Paul found himself in familiar lodgings—sitting in a Roman prison.

From the time Saul of Tarsus became the apostle Paul, trouble had been his middle name. He seemed to bounce from one crisis to the next. It was always something. And tough as he was, as strong in spirit as he may have been, Paul was still human; it would appear from the circumstances and from what the Lord said to His servant, that he was feeling down and discouraged by it all.

Yes, he knew heaven awaited him...eventually. But he was also a flesh-and-blood man, and couldn't help but be concerned about his future. And so in verse 11 we read these wonderful words:

> But the following night the Lord stood by him and said, "Be of good cheer, Paul; for as you have testified for Me in Jerusalem, so you must also bear witness at Rome."

On first reading, you might wonder if those were the words Paul really wanted to hear. You're in a dungeon (it can't get much lower than that) and someone comes to you and says, "Cheer up!"

It's not always such a good idea to go someone who is feeling down and say, "Put on a happy face. Smile awhile." Glib words like that don't often comfort—and can actually make things worse.

I'm not critiquing what Jesus said to Paul; I would like to *clarify* what He said to His discouraged servant. The fact is, "cheer" or "cheerfulness" is not really the best definition of the word that is used here. You might say that cheerfulness would be the *outcome* of what Jesus actually commanded here.

You see, our Lord never commanded people to be cheerful. He didn't go to someone with a disability and say, "Be cheerful. Smile. Snap out of it." No! He had true compassion, reached out to them in their agony, and sometimes shared the agony with them.

A better translation of the Lord's words to Paul would be, "Paul, be of good courage."

That's the operative word. *Courage.* And courage seems to be in short supply these days, doesn't it? What is courage? Courage, also known as *bravery* or *fortitude*, is the ability to confront fear, pain, risk, danger, uncertainty or intimidation. Physical courage is bravery in the face of physical pain, hardship, or even the threat of death.

I think you and I tend to imagine that some people are simply "more courageous" than others. But that isn't necessarily the case. It was Mark Twain who said, "Courage is the mastery of fear. Not the absence of fear."

Then again, what some people call "courage" is really more akin to insanity! I remember when I was a kid growing up it seemed like I always had one friend who was willing to do *anything*. Maybe you've known people like that, too. They usually have nicknames like Animal, Psycho, Hot Dog…or maybe just Fool. Most of those guys are no longer with us. (And they are usually guys. Rarely girls. Girls are smarter than that.) But these are the guys who always try it first, whatever "it" happens to be. *Walking across a railroad trestle. Jumping off the roof. Driving with no hands.* That stuff isn't courage, it's just a shortage of common sense.

True courage is overcoming your fear in the face of adversity. As one person has said, "Courage is fear that has said its prayers." And we've all seen that kind of authentic, admirable courage on display from time to time—especially among those in our military, in law enforcement, and in our fire and rescue units. We've heard so many stories of heroism over the years of those that have laid down their lives for others.

Not long ago, I told a story in the pulpit about a courageous mother named Patsy Lawson who lived up in the mountains in a town called Running Springs, and commuted to her job in the Los Angeles area. She was coming down the hill with her two children—five-year-old Susan and two year old Gerald—to drop them off in daycare before she went to her teaching job.

On the way, however, she lost control of her car and it crashed upside down in a cold mountain stream. The husband, alarmed at his wife's absence, searched frantically for her, finally spotting her car in the stream. The little girl died in the accident, but the two-year-old survived, held up out of the water by his mother.

For up to four or five hours, as she was dying, she held her little boy above the water so he could breathe. And when they found her, her arms were locked in that position. She didn't make it, but her boy lived.

After I told that story, the boy himself—now a young man—contacted us. He wanted us to know that he was doing well, and that he had become a Christian. What an example of courage he has had in his life!

We need such courage today. But it isn't all about running into a burning building to save someone or throwing yourself on a grenade to protect your buddies. There is moral courage, as well—courage to stand up for what's right. It takes courage to go against the whole current of our culture, and do the right thing today. It takes courage to follow the commands of Scripture, and to stand by what the Bible teaches.

We're living in a time when it's not popular to say that God's definition of marriage is between a man and a woman. This is an era when it's not popular to say that life begins at conception, and that every child, regardless of the circumstances that led to their conception, ought to have a right to live. It takes courage to stand up for those things.

It takes courage to honor your marriage vows today, when people all around us divorce at the first sign of hardship or trials. It takes courage today to remain sexually pure as a single person, waiting until you meet that right person to whom you will commit your life. It takes courage to follow Jesus Christ, and to share your faith with other people.

We need courage today. But where do we find it?

Paul found in the presence of the Lord.

Not Alone

But the following night the Lord stood by him....
(Acts 23:11)

We might add four words to the verse of Scripture above: "…*And nobody else did.*" We don't read of anybody from the church of Jerusalem coming to Paul's aid at this point. As far as the local Christians seemed to be concerned, the apostle was on his own with the Romans. It had happened a number of times in the apostle's life. In his final imprisonment, in his very last letter, the apostle wrote these sad words to his young friend Timothy: "The first time I was brought before the judge, no one was with me. Everyone had abandoned me. I hope it will not be counted against them."[90] Another translation says: "No one stood by me. They all ran like scared rabbits."[91]

Have you ever felt that way? As though everyone has abandoned you? Maybe there was a time in your life when your friends—or perhaps even your family—disappointed you. Maybe your husband or your wife let you down. Sometimes we become so discouraged we falsely imagine that even God has let us down.

You can look to people for comfort, and sometimes you'll find it. But I just have to warn you: If you consistently look to people for your comfort and support, you *will* be disappointed. It doesn't matter if it's a friend, a close relative, or even a pastor. Yes, there are good and godly people out there who will help you, lift you, and encourage you at times, and God will work through obedient, Spirit-filled people to do these things for you.

Ultimately, however, you need to look to God for comfort. He will be with you, standing at your side, when all others have faded from the scene.

The fact is, God can compensate by His own loving presence for every earthly loss. Commenting on this desolate moment in Paul's life, the great preacher C. H. Spurgeon wrote: "If all else forsook him Jesus was company enough. If all others despised him, the smile of Jesus was approval enough. If the good cause seemed to be in danger, in the presence of the Master victory was sure. The Lord who stood for him at the cross now stood for him in the prison. It was a dungeon, but the Lord was there. It was dark but the glory of the Lord lit it up with heaven's own splendor." And Spurgeon concludes, "Better to be in a jail with the Lord than to be anywhere else without Him."

Amen! Isn't that true?

I would rather be in the worst place imaginable with the Lord than in the greatest place imaginable without Him. And that was the apostle's experience as well.

God Was More than Aware of Paul's Situation

The Lord came and stood by Paul in the prison of the Roman barracks, and we don't have any record of Him doing an Internet or MapQuest search to track His servant down. The Lord didn't need to hire private investigators to locate Paul. Jesus knew exactly where he was.

John Bunyan, the author of *Pilgrim's Progress*, spent years in prison for his faithfulness in preaching the gospel. At one time a minister came to visit him and said, "Bunyan, the Lord has sent me to you, and I have been looking for you in half of the prisons of England and finally I found you." And Bunyan responded, "Well the Lord must have not sent you, because He has known where I have been all this time. Why didn't He just send you straight to me?" A good point.

He is with us in our prisons. Maybe you are in a literal prison right now. I receive letters quite often from those who are incarcerated for crimes they have committed, and they talk to us about how our publications or our radio broadcasts have helped them in their confinement.

I just heard the story of Michael Franseze, who spent four years in prison. Dubbed by the media as "the prince of the Mafia," he was said to have been one of the fifty wealthiest and most powerful crime bosses in America. In the mid 1980s at his peak, this man was making six to eight million dollars a week. Ultimately, he was busted by the Feds, gave them the information they needed, worked out a plea bargain, and spent four years in prison.

It was while he was behind bars that a guard led him to Christ. He told me when we met that he had listened to our radio broadcast every day while he was incarcerated. Now he is out of prison, and travels around sharing his testimony.

So God can meet you even in an actual prison, behind literal bars of steel. But not all prisons are jails or penitentiaries. A hospital bed or a convalescent home can be a prison. So can an injury or a chronic illness. Old age itself can be very confining, where you find yourself unable to get out or do what you used to do, and you feel bound.

Paul says to all of us as He said to Paul, "Be courageous. You're not alone, and I am fully aware of your suffering."

You might be in a prison cell of mourning because of the loss of a loved one through death. Jesus is there with you…and with me as well. He understands what you're going through, and He knows what lies ahead for you.

Jesus came to Paul in his hour of great trial, because He knew His servant needed a special word, a special touch, and a special impartation of strength. Locked in that prison cell as he was, Paul didn't know what was really going on at that point. He didn't know that there were forty men who had taken an oath to not eat or drink until they had killed him.

Sometimes, ignorance really is bliss, isn't it? If you could know everything about your future…would you *want* to? If you could know about every plot made against you or every bad thing that anyone has ever said against you, would you want to have that information in your head? I wouldn't. I think it would be quite disillusioning.

Paul didn't know about the plot described in Acts 23:12-15, because at that point, he didn't *need* to know. God reveals to us as much as we need to know when we need to know it. Not necessarily more, and certainly not less.

The important thing is not that you know, but that *He* knows. And He surely does. Your troubles, though unexpected to you, come as no surprise to God.

In the military, they have a term that describes this deliberate exclusion from certain facts. They call it a "need-to-know" basis. So a subordinate might come to his commanding officer and say, "What's going on with this mission?" And the officer might reply, "This mission is on a need-to-know basis, and you don't need to know!"

In a similar way, sometimes we will come to God and say, "What's going on with these events in my life? What's this all about?" And God may reply, You don't need to know right now. But in time, I will make it known to you."

The Bible says in Romans 8:28, "We know that all things work together for good to those that love God and are the called according to His purpose." It doesn't say we will *see* all things work together…. Because we can't always see (or even imagine) how certain things could result in good for anybody. But we can *know* that they will—by faith—and that God will give us more details when He is ready. Until that time, we must trust.

God had a Future for Paul

"Take courage! As you have testified about me in Jerusalem, so you must also testify in Rome."[92]

Jesus reminded Paul that He knew what he was doing in Jerusalem—and approved it. That would have been especially comforting for Paul to hear, because his trip had been a little controversial. On his journey, several believers had warned him that trouble lay ahead in that direction. At the home of Philip the evangelist in Caesarea, Agabus had warned him very specifically what would come down if he went ahead with the trip.

But he went ahead anyway.

Had he blown it? Missed the Lord's will?

Apparently not, because the Lord Himself commended Paul for giving witness in Jerusalem. Our task as believers, our job, if you will, is to obey the leading of the Holy Spirit. If you do that, you can always anticipate opposition. And when it's all said and done, what God wants from us is not success as much as faithfulness. Results and fruit are His responsibility. Faithfulness and obedience are ours.

Besides, what *is* success, anyway? Many of us tend to gauge success as "the bigger, the better." If it's big and popular, then it must be good.

But time has a way of sorting things out, doesn't it? What may be deemed a success today may be looked back on as a failure in the future. What may be looked upon today as a failure may be regarded as a success in days to come. You don't know until the dust settles, do you? And in that final day when we stand before Him, Jesus is *not* going to say, "Well done, good and *successful* servant." No, what He will say is, "Well done good and faithful servant."

Faithfulness is what counts in God's kingdom.

Even so, as Paul sat there in that prison, you have to wonder if he might have been second-guessing himself just a little. *Should I have listened to Agabus and cancelled my trip? Did I miss God's will somehow? Did I blow it?* And then Jesus comes to him and says, in effect, "I know what's going on here, Paul. I've seen your fearlessness and your faithfulness. You have done well. And you know what? We'll have some adventures together in the future. How about Rome? How about a testimony before Caesar? Be of good courage, son, I still have work for you to do."

I think that Jeremiah 29:11 must be a favorite verse for almost everyone.

> For I know the thoughts that I think toward you, says the LORD, thoughts of peace and not of evil, to give you a future and a hope.

In its context, that verse was given to the Jewish nation when they were captives in Babylon. Certainly as a conquered and displaced people they were discouraged, most likely wondering if they would ever be free again to worship God as they once had. And the Lord spoke to them and said, "I am thinking about you—good thoughts! I want to give you a future and a hope."

In our lives as well, no matter what we may be going through, God is aware of our situation, and thinking thoughts about our future. Now imagine that Jeremiah 29:11 saying: "I know the single thought that I once had toward you," says the Lord. That would still be pretty amazing, wouldn't it? The Almighty Creator of the universe took the time to think even one thought about little *me*? But that's not what the verse. God says, "I know the *thoughts* that I think." So it's not only past tense, but it is present and future.

How many thoughts does He think toward us?

How high can you count?

In Psalm 40 verse 5 we are told, "Many, O LORD my God, are Your wonderful works which You have done; and Your thoughts toward us cannot be recounted to You in order; if I would declare and speak of them, they are more than can be numbered."

Over in Psalm 139, we read:

> How precious it is, Lord, to realize that you are thinking about me constantly! I can't even count how many times a day your thoughts turn toward me. And when I waken in the morning, you are still thinking of me! (TLB)

His thoughts toward you are innumerable.

And they are *good* thoughts.

The Lord speaks of "thoughts of peace and not of evil, to give you a future and a hope." No matter what your circumstances might be telling you now—whether it's divorce, bankruptcy, or cancer—there is a boundless future and a wonderful hope for every son or daughter of God. By the way, the word translated "future" in Jeremiah 29:11 could be translated "an expected end," or "a ground of hope."

The Lord was saying to Paul, "Keep your courage up! There's going to be a good outcome here. Things are moving toward completion, and I still have some things for you to accomplish."

You need to know that, too. You are a work in progress, and God isn't finished with you yet. He is the author and finisher of your faith, and you are still like wet clay in His hands…a half-written song…a half-done painting.

As an artist, I have loved to sketch and draw since I was a little boy. What I like to do most is to draw caricatures of people. Sometimes someone will say, "Draw me, draw me!" But then they don't necessarily like what I draw! Why? Because a caricature is not a lifelike rendering. (I'm not that good. A caricature is usually an exaggeration, designed to make a person laugh.)

Sometimes, however, I'm in the middle of a drawing and someone will look over my shoulder and say, "Oh—wait. You need to do this. Change that. Adjust it over here."

Hey, I may only be a cartoonist, but I know what I'm doing! I know what I have in my mind's eye, and what the outcome will be. So you have to let me finish my work.

In the same way, we see God working in our lives and we see a brush stroke here, a dash of color there, and maybe the suggestion of a line or two. And we say, "Wait. What's this? I don't know if I agree with how this is taking shape."

Step back. Give God room. He is the Master Artist, the Master Craftsman. There will be a completion, and an expected end. God is still at work in your life and *ultimately*, it's going to be very, very good.

He has a future for you.

The question might arise, what about the person who doesn't get out of prison? What about the person who isn't healed? What about the person who dies?

The plan is still good, my friend. The future is still secure.

Paul himself, though he survived this prison and went on with his ministry, eventually found himself imprisoned again, in Rome. Church history tells us that he may have appeared before Nero, and that he was ultimately beheaded for his faith.

So what's up with that? *A future and a hope?* Beheaded? How does that work?

I will tell you how it works. It was the expected end. And it ushered Paul immediately into the place he most wanted to be—into the presence of the Lord he loved and served. Sometimes we lose sight of the fact that our ultimate goal is not just a comfortable life here on earth. It is an eternal life in heaven.

We became way to focused on the here and now, and not enough on the "bye and bye."

And the Lord says to us, "I have a bigger plan for you than your convenience and ease. I have a bigger objective here, and that is to shape and form you into the very image of my precious Son."

Ultimately, all loose ends are tied together.

Ultimately, the sculpture is completed and the painting is done.

But until that day comes, it's a waste of time and energy to second-guess an Artist whose skill is far beyond our understanding.

All that precedes our future life in heaven is but a glimpse of things to come. We tend to think of life on earth as "the real thing," and heaven as vague, misty, and surreal. But it's the opposite. That's why C. S. Lewis referred to our time on earth as "the shadowlands." Earth is a pale version of heaven, not the other way around. Heaven is the real thing, earth is effectively the copy. We are told in Hebrews 8:5, "They serve in a place of worship that is only a copy, a shadow of the real one in heaven."

Again, to quote C. S. Lewis: "The hills and valleys of heaven will be to those you now experience not as a copy is to an original, nor as a substitute is to the genuine article, but as the flower to the root, or the diamond to the coal."[93]

I am not suggesting life is nothing more than an extended misery until we finally leave it and enter heaven. Life can be wonderful and filled with joy. You can be going through a bad thing today that will be turned into a good thing tomorrow. But ultimate joy will come when we see the Lord in heaven, and we must not lose sight of that.

God had a future for Paul, and He has a future for you as well. So have courage. Be of good cheer. God is with you, standing by your side, preparing you for a certain future.

And never forget: The best is yet to come.

EIGHTEEN
The "Almost Christian"

Almost.

It's an interesting term.

It's a word we sometimes use to give ourselves a little time, when we're not quite ready to commit. For instance, maybe you sit down in a restaurant, pick up a menu, and before you even have a chance to glance at it, the server comes back and says, "Do you know what you would like to order today?"

And you say, "Well…almost."

You say that because you're not sure yet.

Or maybe you're a husband waiting for your wife to come out, because you should have left for your dinner ten minutes ago. You say to her, "Are you ready yet?"

"Almost," she says. (Guys, you know what that means, don't you? One hour minimum.)

Or maybe you're late for a meeting, and your boss calls you at home, wakes you up and says, "Where are you?" And you say, "I'm almost there." Which could mean that you haven't even climbed out of bed yet, because your alarm didn't go off.

Almost is a word that we sometimes couple with procrastination. I'm almost ready to decide…but not quite yet.

There are certain words that don't work with almost. Like "almost pregnant." That's a term that simply won't fly, because you either are, or you aren't.

It's not any good to say, my team almost won the Super Bowl—even if they only lost by two points. It really doesn't matter how many points they lost by. The winner is the winner, so you can't "almost win."

Here's another word that doesn't fit with the word "almost." *Christian.*

You're either a Christian or you're not. Yes, you may be well on your way to becoming a Christian, as you investigate the claims of Christ. But "almost" doesn't cut it. Especially with God.

In this chapter, however, we're going to look at someone who tried to attach the word *almost* to the word *Christian*. When the apostle Paul presented the gospel to him, Herod Agrippa said, "You almost persuade me to become a Christian."

Almost. Apparently Agrippa had been moved by Paul's powerful and persuasive presentation of the gospel. But then, as we will see, he turned and walked away from it. He came close, but not close enough. He was the "almost Christian."

I wonder how many "almost Christians" we have today in our country. Despite a recent rash of books by avowed atheists attacking the Christian faith, most Americans today still claim to believe in God. A recent survey revealed that 80 percent of Americans believe in God, 75 percent believe in miracles, 73 percent believe in heaven, and 71 percent say that Jesus is the Son of God. Seven out of ten believe that Jesus rose from the dead, and that the Bible is all—or at least in part—the Word of God.

But then a recent Barna poll revealed the following. Half of Americans who call themselves Christians don't really believe that Satan exists. And fully one-third are confident that Jesus sinned while He was on the earth. In addition, 25 percent dismiss the idea that the Bible is accurate in all the principles it teaches.

My response to numbers like that is to say that Christianity is not a buffet. It's not a salad bar, where you pick this or that ingredient and leave out the things that don't appeal to you. "*Let's see…. I'll have a helping of forgiveness and a little side of mercy. And I'm going to pass on the conviction and the guilt. I'm on a guilt-free diet you know!*"

No, the Bible doesn't leave us any such option. In effect, Jesus Christ offers a package deal that you either accept or reject. There's no negotiation of terms, and you don't get to vote one way or another. It is God who establishes the terms and sets up the rules, and you either buy in or you don't. It's as simple as that. And you don't have the option of editing out the parts of Scripture you don't like.

A number of years ago I actually had someone ask me the question, "Greg, what do you do when you come across a verse in the Bible you don't agree with?"

I found it humorous that he would even ask me such a question.

A Bible verse I don't agree with?

I said, "Well, if I don't agree with it, then I change my opinion, because I'm obviously wrong!"

It's not for us to agree or disagree with the Bible. Yes, it's entirely possible that we might not understand a particular verse of Scripture, but there really is no place for us to "disagree with it," as it is all inspired and "breathed" by God Himself.

The Bible is our very source of truth, and we adjust our beliefs according to what the Scripture teaches. That's what it means to be a believer.

I believe there are many people calling themselves Christians today who may not be believers at all. In 2 Corinthians 13:5, Paul writes: "Check up on yourselves. Are you really Christians? Do you pass the test? Do you feel Christ's presence and power more and more within you? Or are you just pretending to be Christians when actually you aren't at all?" (TLB).

Paul says, "Do a self-exam. And you'd better make sure you are what you say you are." Or in other words, "Are you really a Christian according to what the Bible says, or are you an 'almost Christian'?"

What distinguishes a believer from a nonbeliever or a pseudo believer or a pretending believer? Does it all boil down to what you *believe?*

Not necessarily! You can believe that Jesus Christ is the Son of God and the Bible to be the Word of God, and still not be a Christian. Listen to what James says about the "faith" of demons: "You believe that there is one God. You do well. Even the demons believe—and tremble!" (James 2:19).

Simply believing in the truth of the Bible or the identity of the Son of God doesn't mean I'm a Christian. Again, mere intellectual assent to certain truths isn't all there is. Saving faith has to go beyond that.

The fact is, you can read the Bible, pray, keep the Ten Commandments to the best of your ability, attend church on a regular basis, and even be baptized, yet still not necessarily be a Christian.

I'll take it a step even further. You can make some visible changes in your life that would *look like* conversion to some, and not necessarily be a Christian.

So you say, "All right. Now I'm a little concerned about myself. How can I know if I am really a Christian?"

Let's go back to our story in the book of Acts, and learn about what it means to be a real believer.

Trouble and More Trouble

As we have noted, Paul's middle name could have been "Trouble."

He encountered it wherever he went, wherever he turned. When he traveled, he seemed to go from hot spot to hot spot. Once again, in Acts 23, he had been arrested and incarcerated for preaching the gospel. And while he was in that Roman lockup, his nephew heard of a plot that had been hatched against his Uncle Paul, went to call on him in his prison cell, and delivered the news.

Forty men had taken a vow that they would not eat or drink till they killed Paul. So Paul told his young relative, "Please, go tell that Roman man in charge of me what you just heard." When he reported his news to the centurion, you can tell right away that the Roman accepted the young man's words; it was a credible threat, and he decided he needed to get Paul out of Jerusalem.

That night under the cover of darkness, with 370 Roman soldiers guarding him, the apostle was transported to Caesarea, over on the Mediterranean Sea. Upon arriving in this Roman colony, he was placed under the command of the governor there, whose name happened to be Felix.

Felix the Roman governor really didn't know what to do with Paul. He brought him into a public gathering, and Paul's accusers came with their false accusations and lies. They had brought along with them a silver-tongued orator named Tertullus to present their list of bogus accusations against the great apostle.

When Paul's turn to speak came, he (as always) gave a brilliant presentation of the gospel of Jesus Christ.

Felix had never seen anyone like Paul before. So confident. So sure. So bold, despite his circumstances. Intrigued, Felix, along with his wife Drusilla, spent private time with Paul.

Drusilla happened to be Felix's third wife, and he had stolen her from another. Something in him wanted to know more about what this passionate Jew was saying, and Paul—never one to pull his punches—laid it out. The Bible tells us in Acts 24:25, "As he reasoned with them about righteousness and self-control and the judgment to come, Felix was terrified. 'Go away for now,' he replied. 'When it is more convenient, I'll call for you again.'"

I think Felix had really wanted to know more, but when Paul got down to the brass tacks, it made the loose-living governor very, very uncomfortable; talking about morality and integrity—not to mention God's judgment—weren't topics he was used to dealing with. So Felix said, "Okay. Stop. Time out. I think that's enough for now."

Two years passed, and Paul remained incarcerated. The Bible says Felix had been hoping Paul might pay him off, so he could release him. But no bribe was coming. So Felix's term came to end, and he was replaced by another Roman governor by the name of Festus.

As with all politicians, Festus knew very well that he would inherit a number of hot potatoes from his predecessor. And one of those left-over problems was named Paul.

As with Felix before him, Festus didn't have a clue what to do with the apostle. As it turned out, however, the Jewish puppet king Herod Agrippa and his sister Bernice were in town to congratulate Festus on his appointment as governor of Caesarea.

This Herod was from a long line of wicked men—all known for their cruel, God-defying ways. Of course there was Grandpa Herod, the first of the lot, who had met with the wise men searching for the "king of the Jews," and had been responsible for the execution of the baby Jewish boys in Bethlehem and its environs. Herod the Great, as he was called, was a paranoid tyrant. He had been given the title "King of the Jews" by Rome, and didn't want anyone to threaten his position.

His son Antipas was the Herod responsible for beheading John the Baptist. Herod Agrippa, the man in this story, was the son of Antipas.

So this latest Herod comes to town to congratulate (butter up) the latest Roman governor, Festus, and he is invited to hear a most unusual prisoner give his defense. The royal party arrived with a lot of pomp and circumstance, dressed in their robes of state and surrounded by soldiers in their dress uniforms. It was quite the occasion.

Then Paul was shown into the room, his chains clanking, and no doubt wearing a ragged, faded old robe—perhaps blood-stained from his many beatings.

Walking into the hall, he took note of the dignitaries in all their finery…and I don't think he was intimidated one little bit. He saw it as yet one more opportunity to bring the gospel.

Paul's presentation of the Good News to these VIPs—Festus, Agrippa, Bernice, and the like—was a wonderful example of how to declare the salvation message to anyone, whether famous or unknown, whether a big crowd or a single individual. These are principles we all can use in our witness.

Positive Principles for Sharing the Good News

#1: Find common ground and build a bridge to your listener.

> Then Agrippa said to Paul, "You may speak in your defense."
>
> So Paul, with a gesture of his hand, started his defense: "I am fortunate, King Agrippa, that you are the one hearing my defense against all these accusations made by the Jewish leaders, for I know you are an expert on Jewish customs and controversies. Now please listen to me patiently!" (Acts 26:1-3, NLT)

This wasn't empty flattery on Paul's part, but it was diplomatic. Agrippa was indeed steeped in the ways of the Jews, as was their secular ruler, appointed by Rome. It was he, for instance, who would appoint the high priest. So he knew all about Jewish culture and custom, and was aware of the teachings of the Jewish prophets.

It's also worth noting that Agrippa was an immoral man, rumored to be in an incestuous relationship with his sister. Paul, of course, could have brought this up. He could have said, "You're one wicked man, Agrippa. And everyone knows it." But he didn't do that; he was respectful, and built a bridge instead.

Sometimes I think Christians unnecessarily offend their listeners when the present the gospel. They insult them, and that simply isn't necessary. In Colossians 4, Paul counsels us to let our speech be seasoned with a little salt—not horseradish. There is an inherent offense in the message of the gospel already (as you point out that people are sinners and in need of salvation), so we don't have to add to that offense by being rude or condescending. Let's share the message biblically, understandably, lovingly, and compassionately.

It has been said, "No one should ever preach on the topic of hell without a tear in his eye." Yet I have seen some preachers talk about hell and almost seem delighted by the fact that people are going there.

Yes, you can certainly warn of consequences and judgment, but you can do so with humility and compassion.

When Jesus was with the Samaritan woman at the well, He could have immediately torn into her about her life of immorality and scandal. She was certainly known for it. Yet He didn't confront her initially about that. He appealed to her inner thirst. Ultimately, of course, He did confront her with her sin, and there is a place for that.

But He first built a bridge.

He first established a dialogue.

Some people burn the bridge before they even get it built!

#2: Use your personal testimony to build that bridge.

As you read through the book of Acts and look at the messages Paul gave to people like Agrippa, Felix, and Festus, you will find he almost always started with his own personal story.

There is interest and power in the telling of that story, but we ought to observe some cautions, too.

First, don't glorify or exaggerate your past. Accuracy and truthfulness are very important. I have noticed that some people's accounts of their conversion seem to change with the passing of time. I will hear their testimony, and then ten years later I'll hear it again and think to myself, *Wow. It's a little more dramatic than it used to be.* But there's no need for that.

Just tell your story the way it happened, whether you consider it compelling or not. Really, it doesn't matter if it's not particularly dramatic or wouldn't make a good movie. No matter what our background, we were all sinners, separated from God, and saved and forgiven by Jesus Christ. Your story is valid, whatever it is, because it will relate to someone else who needs to hear about his or her need for Jesus Christ.

Another thing about your testimony. Don't boast about what you "gave up for God," but rather about what God gave up for you. I've heard some people tell how they came to faith, and they go on and on about the great sacrifices they made when they gave their hearts to Christ. Sometimes they actually make their past sound more appealing than their present, as they recount the stories of what they used to do and all the high times they used to have in their old life.

I like the way Paul summed up his past in Philippians 3:

> The very credentials these people are waving around as something special, I'm tearing up and throwing out with the trash—along with everything else I used to take credit for. And why? Because of Christ. Yes, all the things I once thought were so important are gone from my life. Compared to the high privilege of knowing Christ Jesus as my Master, firsthand, everything I once thought I had going for me is insignificant—dog dung. I've dumped it all in the trash so that I could embrace Christ and be embraced by him. [94]

So don't glorify or exaggerate your past, or make it sound better than the present. And if you really think that it was, then you don't understand what God has done for you.

Finally, just remember this: It's not about you, it's about Him. The only reason for telling my story in the first place is to point to *His* story. My testimony is just a bridge, not the destination. The destination is Jesus Christ.

In Acts 26, Paul uses the fascinating details of his own dramatic conversion to build that bridge to his listeners.

> "I used to believe that I ought to do everything I could to oppose the followers of Jesus of Nazareth. Authorized by the leading priests, I caused many of the believers in Jerusalem to be sent to prison. And I cast my vote against them when they were condemned to death. Many times I had them whipped in the synagogues to try to get them to curse Christ. I was so violently opposed to them that I even hounded them in distant cities of foreign lands.
>
> "One day I was on such a mission to Damascus, armed with the authority and commission of the leading priests. About noon, Your Majesty, a light from heaven brighter than the sun shone down on me and my companions. We all fell down, and I heard a voice saying to me in Aramaic, 'Saul, Saul, why are you persecuting me? It is hard for you to fight against my will.'

"'Who are you, sir?' I asked.

"And the Lord replied, 'I am Jesus, the one you are persecuting. Now stand up! For I have appeared to you to appoint you as my servant and my witness. You are to tell the world about this experience and about other times I will appear to you. And I will protect you from both your own people and the Gentiles. Yes, I am going to send you to the Gentiles, to open their eyes so they may turn from darkness to light, and from the power of Satan to God. Then they will receive forgiveness for their sins and be given a place among God's people, who are set apart by faith in me.'" (vv. 9-18, NLT)

Earlier in the chapter, I spoke about "almost Christians"—those who may be doing religious or spiritual things, and yet haven't experienced a genuine conversion to Jesus Christ.

"All right, then," someone might reply, "what exactly *do* you need to do to be a Christian?" The answer comes from the Lord Himself, as quoted by the apostle. Here was Paul's calling in a nutshell: "*To open their eyes, so they may turn from darkness to light and from the power of Satan to God. Then they will receive forgiveness for their sins and be given a place among God's people, who are set apart by faith in Me.*"

This is the essential gospel message—what needs to happen for a person to come to faith.

First, your eyes must be opened.

The Bible teaches that prior to becoming Christians, we are spiritually blind. The apostle Paul wrote in 2 Corinthians 4:3–4: "If the Good News we preach is veiled from anyone, it is a sign that they are perishing. Satan, the god of this evil world, has blinded the minds of those who don't believe, so they are unable to see the glorious light of the Good News that is shining upon them."

So we need to pray that God will open people's eyes spiritually when we tell them the Good News. In his Ephesian letter, Paul prayed that his readers would have the eyes of their hearts opened. The fact is, there is nothing I can say, or you can say, that will *make* a person believe. I have had people come up to me and say, "Greg, what's the *one thing* I can say to my non-believing friends to make them become Christians?"

But there is no "one thing." I have no such truth, nor does anyone else.

Even though I have had the great privilege of preaching the Gospel to millions of people, conversion is still a mystery to me. I have seen it happen it many, many times, and I still don't fully comprehend it. To think that He would use someone as foolish as me—or you—to simply articulate a message, and then have God's Holy Spirit make that resonate with the listener? How amazing. And how wonderful.

I can't explain how it takes place, but I have seen it happen time after time. Even when I am speaking! I will watch the reactions of people in a service, and sometimes I can pick out the nonbelievers as I speak. There are telltale signs. Sometimes you can actually see God's Holy Spirit opening their eyes to the truth of the gospel. You can read it in their faces. And then, sure enough, when the invitation comes, you see those very people come forward to receive Christ. But it only happens as the Lord opens their eyes.

Second, you have to turn from darkness to light.

Here's how it works: Only God can open your eyes; only you can turn from darkness to light. Only God can make you aware of your need for Christ; only you can put your faith in Christ. God won't do it for you. He has given you a free will, and it's up to you to respond and decide.

What does it mean to turn from darkness to light? Paul answers that in Romans 13.

> Wake up, for...the night is almost gone; the day of salvation will soon be here. So don't live in darkness. Get rid of your evil deeds. Shed them like dirty clothes. Clothe yourselves with the armor of right living, as those who live in the light. We should be decent and true in everything we do, so that everyone can approve of our behavior. Don't participate in wild parties and getting drunk, or in adultery and immoral living, or in fighting and jealousy. But let the Lord Jesus Christ take control of you, and don't think of ways to indulge your evil desires. (vv. 11-14, NLT)

How clear is that? The problem arises when people try to live in two worlds. They know and believe what is true, but they haven't let Jesus Christ control their lives or put to death their evil desires. In other words, though they have seen and acknowledged the light, they haven't yet turned from darkness. They are almost Christians.

So Paul builds a bridge, shares his personal testimony, and now he gets down to the bottom line: preaching Christ and His crucifixion, death, and resurrection.

> "I teach nothing except what the prophets and Moses said would happen—that the Messiah would suffer and be the first to rise from the dead as a light to Jews and Gentiles alike." (vv. 22-23, NLT)

Whenever you have the opportunity to present the gospel to someone, make a beeline to the cross. The power of the message is in the account of the life, death, and resurrection of Jesus. That's why Paul wrote in Corinthians, "I resolved to know nothing while I was with you except Jesus Christ and him crucified."[95]

As Paul reaches this all-important bottom line, Governor Festus suddenly erupts, interrupting him mid-sentence.

> Festus shouted, "Paul, you are insane. Too much study has made you crazy!"

> But Paul replied, "I am not insane, Most Excellent Festus. I am speaking the sober truth. And King Agrippa knows about these things. I speak frankly, for I am sure these events are all familiar to him, for they were not done in a corner! King Agrippa, do you believe the prophets? I know you do...." (vv. 24-27, NLT)

I think there must have been an audible gasp in the room as Paul counters the governor, then makes a direct appeal to the king. You could probably hear people whispering, "Did he just say that to Festus? And did he just say that to Agrippa?" With the merest sweep of the hand, either one of these guys could have had Paul summarily executed. But he took them both on, challenging them.

> "You believe the prophets, don't you, King Agrippa? Don't answer that—I know you believe." (Acts 26:27, THE MESSAGE)

I love Agrippa's response in verse 28: "'You almost persuade me to become a Christian.'" Or more literally, "Do you think you can make me a Christian so quickly?"

Paul must have smiled a little here, because that was certainly the idea! The fact is, a person can become a Christian in a flash. It's not a long, drawn-out process. Some people might say, "Well, you know, I'm in the process of converting to Christianity." Coming back to what I said earlier, you're either a Christian or you are not. You are not "converting"; you are either converted or you are not converted. But it can happen so fast you can't even measure it by human time.

Paul certainly did think Agrippa could become a Christian. Why not? Hadn't Saul of Tarsus become a Christian—and what could have been more startling than that? Even Caesar could be converted, and Paul expected to have an audience with the emperor, because he had appealed to him. Unfortunately, we don't have a record of the conversation he had with the emperor of Rome. But we do know from history that the Caesar on the throne at that point was one of the most wicked of the lot: Nero. This was the man, you may recall, who was responsible for the burning of Rome and the radical persecution of Christians.

Paul, however, was utterly fearless. As far as he was concerned anyone was eligible for the kingdom. Anyone could believe. Anyone can be transformed. If someone like him could be changed, certainly anyone else could as well.

To Agrippa's semi-sarcastic retort about becoming a Christian so quickly, Paul responded: "'Whether quickly or not, I pray to God that both you and everyone here in this audience might become the same as I am, except for these chains'" (v. 29, NLT).

With that last comment, he probably held up his arms with the shackles on them. He was saying, "You may be royalty and live a privileged life. But I wish you could stand where I am standing, because I have peace, confidence, and hope. And I don't think you have those things."

With that, Agrippa and Bernice left the room. Agrippa had come so close to opening his heart…so close, but so far. He was an almost Christian.

Truths to Consider

It's not enough to just be exposed to truth. We must act on it.

Constant exposure to the truth without ever acting on it can harden any heart. You want to know the easiest place to get a hardened heart?

Your church.

"In church?" you say. "I thought you were going to say in a bar or night club or out partying with friends."

Here's what I mean: The same truth that will set one person free can cause another to become more hardened against things of God. It matters a great deal how you listen and respond to the proclamation of God's Word, and where your heart is at in the presence of God's people worshipping all around you. Maybe you've heard the old expression, "The same sun that softens the wax also hardens the clay." It's true. And by the same token, the same truth that liberates one causes another to shrug his shoulders and say, "I've heard that before."

Okay, so you've heard it before. But have you ever responded to that truth? Have you ever taken it in? Or you just a well-instructed nonbeliever?

The truth is, some people in church every Sunday may be further away from the kingdom of God than the guy who hangs out in the bar every day and never darkens the Church door. Why? Because the guy in the bar who hears a clear gospel presentation may believe on the spot. But the guy who has heard it his whole life and thinks he knows it all, might become so hardened and resistant that he'll go right on saying no to Jesus…for the rest of his life.

None of us want to end up as an almost Christian…

…*like Herod Agrippa, who knew the prophets, listened to Paul, and was "almost persuaded" (but not quite)*

…*or like the rich young ruler, who actually knelt before Jesus and*

wanted so much to follow Him, but couldn't bring himself to pay the price
    …or like Judas Iscariot, who walked, laughed, dreamed, talked, ate, and slept in the immediate presence of Jesus Christ, yet ended up betraying Him for thirty pieces of silver.

Share, bridge, engage, and transition.

As we share this most important message in all of life, we should try to first build bridge of communication, as Paul did—not carelessly or deliberately burn it before we even begin. Engage your listener with your own personal story—but make sure that your story points to the ultimate story, the greatest story ever told: the life, death, and resurrection of Jesus Christ.

Only God can open the eyes and ears of the listener.

Only He can open a heart. All we can do is to build a bridge, give witness to what we have seen and heard, tell the story as best we know how, and then step back and let Him do what only He can do.

NINETEEN
Surviving Life's Shipwrecks

I have never been literally shipwrecked, but I have been through some pretty rough seas.

I remember years ago being on one of those Bible study cruises with a group of people from our church.

My good friend, Pastor Raul Ries was speaking one night when the ship ran into some really rough water, with waves of twenty-five to thirty feet. It was a big cruise ship, but it was really being pitched around.

Pastor Raul was doing his best to keep the message going, but it was a losing effort. He would say, "Look down at verse 4," and we would glance down—but then look up really fast because it made you sick to look down. Nobody could really figure out what Raul was preaching, and I don't think he could, either. He was obviously disoriented, and it seemed like he changed the topic of the sermon about fifteen times.

In the meantime, people were getting sick and lurching out the room. My wife Cathe (who had turned an interesting shade of green) said, "Take Jonathan back to the room," and ran out the door. That was fine, but then Jonathan got sick, too.

Let's just say Raul gave an early benediction and ended the service before it really ever got started.

That wasn't a shipwreck, it was only rough seas.

We've all had our share of rough seas, haven't we? I've had my share of hardships in life. More than many? Perhaps. But not as many as some. I remember thinking not that long ago that maybe the days of big shipwrecks in my life were over. Oh, I know there will always be some difficulties, challenges, and trials in the Christian life. But I'd found myself hoping that I might somehow escape any big traumatic events through my remaining years. You know…relative smooth sailing the rest of the way to heaven. But of course, that was not to be with the unexpected death of our oldest son Christopher. That was to be so far the worst shipwreck of our lives, if you want to call it that. It was certainly the most traumatic and difficult time I have ever experienced.

The book of Acts records the dramatic details of the apostle Paul's shipwreck in Acts 27. But apparently, that wasn't his first experience "on the rocks." In his letter to the Christians in Corinth, he relates: "Three times I was shipwrecked. Once I spent a whole night and a day adrift at sea" (2 Corinthians 11:25, NLT).

Travel by sea in those days was primitive and harsh. You took your life into your own hands when you boarded one of these first-century sailing vessels. And Paul tells us, "Trust me. I've been through it. I know more than I ever wanted to know about shipwrecks."

Maybe some of the modern conveniences of the twenty-first century have made traveling a little more safe and convenient but in some way shape or form, every one of us will face shipwrecks. That's the reality of life on this planet: I hate to break this to you, but the fact of the matter is you're either coming out of a storm or about to go into one. I know that sounds rather harsh to some, but I do believe it's basically true.

Now, don't misunderstand what I am stating here. There will be those wonderful stretches of smooth sailing, when the skies are blue and the sun is shining. Those golden seasons may go on for weeks, months, and sometimes even years. In God's grace and kindness, you're going to have some beautiful moments in your life in between the storms. Not all the winds that blow in life are necessarily devastating.

In one instance of the ship's log in the book of Acts, the text says,

"The south wind blew softly." Thank God for those moments, when the breezes are gentle and the sun is warm on your shoulders. But we all know—or ought to know—that there will be storms just over the horizon. Jesus Himself said so. He said, "In this world you will have trouble" (John 16:33, NIV).

Sometimes people think that when they're in the will of God, they'll always have smooth sailing and calm seas. That certainly *wasn't* true for the apostle Paul! In the course of his ministry, he seemed to face every kind of adversity imaginable. He had so many enemies jealous of his success that they would actually follow him around and seek to undermine him, hoping to destroy him. He experienced beating after savage beating at the hands of his many adversaries, and spent years of his life in harsh confinement. And on top of it all, he had a personal physical disability that the Lord had declined to heal.

Paul wrote in 2 Corinthians 4:8-9, "We are pressed on every side by troubles, but not crushed and broken. We are perplexed because we don't know why things happen as they do, but we don't give up and quit. We are hunted down, but God never abandons us. We get knocked down, but we get up again and keep going" (TLB).

A lot of preachers love to focus on that "prosperity" topic. And sometimes I think they have hijacked a legitimate biblical term. After all, God wants His sons and daughters to prosper. He wants you to experience prosperity. But what does that really mean? That you'll never get sick? That you'll never have problems? That you'll never run out of money?

No, that's not what the Bible means by "prosperity."

Five years before making his journey to Rome, Paul wrote the believers there and said in Romans 1:10, "Making requests, I am asking you to pray, if by any means now at length I might have a prosperous journey by the will of God to come to you." In other words, "Hey, would you guys pray for me? I'm coming your way. And pray that the Lord gives me a prosperous journey by the will of God."

Did God answer his prayer? Yes.

He did make it to Rome, and had an amazing ministry there of preaching, teaching, discipleship, and writing. He just hadn't understood that *getting* to Rome would mean false accusations, arrest, incarceration, and chains. He couldn't have foreseen that it would involve hurricane force winds at sea, shipwreck on an island, and the bite of a poisonous viper on the way.

The reality is you can live a prosperous life in the will of God and still face fierce personal conflict and adversity. Paul went through shipwreck on his way to Rome, but he had a prosperous journey by the will of God *because of what it ultimately accomplished*. So that's a different definition of prosperity than we might normally think of.

Facing storms and shipwrecks in our lives really isn't a matter of "if," it is a matter of "when." So it's time for us to get our sea legs under us. Rather than trying to avoid the storms of life, we need to learn how to get *through* them. How to survive them. And how to learn the lessons that we can only learn in such times and such places.

It has been said, "You can't direct the wind, but you can adjust your sails." I can't control all the elements of my world. In fact, I can't control very many of them at all. I can't control my environment. I can't control the circumstances that come my way. I can't keep people from opposing me or undermining me or seeking to harm me. But I can control my *reaction* to them. I can adjust my sails. And adapt.

When hardship hits you can get mad and bitter at God, or you can completely surrender and say, "Lord, I'm going to trust You no matter what."

It is our choice what we do with our sails when storms come our way.

A Journey to Rome

The apostle Paul was in a shipwreck on the way to Rome. But why was he even going to Rome? Because after two years of unjust incarceration under two Roman governors, Paul made a legal appeal to Caesar himself. As a Roman citizen from Tarsus, he had the privilege.

Once he had made that appeal, official Rome would do all it could to get him there. Governor Festus told him: "You have appealed to Caesar? To Caesar you shall go!" (Acts 25:12).

Transportation in those days, however, was an interesting prospect to say the least. Paul sailed from Caesarea in a ship bound for Rome. He was joined on board by some other prisoners, the soldiers who were guarding them, and a centurion named Julius.

As they began their journey on this primitive little ship, Paul knew that bad times were coming. Almost from the start, the small sailing vessel had to contend with uncooperative weather and belligerent winds. Dr. Luke, the author of the book of Acts, traveled with Paul on this voyage, and penned these words in his journal.

> We had several days of rough sailing, and after great difficulty we finally neared Cnidus. But the wind was against us, so we sailed down to the leeward side of Crete, past the cape of Salmone. We struggled along the coast with great difficulty and finally arrived at Fair Havens, near the city of Lasea. We had lost a lot of time. The weather was becoming dangerous for long voyages by then because it was so late in the fall…. (Acts 27:7-9, NLT)

No one really wanted to stay the winter in Fair Havens. It was apparently a poor harbor and (who knows?), maybe the accommodations and restaurants weren't so great there, either.

Luke writes that "Most of the crew wanted to go to Phoenix, farther up the coast of Crete, and spend the winter there. Phoenix was a good harbor with only a southwest and northwest exposure" (Acts 27:12, nlt). That made sense to the crew. Who wouldn't want to winter in Phoenix!

Paul, however, warned them that serious trouble was ahead if they put out to sea again. But why should they heed the words of prisoner?

So they set sail…and got slammed by a monster storm. Was it a Category 5, like Hurricane Katrina? The Bible doesn't say. But it was plenty bad enough, and the little Roman prison ship was no Queen Mary.

After days of being driven and battered by the storm, Luke wrote:

The next day, as gale-force winds continued to batter the ship, the crew began throwing the cargo overboard. The following day they even threw out the ship's equipment and anything else they could lay their hands on. The terrible storm raged unabated for many days, blotting out the sun and the stars, until at last all hope was gone. (vv. 18-20, NLT)

"I Told You So...."

Apparently, the apostle Paul wasn't above saying, "I told you so."

In a severe storm at sea, after all the cargo had been jettisoned and the crew had given up hope of even surviving, Paul reminded them that he had warned them before they ever set out.

The Bible records his words, most likely shouted into the wind on that wild, stormy day at sea: "*Men, you should have listened to me in the first place and not left Crete*. You would have avoided all this damage and loss. But take courage! None of you will lose your lives, even though the ship will go down. For last night an angel of the God to whom I belong and whom I serve stood beside me, and he said, 'Don't be afraid, Paul, for you will surely stand trial before Caesar! What's more, God in his goodness has granted safety to everyone sailing with you.' So take courage! For I believe God. It will be just as he said. But we will be shipwrecked on an island" (Acts 27:21-25, NLT).

Paul knew a storm was coming when the others didn't. How did he know that? The Lord's angel had stood next to him at night and gave him that sure word. Initially, the captain and the centurion in charge rejected Paul's counsel. When the apostle warned them about the trials and troubles ahead, they blew him off. "You're just a landlubber. A preacher. What do you know? This is what we do for a living. We'll be fine. Just get on board."

But now, in grave danger and at their wits end, they suddenly found Paul the landlubber's opinions interesting and relevant!

The truth is, as Christians who believe our Bible, we know things nonbelievers don't know. We know that circumstances in our nation and world will eventually go from bad to worse—much worse. We know that Washington doesn't have the answers, and that government doesn't have the solutions to life's greatest dilemmas and needs. We know that man in his own wisdom will always make a mess of things. We know that an Antichrist will come on the scene one day with new answers for world peace and a prosperous global economy, and that just about everybody will buy into his formulas for success. He'll offer military solutions, economic solutions, and new religious ideas designed to help us "set aside our differences and pull together."

Yes, because we read and believe our Bible, Christians know what is coming down in the days to come. And we also know that earth doesn't have what we are looking for. Not even close. That's why we, like Abraham, are looking for a city that has foundations, whose builder and maker is God Himself.

God revealed to Paul something that nonbelievers didn't know, and He has done the same for us. He is able to take a situation of pain and hardship and use it as an opportunity to point people to salvation and new life in His Son. And God gives us that same platform.

As I write these words, our nation suffers from a deeply troubled economy, and even the experts can't agree on how to resolve the problems we're facing. People are losing hope. And some of those discouraged, disillusioned people out there will begin to reevaluate what really matters in life, and their relationship with God. This can be an opportunity for us to speak up, offer a word of true and lasting hope, and point people to Christ.

Paul had said, "Guys, listen up. An angel of the Lord appeared to me and told me about what's going to happen in the next few days. First of all, know this: we're going to get through this together. Every one of us! We're going to survive the storm." But then he dropped the bombshell. "*But we will be shipwrecked on an island.*"

In other words, healing, hope, help, and rescue were on the horizon, but the storm wasn't over. And there was a shipwreck ahead.

On one occasion, Jesus said to His disciples, "Let's go over to the other side." So they boarded their little boat to cruise across the Sea of Galilee—which is really a very large freshwater lake known for storms rising up without warning. And sure enough, a storm came roaring out of nowhere. This one was a doozy, because even the seasoned sailors despaired of life. And what was Jesus doing? He was sound asleep in the stern. Waking Him, they yelled, "Teacher don't you care that we are perishing?" (See Mark 4).

It was really more like an accusation. "Hey Lord, are You paying attention? Don't You care that we're going through this? Wake up and do something!" Jesus stood up, and rebuked both the storm *and* His boys. To the storm He said, "Peace! Be still!" And of course it instantly obeyed. But to His own followers He said, "Why are you so fearful? Why is it you have no faith?" Or literally, "Why are you so timid and fearful? Boys, haven't you learned anything? Remember what I said? '*Let's cross over to the other side.*' I didn't say, 'Let's go to the middle of the Sea of Galilee and drown!'"

The fact is, Jesus never promised calm seas and smooth sailing. But He did promise a safe passage. He told them they would make it to the other side.

Listen…it is better to be in a storm with Jesus than anywhere else without Him! I would rather be in a rowboat with Jesus in the middle of a hurricane than a thousand miles inland without Him. I would rather be in a lion's den…or a prison…or a hospital…or even a shipwreck with Jesus than in any other situation without Him. As long as I know the Lord is there, I can get through *anything*.

Four Handholds in a Storm

Paul's confidence and hope was built on four principles, solid truths that we can apply to the storms in our life, whatever they may be. What are those principles?

#1: God was with him.

Paul was conscious of the presence of God in the face of danger. In verse 23 he wrote, "Last night an angel of the God to whom I belong and whom I serve stood beside me."

Yes, there was the storm, and a shipwreck loomed just ahead. Paul knew that. But as long as Jesus would be there, too, he didn't have a worry in the world.

And He is with us in our storms as well.

We've already spoken in this book of Paul's "thorn in the flesh," that he mentions in 2 Corinthians 12. It could have been some kind of disability, something he'd been born with. More likely, it was something he incurred later in life as a result of his many beatings, his shipwrecks, or the time he was stoned and left for dead.

Whatever it was, it bothered him greatly—to the point that he asked the Lord to take it away on three separate occasions. Each time, however, the Lord said no, telling Paul, "My grace is sufficient for you." Effectively Jesus was saying, "Paul, I'm not giving you healing this time. I'm giving you Me. I'm giving you My presence, and that is My answer to you."

Sometimes when we have physical afflictions, the healing will come. By all means pray for it, and pray more than once. Ask the Lord to touch you, heal you, and restore you. But there are times in our lives, too, when He will say, "My grace is sufficient." And instead of a healing He will personally be there for you in a unique and sufficient way.

A. B. Simpson wrote: "Once it was the blessing. Now it is the Lord. Once it was the feeling. Now it is His Word. Once His gifts I wanted. Now the Giver alone. Once I sought healing. Now Himself alone."

God is with you regardless of what storm—even shipwreck—you may be enduring right now. You are not alone.

I've been teaching my granddaughter Stella a new Bible verse. She knows three now—which isn't bad for two and a half years old. The new one is: "Jesus said, 'I will never leave you or forsake you.'"

Stella is doing pretty well with it, even though she says "porsake" instead of "forsake." I don't think she even understands what it means yet. But that's okay; she is hearing God's Word and getting it into her little heart.

What a truth to hang onto! What a handhold in any storm. He will never leave or forsake you…even when tragedy hits…even when your company downsizes, and you get the dreaded pink slip…even when the doctor calls and says, "The test results are back, and I need you to come to my office immediately"…even when the phone rings and someone says, "There's been an accident."

You are not alone. The Lord is standing next to you. He cares. He will be there.

#2: He belonged to God.

"For there stood by me this night an angel of the God to whom I belong and whom I serve…." (v. 23)

Paul spoke of "the God to whom I belong." In the Song of Solomon we read, "My beloved is mine and I am his." As a Christian, you belong to the Lord. You are His.

There are a number of analogies the Lord uses to show how we belong to God. For instance, we are called "the bride of Christ."

My bride is Cathe. I call her my wife, and she calls me her husband. She belongs to me and I belong to her. That's just the way it works. We belong to each other.

The Bible also compares us to sheep that belong to a shepherd. In John chapter 10, Jesus affirmed that He is the Good Shepherd and that we are His sheep. Sometimes we romanticize this wooly little animal, the sheep. They look so charming out there in the green grass, under the watchful eye of the shepherd. But we should also bear in mind that they are one of the stupidest animals on the face of the earth. It should not inflate you with pride to hear that you are compared to a dumb, defenseless sheep.

We are also compared to children belonging to a father. Romans 8:15 says, "God has not given us the spirit of bondage again to fear, but one of adoption whereby we cry, 'Abba Father.'" *Abba* was an affectionate cry of a Hebrew child. Even if you go to Israel today you will see a little child cry out, "Abba" to their fathers. We might say, "Daddy," or "Papa." It's a close, affectionate, endearing term. And we have that kind of access and closeness with our Father God.

My two sons have always had access to me. They didn't have to make an appointment to meet with Dad, they just walked up and started talking to me. That's the way it is with Jonathan to this very day. And if I'm in a crowded room talking to a lot of people and my little granddaughter comes walking in and yells out, "Papa"…well, the conversation's over. I'm going to pick up that little lady and go play with her. Maybe even with dolls! That's the kind of relationship that we have, and that's the kind of access she has. She is welcome to approach me *whenever*, and she knows that.

Finally, we are compared in the Bible to God's actual property. We read in 1 Corinthians 6:19, "You are not your own." In the original language it could be translated, "You are not your own property. You are bought with a price." He has reassured us of this by putting His own seal on us, as a king might seal his property with his signet ring on wax. We are told in 2 Corinthians 1:22 (NLT), "He has identified us as his own by placing the Holy Spirit in our hearts as the first installment of everything he will give us."

I belong to God. I have been bought and paid for, and I am His.

I heard the story of an older gentleman who was known for his godly life. Someone once asked him, "Old man, what do you do when you get tempted?"

He smiled and replied, "Well, I just look up to heaven and say, 'Lord, your property is in danger.'"

You are God's bride. You are His child. You are His sheep. You are His property. And like Paul, you too can say, "I belong to God."

#3: He was doing the will of God.

Paul could have a calm heart in the middle of the mother of all storms, because he knew he was in the center of God's will for his life. He was on business for God.

In his prison cell back in Caesarea, Jesus Himself had stood by Paul and said, "Be of good cheer, Paul; for as you have testified for Me in Jerusalem, so you must also bear witness at Rome" (Acts 23:11). Then, in the middle of the storm out at sea, an angel stood by Paul with this message from God: "Do not be afraid, Paul; you must be brought before Caesar...." (Acts 27:24).

Paul had heaven's business to transact in Rome, and he knew that God would get him through any difficulty along the way. He was walking in God's plan, and he knew that it was God's responsibility to get him through—rough seas or not!

The same is true of our service to the King. No, we aren't assured of smooth sailing, and we're not promised immunity from shipwrecks (or viper bites![96]) along the way. But we are definitely assured of a safe arrival. Know this: *As long as God has work for us to do here on earth, we will be here to do it.* God will preserve us to do it. And when that work is done it is done, and He'll bring us home to heaven…not a moment too soon, and not a moment too late.

#4: He believed in God.

In verse 25, Paul said, "So take courage! For I believe God. It will be just as he said" (NLT).

I love those words. These are not the words of a person in denial, but one who is very much in touch with reality. Paul said this as they were still in the storm, still being tossed around like a cork on those massive waves, still plunging through the sea without the light of sun, moon, or stars, and with everyone on board in despair of their very lives.

The Lord Himself had reassured Paul, and Paul believed in God! This wasn't mind over matter, it was faith over circumstances. Paul was fully convinced of the faithfulness of God, and was sustained by that conviction. He had seen the Lord take care of them up to this point and he was confident the Lord would carry him through, and that he would get to the other side.

In Luke 5 there is a story of Jesus speaking to a large crowd of people on the shore of the Sea of Galilee. And because the crowd kept pressing in on Him, Jesus asked Simon Peter if He could borrow his fishing boat as sort of a floating pulpit. Peter agreed, the Lord launched out a little bit from the shore, and kept on speaking.

Luke picks up the story:

> When He had stopped speaking, He said to Simon, "Launch out into the deep and let down your nets for a catch."
>
> But Simon answered and said to Him, "Master, we have toiled all night and caught nothing; nevertheless at Your word I will let down the net" (Luke 5:4-5).

When Simon Peter addressed the Lord, he used a nautical term that could have been translated, "We have toiled all night and caught nothing, nevertheless, *Master or Captain of this boat*, we will do it."

Was he being sarcastic or reverential? Did he really think this "land-lubber" rabbi called Jesus would know more about fish and the Sea of Galilee than he did, a seasoned fisherman?

I don't know what his tone of voice might have been as he said those words. But I know this much: When they launched out into the deep, there were so many fish in their nets that the nets began to break and the boat began to sink beneath the weight of the catch of the day. And then another boat was brought up alongside, and it was overwhelmed with fish as well.

Totally amazed, Peter fell on his knees before Jesus and said to Him, "Depart from me, for I am a sinful man, O Lord!" Effectively he was saying to Jesus, "Don't waste Your time on me. I'm going to disappoint You and let You down. I'm not going to measure up. Don't even bother with me, Jesus."

And Jesus replied: "Do not be afraid. From now on you will catch men" (v. 10).

Is Jesus the Captain of your boat? Let Him be that for you. Let Him take control. Row where He says to row, fish where He says to fish, and trust Him to get you through the roughest of seas. Jesus was the captain of Paul's boat—*even in the storm*—and that gave Paul complete confidence.

Paul told everyone on board: "So take courage! For I believe God. It will be just as he said. But we will be shipwrecked on an island" (vv. 25-26, NLT).

I love the way that Paul always ended up running everything! There he was, a prisoner on a Roman ship, and he ends up giving orders to the centurion and the soldiers (see verse 30-36). They listened to Paul because he spoke as one who had authority beyond his own. Everyone had seen how God was with him.

No matter how desperate or dire his situation, Paul never seemed to be under the control of circumstances. He wrote in Philippians 4:12–13, "I know how to live on almost nothing or with everything. I have learned the secret of contentment in every situation, whether it be a full stomach or hunger, plenty or want; for I can do everything God asks me to with the help of Christ who gives me the strength and power" (TLB).

When the ship beached short of the shoreline, everyone swam to shore or rode the surf in on boards. (Was this the first instance of surfing in human history?) Everyone arrived safely on the beach, exactly as God had promised through Paul.

Paul eventually did make it to Rome. And after a peaceful season under house arrest in rented lodgings in Rome (described in Acts 28), tradition tells us that he ended up in the Mamertine Prison—a cold, dark dungeon with no windows, only a hole through which food could be lowered.

Although it is not recorded in Scripture, tradition further tells us that Paul finally did receive his audience with the emperor—Caesar Nero—just as the Lord said he would.

As Paul's life came to an end in that black dungeon, he might have found himself looking back on imprisonment after imprisonment, beating after beating, rejection after rejection.

Not Paul! In his final epistle, 2 Timothy, the apostle reflected on a life of triumph and victory. He told Timothy, "I have fought the good fight, I have finished the race, I have kept the faith. Finally, there is laid up for me the crown of righteousness, which the Lord, the righteous Judge, will give me on that Day" (2 Timothy 4:7-8).

In another translation we read the words:

> You take over. I'm about to die, my life an offering on God's altar. This is the only race worth running. I've run hard right to the finish, believed all the way. All that's left now is the shouting—God's applause![97]

Not Just Another Chapter

This has not been "just another chapter in a book" for me. These aren't pious platitudes casually dispensed from Greg Laurie's ivory tower. These are truths freshly learned in a great life storm that we have endured as a family.

And I can tell you we have come through this shipwreck of shock, loss, grief, and sorrow, and we have found these principles to be true. At our lowest moments, it has been the Lord's presence that has sustained us.

More than anything else, it is His presence that has seen me through. When I say that the Lord is with me, I'm not talking in religious jargon or poetic language. I mean He is with me. Literally. Constantly. Personally. A day at a time, an hour at a time, and sometimes a moment at a time. How could I have even endured without the strong conviction of His nearness?

We recognize that our son Christopher belongs to God, and that He is with the Lord. And we recognize that we belong to God, too, every member of our family. We are seeking to do the will of God, and to glorify Him in any way we can, until we will all be reunited on the Other Side.

We choose to believe in God—His goodness, His grace, His provision, and His perfect plan. As I said earlier, you can't direct the wind, but you can adjust your sails.

Life will throw its curve balls at every one of us. We will all face times when we say, "I don't get this. Everything was tracking along in my life until this, and this makes no sense at all."

You might even say, "God, why?"

That's okay, you can do that. Just don't expect an answer. It's not because there isn't an answer, it's because even if He gave it to you, you wouldn't get it. It's like me trying to explain things to little Stella. She loves me and trusts me, but there are many things that simply don't make sense to her at age two and a half. She's still a little girl, and she's not able to grasp some things yet.

It's the same way with our infinite God. He could explain and explain something to finite Greg, and Greg will still say, "Lord, I don't understand." So He says to me, "Greg, I love you and I will be with you, helping you through this dark time and this dark place. That is My answer for you. I am your answer."

It's the best offer I could ever imagine. And even though I still don't like rough seas, I'd rather be in a shipwreck with Jesus than in a cruise ship with anyone else.

NOTES

[1] 2 Timothy 3:16
[2] See Acts 17:6
[3] Acts 2:39
[4] Acts 2:13, PHILLIPS
[5] THE MESSAGE
[6] 1 Corinthians 15:33, NIV
[7] 2 Timothy 3:17, PHILLIPS
[8] See Isaiah 55:11
[9] 1 Corinthians 2:2, NIV
[10] Matthew 16:18
[11] See Matthew 14:24-30
[12] 1 Samuel 16:7
[13] 1 Peter 2:4-5
[14] Ephesians 1:12, NIV
[15] John 15:8
[16] See Matthew 28:18-20
[17] 1 Peter 5:5, TLB
[18] Matthew 18:20
[19] See Psalm 22:3, KJV
[20] NIV
[21] 1 Corinthians 11:28-29, NIV
[22] Isaiah 53:11, TLB
[23] Acts 4:13
[24] See 2 Timothy 4:2
[25] John 4:35, NIV
[26] Luke 6:26, NIV
[27] Matthew 5:10

[28] James 3:2, NIV
[29] Romans 7:15-19, NLT
[30] 1 Thessalonians 5:19
[31] Hebrews 2:3, NIV
[32] PHILLIPS
[33] THE MESSAGE
[34] NIV
[35] 2 Corinthians 5:8
[36] Matthew 10:32, NIV
[37] Ecclesiastes 3:2
[38] Hebrews 9:27, KJV
[39] Luke 15:7
[40] Psalm 126:5-6, TLB
[41] Hebrews 1:14, NIV
[42] Psalm 34:7
[43] Hebrews 13:1-2
[44] NLT
[45] Isaiah 55:11
[46] Daniel J. Boorstin
[47] NKJV
[48] Esther 4:13-14, THE MESSAGE
[49] *Paul: A Man of Grace and Grit*
[50] Acts 21:39, NIV
[51] Acts 1:8, NIV
[52] 2 Timothy 3:12
[53] Philippians 3:10, New International Version
[54] See Acts 14:19; 2 Corinthians 12:1-6
[55] 2 Corinthians 12:2, 4
[56] Acts 8:1
[57] John 3:16
[58] Jeremiah 29:12-14, Matthew 7:7-8, TLB
[59] Luke 22:44
[60] THE MESSAGE
[61] Matthew 7:7
[62] Mark 9:24
[63] Hebrews 11:6, NIV
[64] 2 Timothy 2:3
[65] TLB
[66] NIV
[67] Romans 5:2-5, NLT

[68] Psalm 119:67, 71
[69] 2 Timothy 3:12
[70] Proverbs 16:18
[71] See Luke 17:11-19
[72] Jeremiah 10:23, NASB
[73] Colossians 3:15
[74] Acts 16:13, NIV
[75] 1 Peter 5:7; Psalm 55:22
[76] See Psalm 22:3, NKJV
[77] Matthew 18:20
[78] Acts 16:26, NIV
[79] THE MESSAGE
[80] Colossians 4:6
[81] Romans 2:4
[82] 1 Corinthians 2:2, NASB
[83] John 3:16
[84] Psalm 90:12, NIV
[85] Michael Josephson
[86] THE MESSAGE
[87] THE MESSAGE
[88] 1 John 1:3, NIV
[89] THE MESSAGE
[90] 2 Timothy 4:16, NLT
[91] THE MESSAGE
[92] Acts 23:11, NIV
[93] *Letters to Malcolm, Chiefly on Prayer*
[94] Philippians 3:7-9, THE MESSAGE
[95] 2 Corinthians 2:2, NIV
[96] See Acts 28:3-6
[97] 2 Timothy 4:6-8, THE MESSAGE

Other AllenDavid books published by Kerygma Publishing

Visit:

www.kerygmapublishing.com
www.allendavidbooks.com
www.harvest.org